"Nostalgic, romantic, and clear-sighted, too, *Beginner's Luck* brings to life an era that seems further and further away from the present than ever before, as the survivors of communes, collectives, and cults honor the fiftieth anniversary of 1968, the year that shook the United States and the world."

—*Counterpunch*

"In the sixties, I knew a lot of people who wanted to 'Turn on, tune in, and drop out.' Malcolm was the only one of my friends who followed through and was able to sustain himself. This is a fascinating look at the people who did it with him, the challenges they faced, and how they coped."

—Linda Ronstadt, singer and author of *Simple Dreams*

"There's no one better suited than Malcolm Terence to chronicle the mad, ecstatic, rushing fumble towards adulthood that we began together in the 1960s. His acuity and training as a reporter, his compassionate psychenaut's heart, and his innate good humor and total lack of pretension or self-aggrandizement means that the reader has the clearest, least-distorted possible lens through which to regard a period of history, the likes of which we may not see again. I love this book."

—Peter Coyote, author, actor, Zen priest

"In this rollicking new memoir, Malcolm Terence traces the wild sweep and scope of his itinerant life as a journalist, hippie, communard, timber worker, and environmental activist. From his first run-in with the Diggers in 1968 to a life on the Salmon River as a community leader, tribal ally, and environmental activist, he details his struggle to make an honest place in and of the world. A perfect tour guide through commune life, counterculture, and the resistance movements of the late twentieth century, Malcolm bears witness in these pages to a generation determined to create new, more sustainable modes of living."

— Rachel DeWoskin, author of *Foreign Babes in Beijing*, *Blind,* and *Big Girl Small*

"*Beginner's Luck* reads like a well-crafted novel, filled with suspense and surprise, improbable plot twists, and a vivid cast of characters worthy of Dickens. Malcolm Terence takes us on a wild ride into an initially bewildering territory—a colorful place peopled by a raucous collection of young people powered by the fuzzy but fervent principles of free love and free land, gathered here to build a new world in the ashes of the old. If you hang on tight and plunge into the wilderness with Terence, if you suspend disbelief long enough to rush headlong down the river and through the rapids, the journey will become irresistible—in no time the strange will become familiar, and the familiar, strange. Terence is a superb storyteller with the eye of an ethnographer, the romantic heart of a utopian, and a still intact pioneering spirit. His droll wit, compelling charm, and wicked intelligence make him an ideal narrator, wise and credible, able to capture the intensity—the courage and the innocence, the conflicts and contradictions, the utopian dreams of a lovelier time to come clashing with the heavy weight of the old order—that characterizes a committed group of kids determined to become new women and new men in order to build a base toward a more balanced and joyful future."

—Bill Ayers, author of *Fugitive Days* and *Public Enemy*

"Imagine sitting around a cozy room after a rollicking dinner with lifelong friends, listening to stories of communal life in the wilderness: generous, self-mocking, brilliantly written tales by a life-long writer/journalist. Beginner's Luck is the fresh notes from the field about local folks who opened their hearts to the wild-looking hippies and about the indigenous tribal people who might and would become friends and family. Here are the campaigns to protect the original growth forests, to stop the spraying of the land with dioxin, to end the damming of the last of California's wild rivers, to welcome the seasonal good fires that cleanse the underbrush and dead trees, to anticipate home births and deaths, to teach in the one-room schoolhouses. Malcolm Terence has chronicled the crazy experiment to share everything—sexual partners, child-raising, and money—to grow food locally, to bake bread and make tofu, to grow abundant gardens, to can the bounty, and to age with delicious optimism. Read this book and re-imagine."

—Bernardine Dohrn, former leader of the Weather Underground

DISPATCHES

FROM THE

KLAMATH

MOUNTAINS

beginner's luck

MALCOLM TERENCE

Oregon State University Press   Corvallis

Library of Congress Cataloging in Publication

Names: Terence, Malcolm, author.
Title: Beginner's luck : dispatches from the Klamath Mountains / Malcolm Terence.
Other titles: Dispatches from the Klamath Mountains
Description: Corvallis, OR : Oregon State University Press, [2018]
Identifiers: LCCN 2018006157 (print) | LCCN 2018021951 (ebook) | ISBN
    9780870719356 (ebook) | ISBN 9780870719349 (original trade pbk. : alk. paper)
Subjects: LCSH: Terence, Malcolm. | Communal living—California—SiskiyouCounty.
    | Hippies—California—Siskiyou County—Biography. | Mountain life—California—
    Klamath Mountains. | California, Northern—Biography. | Counterculture—California,
    Northern—History—20th century. | Country life—California, Northern. | California,
    Northern—Rural conditions. | Logging—California, Northern—Environmental aspects.
    | Klamath Mountain Region (Calif. and Or.)—Biography.
Classification: LCC HQ971.5.C2 (ebook) | LCC HQ971.5.C2 T47 2018 (print) | DDC
    306.09795/20904—dc23
LC record available at https://lccn.loc.gov/2018006157

♾ This paper meets the requirements of ANSI/NISO Z39.48-1992
(Permanence of Paper).

First published in 2018 by Oregon State University Press
Second printing 2018
Printed in the United States of America

Oregon State University Press
121 The Valley Library
Corvallis OR 97331-4501
541-737-3166 • fax 541-737-3170
www.osupress.oregonstate.edu

for Susan Ring Terence, my wife,
and our incandescent children, Slate Boykin and Erica Kate Terence,
saluting their boundless energy to build our communities

Contents

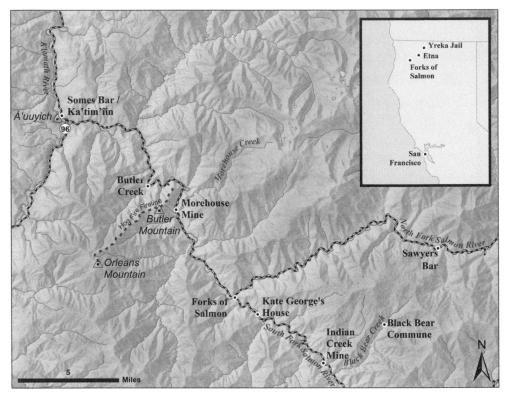

Salmon River Country. GIS design by Jill Beckmann

CHAPTER 1

Hall of Justice

Writers use many devices. I think my favorite is irony, in which the writer pretends to support something that is unsupportable. I'd like to use irony all the time. But I could never be the champ. That title would go to the people who named that building in San Francisco. They named it the Hall of Justice.

I ended up getting all the justice there a person could want because of a brush with a theatrical gang in that town who called themselves the Diggers. They were more theater than gang, but they had allure enough for me. Free food. Wild women. Wild men. It was 1968, and the Diggers had a political analysis that incorporated the fall of capitalism and its replacement by a socialism where everybody would have what they need and rarely need to work.

Certain neighborhoods around Golden Gate Park were full of Digger outposts. My favorite was a huge Victorian house just up the hill from Kezar Stadium on Willard Street. I'd strayed in there one day when my band—a real band with drums and pianos—was stranded in San Francisco between shows for a few days, and someone had given one of the road managers, or roadies, the address. The roadies are the hired hands who haul and set up the equipment at shows. I did that too, but my official title was business manager. That meant that I negotiated contracts, handled publicity, and hustled bookings. The whole band was organized as a co-op, and I was a voting member. Some of the band members boasted that they were communists, a bold declaration in that era. They named the band "United States of America." I wasn't the only one who liked irony. I guess you could say I was the interface between capitalism and this gang of Reds. Like pop musicians everywhere, they dreamed of getting rich, an ideological contradiction that distracts many revolutionaries the world over.

So together this roadie and I went exploring. We had to climb a steep hill and then a steep set of stairs to get to the door. We caught our breath, and the roadie knocked meekly on the frosted glass door. No answer. He knocked louder. Still nothing. I took over and pounded the door like a cop. It was unlocked, so it swung open, and we stepped in to see a swirl of people in a room down a long hallway. At the top of a stairway a naked woman stood, olive skinned and comfortably voluptuous. She had not seen us and was looking over her shoulder, completing a conversation with someone behind her. "What I need is a good fuck," she said with conviction. Then she headed toward us down the stairs and brushed past us down the hall as though we didn't exist. My companion followed her into the throng. I followed.

The building had three or four floors, a basement, endless hallways, stairwells, and crates of ripening and overripe fruit and vegetables in stacks. The main business there seemed to be vision quests and storing mountains of produce. A few regal women seemed to be actual residents of the place, and a whole parade of visitors, me among them, seemed invited to arrive there, eat there, sleep there, reinvent reality there. I'm not altogether sure whether you can actually reinvent reality, but that did not discourage people at the time.

The focus of it all seemed to be a large room with lumpy cushions along the walls and pieces of small furniture even more nondescript than the cushions. People were readying for some big fete at a concert hall down on Market Street that evening. We asked about Michael Agnello Tierra, who had given us the Willard Street address. Michael had been a brilliant, iconoclastic keyboard player in our band (we had two keyboard players playing at once) who had left just before the start of our latest tour. A long-haired woman named Nina, who wore a flowered sheath dress, looked us over suspiciously. Then she agreed that Michael lived in the house some of the time. After that she diverted her attention to three men who were lugging more crates of produce; she directed them to a porch behind the kitchen. She looked much more athletic than any of the men, and I think she was trying to coax the men into some productive activity. The kitchen was already loaded with crates. All the new boxes, I noticed, were filled with zucchini, a vegetable I'd never cooked and possibly never even eaten before. In one corner of the room, one woman was brushing paint carefully on another. The woman who was the canvas kept giving detailed instructions to the painter with more authority than I would have expected from a person who was standing naked in a crowded room. She was a short redhead and seemed to be one of the regular residents, so I approached her to ask about Michael Tierra. She flashed a huge smile and offered a shake with a painted hand. "I'm Sally Blythe," she said, and explained that Michael and Gail Ericson, Michael's girlfriend from Los Angeles, had just gone to the Free Clinic on Haight Street because Gail was several months pregnant and needed an exam. Then Sally Blythe reached into a small jeweled bag on the floor and offered me a tiny orange pill. I thanked her and started to place it in my pocket. She stopped my hand and said, "You're supposed to swallow it."

The evening, like many parts of 1968, remains a blur. I remember a cavernous dance hall on Market Street and a band. The brass section was composed entirely of angels in dark suits. I remember several tall, smoldering hookahs, the Asian pipes with many smoking tubes, but the orange pill was plenty, and I declined each of the hookahs as they were offered. People were invariably friendly in a way I had not seen in the other cities where our band had toured. And I remember catching a bus late at night with Gail, then five months pregnant, to return to the giant Victorian house. The bus was crowded with others from the dance hall and many would catch my eye and nod with slack-jawed smiles as though they knew me already. Gail, who knew to avoid pills of any color, curled up to sleep as soon as we returned to the Victorian, but I was wide awake, so I sat on the side of her bed for hours and tried to make sense of the day. At some point she stirred and shifted position. Carefully, I lowered my head next to her enlarged belly. We all love to talk to children, so I whispered something to the child growing inside her. I heard or I imagined an answer, also whispered. I responded. We, this chatty fetus and I, talked until near morning when I finally fell asleep. When the child was born, a few months later, her parents named her Shasta, after the snow-covered (but still active) volcano, whose towering beauty dominates the landscape from Redding to the California/Oregon border. I don't know how long I slept, but when I woke, Gail was gone and had covered me with blankets.

—

It was difficult to return to our home base in Los Angeles after this. Our record album, also called *United States of America*, was climbing in the charts and has been rereleased many times since that initial 1968 pressing. Clubs were interested in bookings. But the East Coast tour had been exhausting, and the musicians got into huge arguments more and more of the time. At one club in the East Village, the bandleader gave up arguing and punched the violinist in the nose. He was a good violinist, but his nose couldn't handle a punch and started spouting blood. Just then, the club owner walked into the dressing room and told us we were on in three minutes. If he saw the blood, he pretended not to. I had always wondered why violinists wear that little towel, but it turns out it's good for wiping a bloody nose while you play.

We returned home to Los Angeles, and it seemed diffuse and unfriendly, full of freeways and parking lots, but no place where neighbors walked or met by chance or even traded glances. San Francisco was a collage of neighborhoods, and Haight-Ashbury was just one of them. I thought more and more about the Victorian house. Newspapers were full of stories, most of them shallow or banal, about the Haight Street neighborhood, but the memories of our visit made me impatient with LA and with the idea of a return to New York, where we'd spent the winter.

Midway through a show the next weekend in Orange County, two of our musicians were arrested for smoking a joint in the alley behind the club, and I spent until morning arranging a lawyer and bail bond to get them out. It did not promote renewed harmony in the band. Finally, one day, we had a showdown in our lawyer's office in Beverly Hills. The lawyer was a veteran in entertainment law, but his passion was civil liberties. I think he accepted us as a client well before our prospects were any good because we postured as revolutionaries, both politically and artistically. At this particular meeting, I made a long-winded speech. I invoked the ideals we had espoused early on when we'd formed the band and lamented how we had strayed from them. I don't remember my exact words, but I recall that they were rich in principle and distant from the grinding realpolitik of show biz. Out of the corner of my eye I saw that the lawyer, an old Lefty, had tears welling up. Then I saw that Joseph Byrd, the bandleader, was incensed because I didn't side with him. But I wanted out, and burning bridges seemed the surest way. The next morning, I took my few possessions, threw them into the secondhand Coors beer truck we had used to ferry instruments, and headed back to San Francisco.

The big Victorian seemed no less abuzz when I returned. Michael and Gail introduced me to the regulars, and some of the women flashed flirtatious smiles. The residents were invariably welcoming. They were welcoming to everyone except the occasional visitor who seemed so deranged as to be dangerous. I asked endless questions about the Diggers and learned that they distributed free food, staged free concerts, and published a free newspaper, the *Free News*. The Diggers had invented a philosophy of what society should become, but I'd met many people with philosophies before. What made the Diggers different was that they did more than espouse. They tried it out. Okay, everything should be free. I was ready. Bring it on.

The next afternoon, I arrived as Michael Tierra was yelling at a well-dressed boy and throwing him out of the house. I watched until the shaken young man had walked down the steps, and then I asked Michael what was going on.

"Jacob met that kid on Haight Street. He had a bunch of money from his fraternity brothers at UC Berkeley to score pot, and Jacob offered him a deal," Michael explained.

"So what's the problem?"

Michael explained with great patience: "Jacob brought the kid upstairs here, took the money, and left him while he went off to get the weed. The kid was distracted for a long while by all the women flouncing around, but after a couple of hours he started asking what had happened to Jacob. When no one knew, he started to get loud. That's when I had to throw him out. It's not a big deal. Jacob does this a few times a week."

I acted as though rip-off art was the most ordinary thing in my world, but when Jacob slipped back into the house a day later, this time with no fraternity boy in tow, I told him I wanted to talk. I started by asking about the new society the Diggers were creating. I know this sounds corny, but that was the way people seemed to be talking, and I was trying to blend. Jacob entered the conversation enthusiastically and opened a portfolio of his drawings. They were beautiful, peopled by idealistic and heroic figures from his mind. It was a style not far from art deco, but with more beards and dazzled faces. "That," he said with enthusiasm, "is the world we're making by living it. We live our fantasies. That's how we're making everything free."

"Okay, your drawings are incredible. Some of them I've seen in the *Free News* or in the posters for concerts."

He interrupted. "I only let them use my stuff for free concerts. Stuff for money like the Fillmore, no. They're just trying to make money off the bands, and art needs to be free, just like us."

"I get that," I said. "But yesterday you took money from that college boy and disappeared. Michael finally threw him out."

Jacob smiled as though I was flattering him and nodded in agreement.

"What I don't get," I continued, "is how we can say on one hand that we're building a new free world and how on the other we can rip off some hapless dweeb from Berkeley who's just trying to score some smoke." I know this is a pretty rudimentary way to talk to another adult, but I figured he was addled by the idealism that was widespread then, and maybe by a heroin habit.

Jacob's mouth fell open, and his eyes opened wide. "I never thought of it that way. I'm a junkie, you know, and that's why I do it. But your point is right. How come nobody ever said this to me before? You are pretty good at thinking about stuff."

I shrugged and said, "You got a lot of talent as an artist. Would it work for you to sell some of your art and keep the rest of it free?" I knew that using "got" in that sentence was incorrect grammar, but I'd decided that part of the Digger persona was to talk like a hoodlum, and I was trying hard.

Jacob stared into the distance for a while and finally said, "I met a guy from an ad agency on Montgomery Street last week. He was very cool, and I really did score pot for him. No burns. He told me that I should bring my art by his office to show the art department. But he didn't like the condition of my clothes and said I should spruce up a little. Hey, check out these pictures. These are for the next *Free News*."

I looked at the pictures and tried to imagine them in advertisements. It was a stretch, but it didn't seem any more debased than conning straight kids from Berkeley.

"Didja get that jacket when you were a rock star?" Jacob asked me and began fingering the soft brown coat I was wearing.

"I wasn't a rock musician," I corrected. "I was their business manager, but I did travel with them, so I had to dress the part."

"I like that coat because the leather is rough-out like welders wear," Jacob said. "You know, I used to be a welder. Jeez, if I could wear your coat, it'd be just the thing to get in the door at the ad agency. Can I try it on?"

The Diggers also had a store where everything was free. Remember that, and do not judge me harshly as I tell you that I passed the coat to Jacob. When it fit him perfectly, I told him he could borrow it for the day. It was a nice coat. I can still remember it.

―――――

There were many kinds of people crowding into the Haight in those days. There were longtime bohemians and hippie newbies from towns small and large across America. There were bikers in jackets with the sleeves chopped off and black people from the ghetto neighborhood around Fillmore Street a few blocks away. There were draft dodgers, avoiding the Vietnam War, maybe because of fear, although most I met were plenty brave, but standing up against a war that so many of us opposed. I "dodged" myself, and that's a long story that I'll tell you sometime. There was also no shortage of sightseers and tourists. The streets were lined with hip clothing outlets and cheap food joints selling curries, burgers, tofu and vegetables, pizza, and piroshky, the deep-fried, beef-filled Russian pastries that were my personal favorite. When I walked along the street, cool dudes would murmur to me, "Speed, acid, cheap lids," while looking in the other direction. A "lid" was a measured amount of marijuana, although actual quantity or quality was intentionally vague. Drug use was also the main theme of the storefronts called head shops, full of implements to store and smoke pot and of posters for concerts. The Diggers seemed like particular royalty on the streets, and I walked tall and proud because I was staying in one of their houses. There was an element of counterfeit to this because I'd only been there two weeks, but I'd had no qualms about posing as a rock star in my leather jacket for the previous couple of years. Walking down Haight Street with an understated swagger, no problem.

It wasn't exactly counterfeit for me to imagine myself a Digger. There were no rules. That was practically the first rule. The magazines and newspapers were full of articles about the Diggers. But all it took to be one was to announce it to yourself, I guess. So I did. San Francisco and the hippie scenes across America were full of groups like the Diggers, some of them cults that were dark and worrisome. Most of these were controlled by a charismatic leader. The Diggers didn't seem a dangerous cult even though they had no shortage of charismatics, and they were often featured in the press. Maybe that's what saved the Diggers, that so many of them were so magnetic that serious cultdom never got any traction. Peter Berg could captivate a crowd in a big hall with his breathy, rapid-fire speeches. I met him early on. The most publicized Digger, I remember, was Emmett Grogan, the streetwise-est of New Yorkers transplanted out west. I met him only once, and he seemed so self-absorbed that he did not seem to notice that I was even there. The women of the house, not the Victorian on Willard Street, fluttered about meeting his every need. Maybe Grogan could have started a cult, although he seemed driven by a vision that went beyond mere power. Also, he was distracted by drug addiction, which caused his death a decade later.

The friendliest of the charismatics was Peter Coyote, who could explain nearly anything in the lyric language of a poet. He could describe welding on his motorcycle, a long, high-barred chopper in the style of the Hells Angels, as though he were carving a statue of Carrara marble. Once I watched him describe and then demonstrate a shot of something into his vein, I'm not sure what, with the ritual care of a Japanese flower arranger. "Open the syringe," I remember him saying, "until the blood blossoms like a rose." And there was the rose.

One day I met Freeman House and David Simpson, the people who pieced together the *Free News* on lost-and-found Gestetner mimeograph machines. They explained that they had once mixed LSD, then the psychedelic drug of choice, into the ink, or maybe the blood of someone on LSD into the ink, and that that edition had been a particular favorite on the streets of the city. Both of them were as friendly as Coyote and as magnetic. I told Freeman that I'd read and loved one of his articles when it was reprinted in a national magazine, a story about how our handling of garbage presaged the future of America. Freeman's eyes opened wide. "I write those pieces," he said, "but I never know if anyone ever reads them. Hearing you say you read it is wonderful for me. But how did you know it was me?"

I was a newspaper writer a little, I told him, and addicted to bylines, my own and everybody else's. As soon as I said that, David, an incandescent veteran of the San Francisco Mime Troupe, became even more animated. "You are who we're looking for. Freeman and I are ready to move on to other things. How would you like to take over the *Free News*?"

"But what would I write?"

"We write about our vision of what's happening and what should happen, and people like Jacob supply drawings and designs. It's a great collaboration. Jacob told us he'd met you and that you were a deep thinker, very free."

I puzzled about what my vision was and realized I didn't exactly have one, but it didn't seem like the time to say that. So I just said I'd think about it and let them know. No editor in Los Angeles had ever asked about my "vision," and the idea left me a little dizzy. Like a hallucinogen in the ink.

Later in the day I tried remembering life when I'd worked at the *Los Angeles Times* as a reporter. It had had its own kind of excitement, but there were tense moments. The paper was still in those days run by old, white, very conservative men. I remembered that Frank Haven, the managing editor who'd hired me, had once early on called Sherman Miller, my legendary journalism prof, to complain that I was living in Watts, the heart of the black ghetto, and that I had a black roommate. Miller told me about the call but made no judgment.

My old neighborhood exploded two years later in the 1965 Watts riots. This was many miles from where I'd moved by then, a little low-rent neighborhood at Santa Monica Beach. Buildings in Watts were torched by blacks in anger against the white ruling class. Thirty-four people were killed, and the National Guard was called in. And hundreds of people from Watts flooded out to camp on the beach for the whole five nights of chaos in their neighborhoods. The town next to Santa Monica was Venice, where there was also a large black population, but there was no violence there.

I covered the West Side, including Venice and Santa Monica Beach, and I told my editor I wanted to do a piece about the campouts and the non-violence in Venice. He looked at me with that disdainful look he reserved for bleeding-heart liberals and turned me down. The world was changing faster than the *Times*, and I knew that I would have to go with the world.

Certainly, the world was changing fast along Haight Street. The sidewalk throngs were made up of very young people whom I took to be runaways. That's how I found out about the Hall of Justice. My education came one evening when a tactical squad of the San Francisco Police Department came crashing through the front door of the Victorian. "What have you done with a runaway girl who calls herself Susan Sunshine?" they demanded. But the Haight-Ashbury district was filled with runaway girls. When the women of the house said she wasn't there, the police became enraged and said the missing girl had called her parents in Des Moines and given this address. They barged up the stairs but were blocked at the top by Sally Blythe, the petite redhead who'd been swabbed with body paint when I first met her a few weeks earlier. This time she was wearing clothes.

"You can't come in here without a search warrant," she yelled, and the lead officer, a man with the bulk of a side of beef, shoved her to the ground and lurched past her up the hallway. The next two officers helped her get up and told her she was under arrest for assaulting an officer.

Several of us who had watched it all started yelling in protest as the two officers escorted Sally down the stairs. She cursed them colorfully as they descended. I'd decided years earlier that nobody can curse like Catholics, and Sally was good. We started telling the other cops that we were witnesses, and she hadn't done anything to the officer. They ignored us. Finally, one of us said, "Well, if you take her, you have to take us all." I can't remember now why that seemed like a smart thing to say, but maybe it seemed like something they would have said in the Birmingham bus boycott a few years earlier. Two of the officers smiled at each other, and one of them ordered a police van over the radio.

Our first stop as prisoners was at the Park Station, named probably because it sat in a corner of Golden Gate Park, not far from the large Victorian. They'd corralled four or five men, me included, and as many women. I was led to a cell that already held Michael Tierra, Vinnie Rinaldi, and some young guy I'd never met before. Vinnie lived at the Victorian, and the story was that he slept on an ironing board in the basement. I'd even been shown the ironing board, with a couple of blankets and a pillow neatly folded and stacked alongside. Michael and Vinnie had beautiful voices and started singing freedom songs from the civil rights movement. The others of us joined in. A policeman came back to the cell and said quietly, "You motherfuckers need to shut up."

Michael and Vinnie upped the volume, and the rest of us followed suit. A few songs later two officers came back and yelled that we should stop. When we did not, they threw buckets of cold water on us through the bars and laughed as they walked away. We sang one more song to show that we couldn't be cowed, but summers in San Francisco are famously cold and we began to shiver. Michael finally asked the young guy who he was and why the cops arrested him. He explained nervously that he had met a runaway girl from Des Moines on Haight Street and brought her to the house. He wasn't sure why she'd called her parents.

"So you're the reason the house got busted," growled Michael.

"Hey, I'm sorry. I'll call my dad. Maybe he can get us bailed out. He's got that kind of money." Just then an officer told us we were being transferred to the main jail at the Hall of Justice for booking. "They like music more there," he said with a smirk.

It was dark when we arrived, so I didn't see much of the structure, but our berth was a huge drunk tank, a large unfurnished room with concrete benches along the walls. As the barred door slammed behind us, I realized that there were already twenty or thirty men confined there. Some were passed out; most sat quiet and despondent; a few were mumbling sonorously to themselves. None took notice of us as we shuffled in. Soon two officers escorted me to fingerprinting. They may have a more digital way of recording fingerprints now, but in 1968 it was still roll the finger on the ink pad and then on the paper. An officer guided each finger to make sure there was a clear impression. As he released his grip on each of my fingers, I slid it slightly against the paper to smear the ink. It was a trick he'd seen before. "I want you to read this article, Fuzzhead, and then we're going to try it again." He pointed at a faded article, taped to the table.

"I can't read it. It's too dark," I said.

"It says," he pronounced coldly, "that I can take your fingerprints whether your arm is attached to your body or not. Now, do you want to try it again?" I let him take good prints, and, as I left, he said to the other officer, "Take that dirty, hairy one and throw him in solitary." A few minutes later two new officers emerged and looked around for the dirty, hairy one. Without pausing, they grabbed Michael Tierra, not me, and threw him in solitary.

The next morning, we were ushered into the courtroom of Judge Kennedy, an African American man who comported himself with great dignity. Our free lawyer was new at the business, but he liked the idea of working for the liberation of the storied Diggers. Perhaps he later became a great defense attorney, but he did not manage much that day at our arraignment. Within minutes we were back in our cells, charged with contributing to the delinquency of a minor. There is little to say about jail that has not been said, but I will note that the San Francisco jail, in those days on the upper floors of the Hall of Justice, could have used a heater. Our clothes, soaked the night before during the freedom songs concert, had never dried. The beds were hard steel plates suspended bunk-bed fashion from the walls. They were designed to hold mattresses, which were few and far between. And the steel plates were cold. My sole mission in life became to hustle a mattress and a blanket. I had managed both within two days when word came that the young man had talked his rich dad into making bail for all of us. We were ushered without ceremony across the street to the bail bondsman, a man named Barrish who had sprung Diggers in the past. A sign in his window read, "Don't Perish, Call Barrish."

It was wonderful to be free, but San Francisco suddenly seemed confining. The week before our arrest, I'd joined a group of Diggers on a trip to Los Angeles where they were raising money to purchase some land in the mountains. Real estate wasn't high in my priorities in those days, but Elsa Marley and some others had discovered a place at a real estate office in Siskiyou County. It was one of those places so remote that it'd been for sale for a while. My role on the "LA Run," as it came to be called, was to make introductions to rock stars and to pilot my Coors truck, the one that our band had used to haul equipment. It became branch office and bedroom for the fundraisers. When I got back to the Victorian, a car was leaving for northern California to look at the land, a place called Black Bear Ranch. Black Bear was beautiful, but the police in Siskiyou County had a welcoming routine for hippies in those days. I'll spin tale of that adventure soon enough, but, in brief, I spent two weeks in a jail in Yreka, a casualty of an early round of the culture wars that are still being waged in that county.

I wondered at the time why I was having such trouble with the police. I'd been a reporter on the biggest newspaper in Los Angeles, and several police stations were on my beat. My hair then was buzzed short, and my clothes were from Brooks Brothers. Officers had treated me with polite deference. Now that I had long hair and a scruffy beard, I was suddenly a cop magnet. It started to creep into my head that this is what young guys of color had always faced.

Yreka jail was a pain, of course, but the worst of it was that I missed a court appearance before Judge Kennedy. When I finally returned to San Francisco and its Hall of Justice, the Diggers had recruited a new, more effective lawyer named Mike Stepanian, the sharp cookie that I wished we'd had weeks earlier at the arraignment. Word was that this new lawyer could get us all off and was getting paid by the rich dad. A big crowd of familiar faces swirled in the hall. One of them was a Digger of great imagination named Arthur Lisch. Lisch had written a visionary proclamation for the event and wanted to read it to the judge, but the lawyer said it wasn't necessary, so we prevailed on Arthur to wait. He settled for posting it on a bulletin board outside the courtroom, and then, to prove that money would be valueless when everything was free, he taped dollar bills around it.

Judge Kennedy greeted Stepanian warmly if formally and invited him to approach the bench. They talked in voices I couldn't hear. Then the judge read the names of most of the defendants and declared that charges were dismissed against them. The only names omitted were Sally Blythe's and mine. Everyone crowded around Stepanian outside the courtroom to thank and congratulate him. But I finally pressed into the throng to ask why they'd forgotten to read my name. Stepanian smiled and said, "Kennedy will never dismiss a person who's missed a court date unless they serve a night in jail. Just surrender yourself tonight and he'll dismiss tomorrow. You and Sally Blythe both missed an appearance. Sorry. But I'll be here tomorrow."

"But I have an excuse. I was in jail in Yreka. I couldn't make it."

Stepanian broke into a wide grin, shrugged his broad shoulders in his tailored gray suit, and said, "See you in court tomorrow." He walked away down the hall, stopping only briefly to glance at Arthur Lisch's manifesto on the wall, taking no notice of its garland of dollar bills.

Back at the Victorian, Sally Blythe and I planned our surrender. No need to surrender any earlier than we had to. We'd get there a little before midnight. That would do the trick. We agreed to meet at 9 p.m. and travel together. I spent the day walking in Golden Gate Park, close to the Victorian, but when the afternoon fog came in, I remembered how cold the jail had been. I headed for one of the Haight Street thrift stores for warmer clothes for my return to corrections. The third store had a whole rack of overcoats, so I bought two, one extra large and the other simply huge, so I could wear them both. Neither was as stylish as the leather coat that Jacob had borrowed, but I was better prepared this time for the chilly Hall of Justice than I'd been before. I was satisfied that things would go well.

When I saw Sally in the evening, she was not as self-assured. She suggested that she wouldn't go and they might forget about her. When two of the other Victorian women talked her out of that plan, she began to cry. Then she took me to her room, closed the door behind us. and fished out a small parcel wrapped in twine. She unwrapped it carefully to reveal a hypodermic syringe, a spoon, and the other accessories that addicts called their "fit." She brought out a small cellophane pouch from her underwear and prepared the white powder inside it for an injection. I'd seen this before, but it always unsettled me. She panted in quick, shallow breaths briefly, and then her smile reappeared. Deliberately, she retied the parcel, secreted it under the bed, and told me, "I'm ready. Let's go."

The bus ride to the Hall of Justice was easy, and the building lobby was empty except for a janitor mopping the floor at the far end. With measured, deliberate steps, we boarded the elevator to the floor marked "Jail." This would be a cakewalk. Sally was still smiling, but her smile faded when we found the public entrance to the jail was locked. A sign said it reopened at 9 a.m. She raced to a public phone, but the jail did not answer. Every door on the floor was locked. We dropped down a floor, and it was also deserted. Around one corner, we finally found an open service window labeled "Records," and we rang the bell. A sleepy worker finally appeared, and we explained our plight. He said he couldn't help, but Sally began to cry again; maybe tears were welling in my eyes, too.

"We want to pay our debt to society. Can't you help us?" I said. It was a corny line, but it seemed to work, and he agreed to find our booking records. After a long search he said there was nothing in his office, but Kennedy's court staff might still have them. There was nothing he could do, and he shrugged his shoulders much as Stepanian had done, but without the expensive suit.

We descended to the cold steps outside the Hall of Justice, and I wrapped my two overcoats tighter to keep out the wind. There was little traffic on the street and only a few lights in any building. One of them was a dimly lighted office just across the street. In its window, a neon sign blinked a message in green and red: Don't Perish, Call Barrish. Like lost pilgrims, we crossed the street and entered the office. The secretary looked at us with little interest and motioned us to chairs while she finished a phone call. When we finally explained, she led us back into Barrish's office, and he shook his head and grinned as we unraveled our plight for the third time. Sally almost started to cry again but snuffled back the impulse. "I think I can help," Barrish said. "I have a key to the jail. Kind of goes with the business. Come with me."

We took the elevator again, to a new floor, entered a stairway behind a locked door, and in two flights were in the comforting dim lights of the Hall of Justice jail. The officers knew Barrish and accepted our surrender graciously. Briefly, they tried to take my overcoats, but I clung to them fiercely, so they gave up and led me to a new large cellblock. A trustee led me to my bunk, one with a mattress and a blanket. I slept in relative comfort.

In the morning, I was ushered downstairs to the holding cell just outside Kennedy's courtroom with four black men. Three of them flashed unfriendly glares, but the fourth asked me, "Hey, hippie dude, what's your name?" He nodded approvingly when I told him my name was Malcolm. "You know who Huey Newton is?" Half the graffiti in the Bay Area those days said FREE HUEY, a tribute to the broad reach of the campaign by the Black Panther Party to free their imprisoned leader. I nodded my head yes, trying to look tough, but probably coming across as too anxious to please.

Then he turned to the other three inmates and said, "I was in this cell yesterday, and Huey Newton was here for a court appearance. He was sitting right there where hippie dude is sitting right now. Course, Brother Huey wasn't wearing six overcoats. How come you got so many coats, man?" I started to answer that it was only two coats, but at that moment we were ushered out into the courtroom. We were all ordered to stand, and Judge Kennedy ascended to the bench. Our case was the first on the docket, and our lawyer was called forward.

"Good morning, Mr. Stepanian."

"Good morning, Judge."

"Case against Sally Blythe dismissed. Case against Malcolm Terence dismissed." And Kennedy passed our paperwork to a bailiff. We were free. The inmate who'd shared the Huey Newton story flashed me a covert Power-to-the-People clenched-fist salute, and I was escorted out. Afterward, we shook Stepanian's hand, but he had other cases to tend to, so soon we were left standing in the hallway.

Everywhere there were people. Some were plotting. Some were arguing. Some were crying. A few sat alone, with their hands cradling their heads. Justice had been done. I was angry, overjoyed, crying, and plotting myself, all at once. More than anything I wanted out. I thought of the lazy creek that ran through the commune just beginning at Black Bear Ranch. I looked again at the crowds in the hallway.

"C'mon," Sally urged.

I paused to pluck a few of the dollar bills off Arthur Lisch's manifesto and said, "Let's go get a cup of coffee." As I left, I dropped the overcoats on a chair.

CHAPTER 2

The Recipe for Chimichangas, or How I Saved the Commune

I promised more about the commune. First thing to understand: As a crowd of people intent on building a utopian community in the wilderness, we didn't bring much baggage. I mean physical baggage, like tools and working trucks. There was no shortage of what we call psychic baggage, and some fraction of it was useful. For instance, Michael Tierra, the same guy who was singing in that jail cell, had seemed crazy in LA, but he brought incredible music to the Black Bear commune. Myeba Mindlin and Susan Keese had both lived in the Willard Street Victorian awash in patchouli and tie-dye. They brought links to the San Francisco Diggers with all their Byzantine and poetic grace. Calvin Donley and the other black militants brought Chairman Mao. Most all of us brought great notions of freedom and fantasy. I personally never brought much, but I brought the recipe for chimichangas.

Some people look back and say those early commune years were about art or style, about politics or spiritual growth, but I was there the winters of '68, '69, and more. We all knew that Black Bear was about food. We would sit there in the wintry evenings fingering a copy of Julia Childs's first French cookbook, lusting over dishes that took ingredients we knew we would never see. "Divide ten eggs and set aside the whites," they'd all begin. "Add a gill of thick cream," we'd continue, reading to our companions, with the breathy hushed voices of people reading good pornography aloud.

I admit I was tricked. At first I thought the food was good, but maybe because I spent my first two weeks at Black Bear in that jail cell in Yreka, an overgrown truck stop in northern California. Even lentils tasted good for a while when I got out. That's a whole other story, but let me explain. I'd met Roselee Solow Patron at the Digger base camp in Dunsmuir. Still years ahead of the women's movement, Rose was tall, confident, and assertive—a regal woman. I was especially impressed that she had a huge warm flannel sleeping bag, big enough for two by contemporary standards.

Anyway, Roselee and I were hitchhiking up to Black Bear along what is now Interstate 5 when a young, well-scrubbed hippie couple picked us up in a new model van, the perfect ride. They were easy to talk into a side trip to Black Bear, where we'd never been yet. On the way, we stopped for gas in Etna. (In the soundtrack, ominous foreshadowing music should swell at this point.) While the kid was pumping gas, I went to explore an old Victorian house that was getting demolished next door to Corrigan's Bar. The place had been stripped but good. All that was left was an old kitchen sink tossed in the corner and some broken pipes. I remembered that John Albion had sent word that the Main House plumbing wasn't too good, so I asked the gas pump kid if I could do some salvage. "Why not?" he said. "Everyone else does."

We threw the sink in the truck and headed up to Black Bear, where only a few people were living so far. They were delighted to see us. "We brought groceries," we boasted.

"Did you bring any weed?"

We trudged up to the house with barely a hug when they heard we were herb-free, and Martín dredged out an old box of stems and seeds, to try one more time to winnow out enough green for a welcome-to-the-commune smoke. (Martín was originally called "Marty," as befit his New York roots, but he switched to "Martín," pronounced Spanish style as "Mar-Teen." It may have sounded more California cosmopolitan.) Just then one of the women said, "Jeez, here comes a cop car! How did they know?"

Martín told me to stall out front while he slipped out the back with the shoebox. I confidently walked out to distract these simple rural constables. "How are you fellows?" I said. Big smiles all around.

"Doing fine," they said in unison. These guys are really dumb, I thought to myself.

"Were you in Etna today?" one of them asked.

"Yeah?"

"Did you do anything while you were there?" he asked.

"What's there to do in Etna?" I said. They didn't get the joke. "No, I didn't do anything."

"Didn't you do anything?" he tried again. "You know, like take anything?"

"You mean the sink? You want it back?" These cops had to be the biggest hicks I'd ever met.

One of the hicks pulled a card out of his pocket and read in monotone, "I'd like to advise you of your right to counsel, your right to remain silent, and your right not to be questioned without an attorney."

Maybe they weren't the jerks I'd thought. While I was revising my opinion, my hands were behind my back in hick handcuffs, and I was being ushered into a hick squad car. I spent the night (and the next fourteen nights) in Yreka jail. "Whatchya in for?" asked the inmates, who'd never seen a hippie up close. "Possession of hair," I grumbled. My cellmates looked me over. I had by then grown a huge explosion of fiery red hair and a beard to match. They nodded in approval, maybe of my sarcasm, and maybe of the accuracy of the charges.

But this is the story of how I saved the commune with the recipe for chimichangas, and I'm getting lost in self-pity. I hardly heard from the ranch in lockup. One night the jailor we called Turkeyneck yelled back to us, "Hey, Terence. Your friend Michael called and said his girlfriend had a baby girl. He also said he can't make your bail." Everybody in the cellblock laughed for a while. That was the daughter who'd talked with me that night when she was still in her mother's womb. They named her Shasta Free. Welcome to this world, Shasta.

It was a lousy time to have long hair. I'd already been in jail twice that year on trumped-up this or that, and it wasn't even September. I was starting to compare the cuisine of the different jails. Yreka was way better than either San Francisco's Hall of Justice or LA. But two weeks of cornmeal mush and peanut-butter-and-jelly sandwiches on white bread took their toll. Every morning, just before I woke, I'd have a dream that I was in jail. They'd wake us by clicking on very bright lights. As I woke, I'd think it was all just a dream. Then I'd wake some more and be in jail. Suffice it to say that the days in jail flew by like years. The public defender couldn't remember my name. The trial got put off until the following spring.

I finally got released on O.R., shorthand for "Own Recognizance," which is itself courtroom lingo for "No Bail Required." After all that, I decided the ranch was the safest place to wait for my trial. Fresh air, Roselee's sleeping bag, and no more white bread. I thought I was in heaven. That was early September. By mid-October there were thirty of us living together out in the middle of nowhere, and some of the romance was disappearing. So was the food. One afternoon a handful of us came in for lunch, and it was brown rice served on white rice. And winter had barely started. This was a crisis. We decided to take the Coors truck, all I had left to show for that year in show business, and head out shopping in Eureka. (I know you want to hear more about the year in show business, but this is really a short instructional chapter on making chimichangas so it isn't the place. It is true, though, that story that I once danced with Tina Turner.)

"We," in this case anyway, were John Albion, Richard Marley, and me. We had the truck. We had the need. We didn't have any money. I kept asking John and Richard how we were gonna fill the truck with food or even the gas tank with fuel to get home when we didn't have a cent. I guess they couldn't hear me very well over the roar of the truck. We spent the night at the house of Mike Mullen, a longshoreman friend of Richard's. The next day we ran around meeting local bohemian artists who wanted all the stories about the new Black Bear adventure. And then that afternoon we met a man named Merlin. Merlin had done well in the chemistry business—psychedelic chemistry—and was impressed by our plans. He sized us up, to see if urban hippies could survive in the woods, and I think we passed the test when we crawled under the truck in the Humboldt County mud to readjust the baling wire that held up the muffler. He passed more than a $1,000 to Richard, a huge sum at that time, and asked if we were interested in a backhoe. I didn't know what one was and thought he said "some tobacco," so I couldn't understand why Richard and John got so excited.

We hit every food wholesaler in town, and two days later returned to the ranch with a full load of provisions. That was the first food run, a theatrical event that was eventually elevated to a fine art. This is important because the ingredients for chimichangas for a commune winter are the following:

> 4,000 lbs. Tule Lake wheat
> 1,000 lbs. pinto beans
> 55 gal. vegetable oil
> 300 lbs. onions
> 20 lbs. garlic
> 5 lbs. chili powder
> 1 lb. cheddar cheese (optional)

This also happened to be the contents of the larder.

Start by dividing the wheat. Feed half to the chickens. Grind the rest into flour.

But I'm getting ahead of myself. Not much happened at Black Bear for those first couple of years. It was not until 1970 or so that I remembered chimichangas. The food had gotten better than brown and white rice, but only a little. Sometimes Glenn Lyons and John Salter got a deer, but that would be gone in two days. Glenn and John were both university academics who came to the commune as researchers and, like researchers the world over, had "gone native," as they say. Willis Conrad, one of our first friends on the river, was one of the traditional

Karuk fishermen, and he'd sometimes bring up sacks of fresh-caught salmon. But mostly it was beans and rice. For variety, some nights the beans would be undercooked. We tried cooking things by substitution. Maybe cornstarch would substitute for eggs? So Zoë Leader tried baking brownies with a recipe from the nutritionist Adelle Davis, but without eggs, an ingredient we only dreamed of. They came out of the oven smoking, black, with a texture like roofing material. Zoë had just used up the last chocolate and took off for the woods in disgust. Redwood Kardon came by and tried one. "Not bad. Tastes like really good burnt chocolate." Efrem Korngold tried some too and nodded with approval. Not bad at all. Word spread. By the time Zoë returned, the burned pan was licked clean.

So it was, anyway, our day to cook. Doug Hamilton. Mark Gabriel. Me. We reviewed our choices. White beans and brown rice. Brown beans and white rice. We were artists in our souls, but without much palette. Then I remembered chimichangas. They were in those days found only in Sonora and in southern Arizona where I'd grown up. Nowadays you find them in the frozen grease section of every 7-Eleven in the world. Right next to the microwave. They were just deep-fried burritos, really, but in those days they were a well-kept secret.

So we hauled twenty pounds of wheat up to the Corona Mill hand-grinder in the attic, and Doug started grinding. Mark started a long, painstaking round of guitar tuning. I started telling a story about when Linda Ronstadt was my houseguest. After about a pound of wheat, Doug rebelled. "Howkum you azzholes are just standing around, and I'm getting stuck with all the work?" So I started trading off with him and also held the small table steady, which made it go faster. In guilt, Mark started actually playing guitar and also took turns at the mill.

At that point, Gail Ericson came through, looking for her daughter, Shasta. She gave us an uncharitable look and asked how many grown men it took to grind wheat. We all tried to look as busy as possible. Gail could be awfully ungenerous in those days. I remembered months earlier, when there was some wine and everybody was in a frisky mood, I came over to Gail and quietly asked if she wanted to slip off and make love.

Commune Main House Garden. The building was once the home of John Daggett, the owner of Black Bear Mine who became California's lieutenant governor in 1883. The commune had a large garden and a large goat herd, conflicting land uses that required a good fence. Creek Hanauer designed it, split the pickets from a huge fallen incense cedar, and helped build it. Photo by Jeff Buchin.

"Oh, you mean fuck?" she said in a voice that carried across the room, and she walked away laughing. People turned to me with smirks and then turned away.

When the flour was done, we fired the great US army stove, started the beans, and started making flour tortillas for sixty hungry communards. The beans were already soaked, and we started early. I hated them undercooked. Cover them barely with water. Add onions, garlic, and chili powder. Are you writing this down? When the skins of the beans wrinkle, pour in some oil. Never add salt until they're done. Don't add too much water, and don't cover the pot. As the stack of tortillas grew, a sense of excitement spread through the Main House and then across the ranch. Something new for dinner. We began rolling the beans into the tortillas and dipping them into the hot oil, where they sizzled the same way I remembered at the little place across from the Greyhound station in Tucson. Carol Hamilton and Geba Greenberg began helping us.

Tom Drury (left) and I pause in a cooking job we had in San Francisco. Tom was the best of the cooks at the commune, so I knew I had a winner when he praised my chimichangas. Photo from archive kept by Jeff Buchin.

Michael Tierra slipped away to get elderberry wine that he'd already aged for a week. Then he started playing music with Kenoli Oleari and John Cedar, who were visiting from the Free Bakery collective in Oakland.

Some nights there just wasn't enough food cooked. On nights like that, the big eaters like Redwood or Martín would sit near the children in case one of them fell asleep with their food unfinished. Every one of us would have starved before we shorted the food to a child. But it's also a sin to waste food, and they wanted to be first in line to head off any sinful moment. Everybody in those days was so thin it was a little scary. We're much less scary now.

It was a culinary triumph. We'd cooked way too much, and every morsel was eaten. Some were a little burned, most were perfect, and not one was undercooked.

They made a crunchy, resistant noise as you bit them: hot and dry on the outside, spicy and juicy in the center. "These chingyjamas are great," Elsa Marley said, and she gave me an affectionate kiss. More music. More wine. Tommy Drury, best of the Black Bear cooks, praised my invention. Praise from Tom was praise indeed. Smokers slipped outside to light up and tell much better stories than the nonsmokers ever told. I watched Catherine Thompson Guerra whisper something to Danny Guyer, and they slipped away. Another couple left, arm in arm. Buoyed by my new celebrity, I edged over next to Rhoda Bagno, a beautiful friend of Elsa Marley's, and in my most suave voice asked her if she wanted to fuck. She turned and stared at me. "I don't fuck. I make love," she said, and so there could be no doubt, she turned and walked away.

CHAPTER 3

Escaping Utopia

Redwood and I got cabin fever bad by January of '69. Black Bear was buried in snow, at least three feet deep, and had been that way for many weeks. The mountain pass into the ranch was blanketed with six feet of stupid snow. The county road crew had their hands full managing the main Salmon River Road. We were forgotten. Cabin fever, they say, comes in waves like malaria. In its throes, the commune seemed crowded and chaotic. We needed a cure, the get-out-of-here-for-anywhere-else cure.

"Let's go down to the city," Redwood said to me one evening in the teeming commune Main House.

"Right," I said. "I suggest we fly."

"Roselee has a couple pairs of snowshoes. It'd be easy. We walk to Saw-yers. It's only eight miles. Then hitch to San Francisco," said Redwood. He was from Los Angeles, a graduate of a high school where classes were always half empty on days when the surf was good.

"A great idea. I'll hit up Rose for the snowshoes," I said. I was also from Los Angeles, and Tucson before that. Before that winter, I'd rarely seen snow. Now I was snowed in with a crowd of underfed hippies. When the snows first started, a few people had made Donner Party jokes, references to the pioneers in the winter of 1846–47 who were snowbound in the Sierra Nevada and reverted to cannibalism. After a few weeks, there were no more such jokes.

Two mornings later, just before light, we departed with food and peo-ple's letters in our packs to the cheers of our comrades. It was just three miles uphill, five down, and you were on the road in Sawyers Bar. The uphill went well except that along the way we crossed a stream that wet our snowshoes. After that, they started to cake with snow so we had to kick the ice off every few steps. Finally, we tired of the kicking and just hoisted ten pounds of packed snow with every step. Redwood told me a story about surfing in Santa Monica. Then he told another. Finally, we made the summit and our time seemed good. The sun broke through the overcast. We sat on our snowshoes during lunch and dangled our feet into the snow that was probably deeper than we were tall.

Then we launched what we expected to be the short final leg of the trip. "All downhill from here. Let's hitch all afternoon, and we can be in Frisco by morning," I said. King Oedipus had hubris, that fatal pride the Greeks cherished so much in their drama. I was just ignorant. In LA, we didn't have snow. We didn't even have miles except as numbers on the signs on the freeway.

In a half hour the warming snow began to cake even heavier. The front binding weakened on Redwood's left snowshoe and finally snapped. He began an ungainly kick step to compensate. "Let's kill a seal so I can cut a new binding," he joked, but I could tell he was in pain. Redwood was a big man. He'd played football at Los Angeles High the year they won league. Every half hour he would stop to massage away the cramps that exploded in his left leg. Then every fifteen minutes. "Downhill's not as easy as I hoped," he said, and then he stopped cracking jokes altogether. More than once, Redwood fell and managed to get up with much effort. The third time he disappeared entirely into the deep snow. "Go on. Save yourself," he urged. I dragged him up, and he continued in great pain.

Two miles out of Sawyers it began to snow again. It was slow at first but soon thickened. A breeze came up and blew the flakes around in a way that would have seemed pretty in most other settings. It never became a wind, just little gusts. One mile out it started to grow dark. Days don't last long in January. The last half-light was almost gone when we stumbled across the North Fork bridge into Sawyers. We were coated with snow. Our long hair and beards, which the unfriendly Sawyers Bar folk had found so threatening in the fall when we'd first arrived, were now laced with ice and twigs from overhanging snow-loaded branches. A car approached and caught us in its headlights. It raced by. "That fucker drove right by," I protested.

"Maybe he didn't see us," Redwood said. "Two snow-covered freaks standing in a snowstorm. Hard to see." Then he winced again and began rubbing his left thigh urgently. The next car came, and we waved again. The driver gunned his engine to get by, and his car fishtailed past us in the snow. The tire chains slapped and clanked off in the growing darkness. Redwood didn't speculate whether this driver had seen us. I grumbled curses. We hurried to the small general store, which would close soon.

Outside the store, Brian Bundy was pumping gas into a huge military truck that he'd converted into a utility truck for his goldmining. The store lights were already off, and Brian's headlights barely penetrated the thickening snow. "Hey Brian," Redwood yelled. Brian pretended not to hear.

When we got next to him, I said it again. Brian had visited the previous fall when we hippies had first come into the country, and he and Richard Marley soon were trading stories of their years in the Merchant Marine. Later he came back and traded us a grass rake we had, the kind one pulled behind a tractor, for a Pelton wheel. We really needed a Pelton wheel because it was the turbine one used in those parts to make electricity with water power. At the time, though, it seemed unimaginably high tech, as though a Martian had handed me a computer chip and said it was an essential element of a time travel device. I suspect that this crowd of hippies stirred Brian's imagination, and he cooked up the trade as a social ploy. "Whattcha doing?" he said out of the corner of his mouth, barely turning to face us.

This evening in the gloom and what would soon be a blizzard, on the icy road where all his nosy and disapproving neighbors lived, he was less social than he had been last fall. "Whaddya mean? 'What are we doing?'" I blurted. "We're freezing to death. Give us a hand. We need a place to stay."

"It is a pretty bad day," he conceded, again out of the side of his mouth in little more than a breathy whisper. He still had not turned to look at us, as though pumping diesel fuel took all a man's attention.

"Jeez, Brian," I pleaded. "Redwood's leg's fucked up from the walk. It's a blinding fucking snowstorm. You've been to our place. If we don't get a place to stay, we'll fucking freeze to death before morning." My hysteria froze on my cheeks as it dribbled out of the corners of my eyes. "We'll freeze before the ten o'clock news," I thought to myself.

Brian pondered our plight and then, still not looking away from the gas hose, in a nasal voice we could barely hear, whispered, "My house is on the right, quarter mile downriver, just past the Forest Service station. Don't let people see you come." With that, he jumped in the truck, sparked it into noisy life and rumbled away.

Redwood gave me a pained thumbs-up as Brian and his massive truck were swallowed by the gloom and we stumbled down the road to his place. We nervously climbed the icy stone steps to the front door that we hoped was to the Bundy cabin. Redwood knocked loud on the door. Nothing happened. He knocked again, much louder. The door opened a crack, and Brian peered out, checking in both directions to see if neighbors saw him. No neighbor, no matter how nosy, would be out on a night like this, I thought. This town is really uptight about hippies to have Brian so paranoid about being seen with us. He motioned us in with choppy hurry-up gestures and shoved the door closed behind us. Then, before we could get off our snow-drenched coats, Brian changed.

"Let me help you with those coats," he said. "Come belly up by the stove. It's starting to get cold out there. Are you hungry? Betty! Get these guys some grub. You wanna drink? Of course, you want a drink. Don't worry about the mud. Just sit right here." He poured us each a tumbler of whiskey and poured one for himself, which he emptied. At the door to the next room, two or three young children stole peeks at us, but an adult hand tugged them back to safety. Probably the invisible Betty.

Slowly the warmth from the roaring wood stove crept into my body. I looked around the room and realized it had the style of very old buildings. Wallpaper covered some walls but others were made of barely planed rough-cut planks with newspaper or fabric neatly pressed into the chinks. Everything had a glossy patina from generations of woodsmoke. Brian stuffed another log into the stove even though it was nearly full and grinned at our ecstasy. Old woodsmoke was suddenly the best color in the whole world.

"I guess Betty is busy with the kids," he apologized for his wife's disappearance. "I'll cook something. You guys like eggs?" Redwood and I nodded in slack-jawed bewilderment, still marveling that our life had been saved by this crazed gold miner, this reluctant saint. He disappeared into the kitchen and soon smells of bacon and coffee started to fill the room.

He returned in twenty minutes with platters heaped with the promised "grub." He refilled Redwood's glass with whiskey and his own, then frowned at mine, which was not quite empty. "You don't drink?" he said, perplexed and maybe wondering if he'd saved the wrong kind of person from the snowstorm. I hastily downed the glass and the one after it and maybe more. We ate the food, and he promised more until we told him we were stuffed. I started to fade into a reverie. I remember a little of his stories—how to start a fire in a snowstorm with Ponderosa pinecones, why the inside bend of a river collects more placer gold than the opposite bank, how a whore in Manila stole his shipmate's false teeth. I remember that Betty finally joined us, although she never released her grip on the children and they made little effort to move away from her. But they stared. As our long hair and beards dried and fluffed out, Redwood and I must have looked to them like some kind of dirty roadkill, risen from the dead and brought home by Pop. Betty said she was born in the cabin. I remember that it was first built in the 1850s and that it had survived the three fires that ravaged Sawyers Bar over the years.

I do not remember much else except that we must have drifted off to sleep. We must have lived.

CHAPTER 4

White Bear

The young black men from Oakland who spent one of those winters at the commune came with big affable smiles and polished rifles. I rarely saw them with the rifles that winter, but they made great use of the smiles. They were young, too young to have as many years spent in school as I had when I met them, so it always impressed me that they knew so much more than I knew about so many topics, like history and politics and class war.

And they shared concrete knowledge such as how to shoot a rifle and how to please a woman. (Their secret formula for women was to treat them with respect.) They explained what Mao Tse-tung meant to the Chinese people and what black heroes like Huey Newton and Angela Davis, one then imprisoned and the other a fugitive, meant to them.

The commune was a long way from anywhere else even when the roads weren't buried in snow. Those roads into Black Bear were built for log trucks and bulldozers; they were hard on ordinary cars. Bad roads or no roads, no telephone and long before the internet, the commune was profoundly geographically isolated. But, despite this, it was not politically insular.

The country was in a huge convulsion, political and social, in those years when we started the Black Bear commune. The civil rights movement had already filled our headlines and our minds for much of the 1960s. America was still emerging from decades of rabid anticommunism, a campaign that was employed to attack progressives and labor unions. In the 1964 presidential campaign, Lyndon Johnson said a vote for his opponent was a vote for a land war in Asia. Johnson won by a landslide, but by 1968, our military was waist deep in the Vietnam War, an adventure that gave new, muddy weight to the word "quagmire." Robert Kennedy, the leading antiwar candidate for president, had just been murdered by a gunman in Los Angeles, and another assassin in Memphis had killed Martin Luther King Jr.

The young black men who wintered at the commune—Ken Rogers and Calvin Donley—were gifted organizers, and we were willing students. They were, in effect, delegates from a group called Oakland Direct Action Committee. ODAC founder Mark Comfort was a veteran of organizing in the South and an early mentor to the Black Panther Party in Oakland. He had brought Kenny and Calvin up to the commune to spend the winter and headed back to his work in the Bay Area.

It's important to note that we didn't just have Maoist study groups with the black militants. They immersed themselves in all the parts of life in a thriving hippie commune, from cooking to woodcutting to child care. There were also more personal interactions. For instance, the night I came home unexpectedly after dark from a hay run to Etna, I tiptoed into the little cabin I shared in those days with Roselee. She was, besides the woman with the world's biggest sleeping bag, also my unindicted co-conspirator in the sink robbery. Turned out Roselee had invited Mark Comfort into the sleeping loft for the night. He was a charmer and a sweetheart, and I wasn't expected home for another day. Mark had faced sheriff deputies and Ku Klux Klansmen when he was organizing in the South and their brutal equivalent among police in Oakland, but the situation right then in a sleeping loft when I, the hippie boyfriend, showed up clearly unsettled him. He nervously greeted me with one of those complex insider handshakes that were then the style. He talked faster and more jovially than usual and offered to grab his clothes and leave. I said that he shouldn't worry; hippie women weren't their partner's property at Black Bear. Roselee, sensing the harmony and always the hostess, readjusted the bedding and curled up between us. I never did learn those fancy handshakes.

There were other activists. Anarchists came to Black Bear from the Lower East Side of New York and from Haight-Ashbury. There were war resisters, draft dodgers, and organizers from Students for a Democratic Society. SDS had started in the early 1960s and spread to college campuses across the country with a message of what they called "participatory democracy." They challenged the status quo on local campuses and also in national policy. Harriet Beinfield, one of the SDS people at Black Bear, had friends who had spun off an underground splinter group called the Weathermen. Have you heard of the Weathermen? They named themselves after the lyrics of a Bob Dylan song. Dylan's words didn't always make sense. Despite their poetic title, however, we always felt these people in the underground represented us better than our elected officials. These Weathermen always had too much sense to come to Black Bear, which was in the crosshairs of government scrutiny. Every spring, as soon as the roads into the commune were clear of snow, we'd get a visit from FBI agents looking for them. We'd play dumb and ask the agents what the Weathermen were. "They're antiwar activists who've gone beyond dialogue," was the FBI answer. Here was this guy, this FBI agent, who worked for the same government that was carpet-bombing farmers in Southeast Asia, and that was okay. And this other bunch of people in the underground would now and then figure out how to plant a bomb at a draft board induction center, after hours, when no one was there. That was beyond dialogue.

Even if many of us at the commune didn't come from black militancy or underground collectives, we were also not especially embraced by the river locals, with a few exceptions. In some cases, we were shunned; in most cases, simply ignored. In the rare worst cases we were harassed. In my first few minutes at Black Bear, remember, the deputies had busted me for "stealing" junk plumbing out of that demolished building. I've forgiven them for that because, if I hadn't needed to wait around that first winter for my springtime court date, I might have drifted away from the commune and never tasted Salmon River life. (The only part I haven't forgiven was that insulting probation report. The probation officer wrote, "Terence has grand political delusions, but he seems harmless.")

But the harassment got worse, and the whole of Black Bear was the target. Just the year before, one of the many summer visitors asked us if we'd sell him marijuana. We didn't really have any, so he next said he had some and offered to share it. By then, everybody was convinced that he was either a narcotics officer or some hapless guy who'd gotten arrested for pot himself and was trying to get a lesser charge. He didn't stay long, but two weeks later, at first light, the police showed up with search warrants, many patrol cars, and even a few Child Protection officers, so-called, to take custody of the children.

I confess that I wasn't there when this happened, but I was almost there. The day before, I was hitchhiking back to Black Bear with a Digger woman named Ivory Waterworth from visits in San Francisco and Mendocino. Our last ride of the evening was in Sam George's huge log truck. Everybody revered him and called him Salmon River Sam. Sam was one of the sons of the equally legendary Kate George, who had already befriended us at the commune and who years later became my mentor and landlady. But Sam didn't exactly drop us off at the commune. That would have meant traveling a long, winding dirt road through the mountains, and we were down on the river road. Instead he dropped us off at twilight at the end of the trail where Black Bear Creek pours into the river. It left us with a two-and-a-half hour walk up the trail, and it was already getting dark. We headed up in the dwindling light and even continued a mile or two with nothing but starlight. Finally, it grew so dark that we needed to stop at a wide spot on the trail and sleep for the night without tent or bedrolls. We woke at very first glimmer of morning light, not hard when the bed is a rocky, chilly trail, and resumed the walk into the ranch. In about an hour, we arrived and, to my surprise, found most of the population of the ranch standing out in front of the Main House. That's what we called the house of John Daggett, the man who had owned Black Bear nearly a century earlier when it was a productive gold mine. This was unusual; hippies of that era were mostly late sleepers. Several raced over to tell us that the police had just left. They had hauled off John Glazer and his partner, Susie, plus an unlucky newcomer named Jeff Buchin. There was more, and the early risers were happy to recite it all. Glazer and Susie were the last people who still lived regularly in the Main House that summer. When the police stormed up the front steps, Glazer panicked and threw his small private stash of marijuana out the window. It landed at the feet of the police. He had broken one of the commune's few ironclad rules: no contraband overnight at the Main House. It got worse; he had poached a deer the night before and had hung the carcass in the pantry. That violated Rule #2. We always sensed that police raids were a possibility. Our lives in San Francisco's Haight-Ashbury and the stories from the black militants in Oakland and from the anarchists in New York's Lower East Side had taught us that. The only thing that seemed to draw cops as much as a late-night dough-nut shop was an easy target. Dissenters were an easy target.

Jeff Buchin was actually innocent. He had just shown up after dark, parked his van, and thrown out a sleeping bag on the Main House floor. So all three of them were arrested. To seal it with a kiss, the deputies grabbed several small marijuana plants in the nearby garden. A picture of the sheriff appeared in the Yreka paper with the confiscated plants. Only problem was that actually they had grabbed all our tomato plants. There were no pot plants. Well, another problem was that three people were in jail, but they were eventually released. A state lab sent back word that they couldn't positively identify the plants as pot, which probably means that some forensic botanists in Sacramento had a good laugh in private at the expense of the sheriff. Dunno what happened regarding the deer carcass.

The day after the deputies' visit, some visitors from Berkeley came by to take a look at Black Bear, by then a well-known destination. They were friends of Glenn Lyons from before he left Berkeley. Glenn's visi-tors told us that people in Etna had warned them that vigilantes were going to come and finish the job the deputies had started. Then the vis-itors jumped in their car and sped away. The black militants from Oak-land would have known what to do, but they were gone by then, so we were left to our own devices. We did have some rifles of our own, so we devised a plan to guard the commune entrance night and day. There was a gate across a narrow bridge, and we closed it. Then we found protected positions scattered up the hill where people with rifles could back up the gatekeeper. We waited there the rest of the day and into the evening. Some people left to eat or sleep, but others of us took their positions. This displayed unusual discipline considering our usual do-your-own-thing communard lifestyle. Finally, a little after midnight, a car pulled up. It stopped at the closed gate, and Martín walked into the headlights with a loaded pistol to confront the invaders. He was characteristically fearless. On reflection, this was probably a flawed plan, but just then Richard Marley, who most people thought of as the founder of Black Bear Commune, jumped out of the car. "Whatcha doing?" he yelled in his usual New York inflection, half indignant to be stopped and half delighted to find people awake so late.

Martín yelled up the hill that it was Richard, and the other passengers got out of the car. We quickly realized that Richard had caught a ride with two well-known Hells Angels from the San Francisco chapter. They were from the best-known motorcycle gang in the country in those days and showed up only infrequently at Black Bear. They looked around and nodded approvingly as we came down into the headlights from behind stumps and boulders where we'd been concealed, each carrying a rifle. We all mingled there in the headlights, hugging Richard, getting introduced to the bikers, most of us privately relieved that there had been no vigilantes. Probably, this was not the kind of reception expected by the Angels, who viewed hippies as amusing but harmless. One of them turned to Richard and quietly asked if the gate was always guarded thus. Richard only shrugged noncommittally.

That era of so much political foment in so many directions was also when the United States passed the National Environmental Protection Act, now routinely called NEPA. That law, more than any of the rest of the national environmental momentum, would profoundly affect the wild mountains around the commune, although we did not know it at the time. Much of the American public had grown weary of government projects like the construction of the interstate freeway system that had many adverse outcomes to the communities it plowed through. The new law insisted that an agency had to have scientists study the likely outcomes of a big project before work started and, besides that, had to seek public input. At the time we did not know what that meant, and, I suspect, neither did the agencies. When we first arrived in the mountains around the Salmon River from more urban areas, the landscape had looked pristine, but gradually we realized that some days the main traffic on the river roads was log trucks and long low-boy trailers that hauled massive bulldozers. Between them came a stream of the pale green trucks of US Forest Service employees and four-door crew-cab trucks full of loggers.

We first heard that the Forest Service was going to do clear-cut logging just above our commune in the early spring of 1970, just a few months after the NEPA law went into effect. The name "clear-cut" has a kind of sanitary ring to it. In flatter land, logging had its own set of problems, but trees could be removed, essentially one by one, by equipment like bulldozers and huge rubber-tired skidders. In the steep mountains of northern California, expensive cable systems had just been developed that made this select logging, as the previous flatland approach was called, less commercially competitive. The best profits came from punching a road around the top of a steep mountain side and carving a wide flat spot called a landing. Next came setting up towers for the cable system and then falling every tree below the tower so the giant cables could be moved easily. Select logging, as the name suggests, left at least a fraction of the trees in each unit. Clear-cuts took them all. Once each road was built, one block after another became available until the landscape was transformed into a vast checkerboard of destruction. It was also the base of the local economy.

The word of our own clear-cut came, ironically, while we were working a reforestation project downriver on the tribal reservation in Hoopa. We started the tree planting with the highest of ambitions. I armed myself with Chinese reforestation statistics, told our city friends we were off to restore the planet, and left for Hoopa. Our one misgiving was that we might be stealing jobs from the local Native population. Few Native Americans, though, we found when we got there, would touch the work. The usual crew was recruited among winos off the streets of Eureka on the coast. When we got to the rain-swept site, our apprehensions swelled. It was a sea of mud, smashed trees, and tractor tracks. "Where do we start?" we asked bravely.

But none of our bright preconceptions could survive the three weeks we spent in that wreckage. We'd plant a slope in the morning, and by afternoon it would have slipped, trees and all, toward the muddy creek. The next day it might be gone. It recalled a John Wayne/Susan Hayward movie from the Word War II era of my youth called *The Fighting Seabees*. I remember the bulldozers, broken palm trees, and bomb craters from the film.

But we didn't have any Japanese fighter planes—just professional foresters from the Bureau of Indian Affairs, which was the federal agency in the Department of Interior that, in those days, looked after tribal people on the theory that they couldn't look after themselves. The foresters came every day the weather wasn't too bad to inspect our planting and said they were impressed because we were more painstaking than the winos.

We had long conversations with these BIA foresters about logging, and they would answer our questions and arguments with a mixture of promises of unverifiable technology and boasts of smug Americana. After a while one of us coined the name Tree Pigs, and the name stuck. We'd ask them what percentage of the replanted trees they expected to survive, and they'd say with great authority, "Somewhere between 10 and 90 percent." It was no surprise then that somewhere among the forty-five thousand trees we planted or ditched that spring, our hopes fell and then totally collapsed. Tree planting, we decided, was a total sham and cover-up for the logging corporations, and we were the pawns. Socialist reconstruction it was not. Nor planetary redemption.

Eventually, years later, the Hoopa Tribe took over its own forest operations from the BIA, in a series of stages beginning in the late 1980s. At first the tribe ran basically the same program with different colored jerseys, in the words of Nolan Colegrove, who once headed the program run by the Hoopa Tribe. By the mid-1990s, Nolan explained, the tribe had its own forest plan, and it was crafted to protect resources like sacred places and other values the tribe held dear. Nowadays, they still harvest trees, but at the same time they work to protect plants and animals. They also are reintroducing the use of prescribed fire in the forest as their ancestors had done forever, more or less, until they were forcibly stopped by whites a century ago.

That year, 1970, word of the logging near Black Bear came. We'd always thought of the Forest Service as a protector of the public trust, the people who fed the bear that put out the fires, the nature-protecting branch of the Department of Agriculture, but that same US Forest Service was going to offer a stand of virgin Douglas fir near the commune to the highest bidder. The location of the timber sale was a place called White Bear Mine, a cluster of quickly built cabins on a barely passable road spur not far from us. Story was that the mine had been developed more to lure unwary investors than to find any gold. We were not versed in the mechanics of and possible damages from the proposed logging; we were, in those days, big fans of Nature, spelled with a capital N. That's the same first letter in the word Naïve. But even with aesthetics set aside, we knew the prospective cut lay less than a half mile above the ranch and right on top of the purest of the four streams that converged on our property. Even though our commune was only eighty privately owned acres in the middle of the vast Klamath National Forest, we had entertained a fantasy that we were the owners and protectors of most of the area surrounding us.

The logging site was in a beautiful and healthy watershed, and we made heavy use of it. We hunted and fished and collected herbs and wild greens. Each different kind of tree had its special uses, and the variety seemed endless to our city-dulled eyes: Douglas fir, cedar, sugar pine, ponderosa pine, black oak, live oak, tanoak, chinquapin, madrone, manzanita, white fir, alder, and maple. The oaks, for instance, provided my favorite firewood, and their acorns could be cooked in ways that local Natives still used, plus ways that we were inventing. (In our isolation many hours from the nearest bag of pecans, Black Bear bakers invented Acorn Pie. It was not bad, but it will not put pecan growers out of business.) The forest soil and the vegetative duff that covered it on the steep wooded slopes were as important as the trees and the other vegetation. With the forest cover gone, the deep, succulent topsoil was likely to come running down our streams as sheets of mud during the torrential winter rain and snow. We had learned that the hard way when we planted those trees in Hoopa.

We sent a delegate down to San Francisco to get a heavyweight attorney to stop the cut, but this was before the time when many law firms would take such cases pro bono, and we were broke. So for a year we looked the other way in hopes it would go away. Those were the days when we read signs of disintegration and decay all around us, and many of us believed that if we just stayed stoned long enough the American Empire would collapse at our feet.

It didn't.

Thus began spring of 1971. By the time we faced up to reality, Cal-Pacific Lumber had bought the contract for the trees at premium prices, and cutting could start almost immediately. Cal-Pacific owned the sawmill in Hoopa. A couple of the commune regulars stopped to get details at the Forest Service headquarters, then in Sawyers Bar, one afternoon just after the roads were cleared of snow. They brought home a horror story of what would soon befall the watershed, and we all railed with anger at the listings of this many acres, that many million board feet, and countless miles of so-called road improvements.

Around that time, we were visited by a bunch of hippies from Briceland, a town in south Humboldt County. They'd been burned out by vigilantes. Within a day of the fire, small truckloads of their refugees began showing up at the commune, driving only at night, with haircuts, new names, and a new radical bravado born of oppression. They were going underground, they said, like the Weathermen, and now was the time to kick out the jams. They were going to blow up the Los Angeles Aqueduct, but if we needed help shooting any deputies or loggers they'd be glad to help.

"What have you done so far?" we asked. And one hot-blooded hippie said he'd set fire to the matches section of every Safeway he'd passed on the road to the ranch. The empire must have quaked.

In the forge of this excitement we entered our brief militant phase to preserve the environment. Organic vegetables were set aside for ballistics.

"Would we stand aside for the machinations of pig-Amerika? Would you die to protect the trees?"

"Fuck, no," and "Fuck, yes."

Rifle practice went on daily. We examined one another for deviations from the vengeful norm. We studied books like *Crazy Horse* and *Cheyenne Autumn*, which told the stories of small bands of Natives who held the US Army at bay with their backwoods wiles. We purged soft-hearted liberal sentiments from one another.

One woman allowed as how she didn't like guns very much and would rather not shoot anyone if she didn't have to. So some of us yelled at her and reasoned with her and ostracized her until, a few days later, she came before the group and agreed, in tears, that she would shoot a gun when her turn came. Our young black militant mentors had long since returned to Oakland, so I cannot say if they would have approved, but I doubt it. There is a phenomenon that happens in insular groups in which people are talking only to themselves and as a group can magnify schemes that they would ordinarily discount as an individual. Sociologists call it an echo chamber. There was certainly a lot of echo distortion happening here. Happily, it never got any kind of momentum.

Most of the commune women were as committed to resisting the logging as the men, but more practical and not clouded by macho posturing. Dr. John Salter, the anthropologist who lived on and off at the commune, had spent his life recording Native elders and representing underdogs. He somehow sat in at a women's meeting at the ranch that spring, a well-educated fly on the wall, and took notes of the discussion.

In his notes, one of the women says, "There's an awful lot of loose talk about violence, but I think that's mainly because it all seems far off, months from now, and it's easier to talk violence than it is to do something concrete like going to the city to find free lawyers to get the logging put off or stopped."

Another woman says, "I want to know if I can depend on anybody I live with for my survival and the survival of my children and family. I want to know if it's possible to count on each other for that because I'm not into any suicidal number. If we have to use guns to keep the ranch from being destroyed by clear-cutting, I want to be sure we win."

A third woman offers, "If we have to stop them, I'd take off my clothes and lay down in front of the machines." That may have sounded dumb, but some of us were trying to imagine that we might shoot somebody, so who was dumb?

Another woman, probably the most practical voice at the commune and a mother of two, says, "If these things happen, I want to make certain that our children are where they won't be able to get at them. You know that is one of the first ways they would use to try to get us in line. If trouble starts, we should be ready to move right away."

She had not forgotten, none of us had, that when the deputies came on what we had come to call "The Tomato Plant Bust" they had among them officers from Child Protective Services in Yreka so they could cart away the children. In the end they only took three unlucky adults and that sack of tomato plants.

One morning, I remember, we shouldered our ramshackle rifles and hiked up the mountain to study the terrain and hunt for herbs. As we walked, we talked, broke shelf fungus off the trees, and kicked appreciatively at the deep, rich leaf mold. Many of the trees approached two hundred feet in height and six feet across at the base.

But I was starting to go through changes. I already doubted whether we would risk death to save a tree, regardless of its majesty. Also, how could you shoot some poor logger who's only working for a rich guy who isn't not even there? That's what wars were about. When we reached the top of the stand marked for the impending clear-cut, Peter Berg, the theorist of our band, gathered us together. Berg was the dazzling orator of the San Francisco Diggers who'd wintered with us, and he tried to egg on our rage. He told a story of Mexican peasants who, when the outrages of taxation or corrupt law became too oppressive, would march to the capitol to protest.

"Right on," we cheered, half-hearted.

"When they got to the capitol, they were all killed by the *federales*," Berg continued, "but they had made a passionate stand." Our doubts swelled, and we traded nervous glances. Thus passed our militant phase, like the morning fog when the sun burns through. Many people in that era were espousing nonviolence because of its morality. I think we embraced it because we didn't know anything else that would work.

It was many months later that we had to come to terms with the actual logging. These months did not pass, of course, in absolute isolation. We carried on an endless frustrating dialogue with the employees of the Forest Service. They had an answer for everything. The trees, they said, had grown past their prime and had entered something called "negative growth rate" where profits declined as the old-growth giants toppled. But the fallen snags decay into topsoil, we said, and clear-cutting could only cause gross erosion in a steep area. They'd dip into bottomless latrines of self-justifying statistics to show that the world would be a sorry place without clear-cut logging.

Against their sliding scales and double talk there was little we could say. In our moments of anger we'd call the Forest Service employees pimps and liars, but they'd just shuffle around and say they were caught in the middle, that the loggers thought they were too ardent in their protection of the woods. If we confronted them with a logging cut that was an obvious disaster, like the earlier clear-cut on our road that had collapsed in a giant landslide, they'd shake their heads in a hollow show of remorse and allow as how they had made some mistakes in the past, but with the new technology . . .

No matter what explanations they assembled or how soothing their assurances, we could not shed the awareness that the lush mountains around us were getting scarred with the angry craters of clear-cut blocks and that each winter the creeks seemed muddier than the year before.

When we finally found a team of San Francisco lawyers to help us, the loggers began to show a genuine interest in our case and would stop us in town to see how we were doing in the courts. They'd wish us luck and warn us that clear-cutting might indeed hurt our water supply. Then they'd offer us a beer, and we'd talk about hunting, and they'd complain about their wives—all ordinary workman chatter. How come, we began to think, we're the revolutionaries, but they're the proletariat? In the parlance of those politically monochromatic times, this was an unforeseen contradiction.

The only thing the loggers seemed to worry about was the persistent possibility that we might sabotage their equipment. Those Cats were expensive, they cautioned, and besides, they'd be out of work if we blew them up. Clear-cutting was bad, they said. No doubt about it. Loggers who'd worked on clear-cuts up a tributary of the Salmon the year before called it, with regret, the Rape of the Little North Fork. Many said the water supplies on their own homesteads had been hurt by upstream logging operations. The people in these mountain towns don't welcome development with open arms, we discovered. The prospect of paving one of the backwoods roads—and the attendant tourist traffic—aroused a reaction among the old-timers much like the idea of logging did in us long-haired hippies. Some of them, we were told, still chopped gaping potholes in the new pavement to slow and terrorize the flatlanders in their camper trucks and low-slung station wagons. In the end, though, they said they had to do the job to make a living. They'd do it as carefully as they could, with the least possible damage.

The starkest confrontation came in late summer of 1971 when the road crew was about to begin the last segment of the road, preface to actual Cutting of Trees. Our big-city attorneys reached a last-minute moratorium agreement with the Forest Service while they chased a temporary injunction in federal court. But the timber company, which was not party to the agreement, was undeterred and wanted to continue the road work.

A friendly emissary from the Forest Service warned us a day early, and it became clear that everyone expected us to stage a civil-rights-type sit-in at the very least. So at daybreak of that next morning a handful of us stopped the crew at the S-curve below the summit by building a campfire in the middle of the road. The equipment operators courteously shut down their Cats, and we strode up to the assemblage. "We wanna talk," we announced, with as much gravity as we could manage.

When they said nothing in return, one of us said, "Our lawyers tell us they have an agreement with your lawyers. They promised to wait for the results of tests to tell how this cut will affect our water supply. That's the key question, and the tests are scheduled to take place in a couple days."

The timber company had actually won the contract with the Forest Service. That company had hired a logging outfit from Orleans. The timber company's representative finally spoke, and he was firm in his response. "We told the Forest Service we'd wait a week, and we've waited two." Then he walked to his truck and radioed for the sheriff. It still takes a long time to get a police response on Salmon River. The headquarters are in Yreka, nearly one hundred miles of mountain roads to the northeast. That day it would take even longer because two communards had altered the road signs to complicate navigation on the maze of logging roads.

Jeff Buchin, the innocent bystander who was arrested in the Tomato Plant Bust, had kindled a small campfire in the middle of the road. Michael Tierra, who'd shared my life in the rock band, then later at the Haight-Ashbury Victorian on Willard Street and now at the commune, sat down next to the fire and carefully opened a leather pouch. He'd been learning herbs from the tribal elders, and he carefully pulled out a bulky fragment of a root, the one the Karuks call *Kishwuf.* He took out his pocket knife and started cutting small shavings into the flames, and the smoke gave our surroundings the smell of a Native house.

John Cedar, a hippie who later became an accomplished timber faller in his own right, walked over to a small cluster of loggers who were standing beyond the row of stalled logging equipment. He started playing his guitar and began singing a popular song of the era with lyrics about tearing down the garden of Eden.

The loggers listened respectfully, and one of them turned his face away as tears began to well up in his eyes. He was a grizzled Karuk tribal member and a Cat-Skinner, as the bulldozer operators are called.

We used that time to lecture the Cal-Pacific rep for two hours about his timber company's betrayal, the destruction of the environment, and his malignant social role. "I'm sorry, but I have a contract with the Forest Service," was his reply to every attack. (We later discovered he was trying at the time to trade his contract for one on another piece of land, any piece, but the Forest Service would not let him off the hook.) We asked the loggers why they risked their necks working in the woods just to enrich a bunch of New York stockholders. They just nodded appreciatively and looked askance at the mill rep's ample waistline.

Then we took on the mill rep more personally. First we reasoned. Then we yelled. He was a liar and a prick and a fascist and a Hun. One of our men offered to settle it all right then, man to man. "You wanna fight?" he screamed about an inch from the rep's face. "You wanna fight right now?"

"I'm sorry, but I have a contract with the Forest Service."

After a few hours it cooled. You can only yell so much. But no matter how far up the ladder you went, there seemed to be nobody there that day empowered to stop a logging show. So we waited there at the summit. We had stopped the roadwork. All of us—hippies, loggers, mill reps, and a half dozen tree pig observers—sat back to wait for the deputies.

The scenario was clear. The cops would arrive, we'd block the work, somebody would read a warning, and we'd be dragged off to jail. But hours passed and no cops. Everybody sat down to lunch. More time and the executive nervously radioed in to see what was happening. An idle logging crew costs a lot of money. The obsequious Forest Service employees tried to reason with us. We told them we had talked it over and decided they were full of shit. A rumor passed around that the police squadron was lost on some backwoods road, that maybe someone had altered the road signs.

Finally, they arrived, six of Yreka's finest in three cars armed with mace and clubs, fingering their holstered pistols. They were ready to beat us to a pulp. The mill rep from the timber company huddled with them while they peered nervously into the surrounding woods. What snipers could be concealed there?

Then the head cop, college boy among the thugs, walked over and asked what our problem was. We launched into a long-winded explanation of the fragility of the forest ecosystem, the dangers of clear-cut logging, about summer's sun and winter's snow. In closing we demanded they arrest the Forest Service and the Cal-Pacific executive for crimes against nature.

Cop leader was awestruck. But he recovered with an equally long explanation of his duty and role, which, though it might differ from his sentiments, was to keep the county road open. This was the response we expected, but since we were just stalling, we babbled for a half hour more in mock seriousness, and over and over he said, in essence, that he wasn't empowered to arrest anyone with property and power.

This was our cue to lie down in front of the Cat, which had sat idle all day. We huddled for a minute, decided we had played the bluff long enough, thanked everybody, and split. Not one of our crew insisted on being arrested. This was strictly show biz. If anyone had seriously considered it, then Michael Tierra would have convinced them otherwise. He had gotten collared in the same bust as me a few years earlier at Willard Street, the one that ended us up in San Francisco's Hall of Justice. And I would have chimed in. Civil disobedience wasn't for kids, and we were still kids in the world of social change.

The cops and the mill rep, who were looking forward to a little bloodletting, were outraged. The logging crew just shrugged. No logs hauled, but also no injuries. It had been an easy day, even entertaining. We had wasted their time, but it was a limited and somehow frustrating victory, for they would surely resume the work the next day.

Osha Neumann, one of our crew that day, had arrived at the ranch with a gang of anarchists from New York's Lower East Side about a year before. He was already a brilliant and provocative muralist, and years later he became an attorney to help poor people in the legal system. After that showdown, he wrote in his journal, "I cannot say to the loggers, 'Clear-cutting seems to destroy some necessary vibrational unity.' I can perhaps say, 'Clear-cutting is bad forestry: there are better ways.' Perhaps this is true. Perhaps not. It's not something that I say naturally. It's something that I have to study up on. I can also say, 'We feel too much forest is cut. It is wasted. The buildings that are built are shoddy, stupid, unnecessary and wastefully constructed. The economy must become more economical, less exploitive. But already the loggers will feel this is vague, utopian, hippie stuff. What do I know, walking around naked all day, puttering in the garden? We are cut off; communication is difficult. I can't tell him to live like me, yet."

Most of our cards were on the table by this point, so we had to take our chances with the San Francisco attorneys and a Nixon-appointed federal judge. Our lawyers tried to sound reassuring, but they always reminded me of that public defender I once had in Yreka who couldn't remember my name from meeting to meeting. In the end the lawyers' brave efforts, like ours, were for naught.

Even when the more sympathetic road builders on the logging crew stalled the work with claims that it was unsafe to continue, the Forest Service was relentless. Impossible or not, the work must go on, they said. They seemed afraid that they would lose power over their domain if we won. The courts upheld the timber sale.

Through the winter we gathered technical data and tried to rally our lawyers for an appeal. They told us our chances were great, but we felt by then that we couldn't believe them. We were right. I think the judges call recesses in cases like this to check their stock portfolios.

After the winter snow was gone, the loggers returned to fall all the giant trees at the White Bear timber sale in a few days. Their crews operate with great skill and swagger. At the time it seemed flavored by an unseemly machismo, but a few years later, after a stint as a logger myself, I realized that they were mostly exhausted by the sheer labor and by the ever-present threat of a disabling accident. A logging crew can do so much more of its devastating work in a few hours than we can offset in years of opposing them, that we needed to call our tactics into question. We hiked back down the road to the commune, after our day of protest theater. The fight over the correct way to log is still going on, and, although our clumsy first round was a loss, the balance has slowly shifted to favor the protection of natural habitat. There is a saying about losing battles, but winning wars; it is scant satisfaction when you've just lost your first battle.

CHAPTER 5

Swimming with the Sharks

It all started when Eldon Cott disrespected the district ranger in public. I guess the "in public" part was his real crime. There was no shortage of people who regularly dissed the ranger in private. Like many of his predecessors and his successors, the ranger was not held in high regard. It happened at a public meeting in 1976 when I was out of town, but we all heard about it. And we all heard that the ranger was going to get even. It wasn't that hard. He had the whole power of the United States Forest Service and the Department of Agriculture. All Eldon had was a tiny cabin on a mining claim at Morehouse Creek on the main stem of the Salmon River. Some people said he'd have been wiser to keep his mouth shut, while other people applauded that he spoke his mind to power. Most of us weren't even sure what he'd said at the public meeting. Maybe it was just his laugh.

Eldon Cott was a large man, but there was nothing intimidating about him. Unless it was the sense that people had that he could read their minds. But he'd never use that for harm. He'd just make a comment and then laugh a deep, rolling belly laugh. Most of us found this disarming and even charming. People said that Eldon later began working as a Santa Claus at high-end department stores and that children loved him. But few of us viewed the world like Ranger Stubblefield, the downriver district ranger. Maybe he took Eldon's laughter as a direct attack, and we all figured any district ranger had to harbor so many nefarious secrets that a mind reader, even a good-natured one, was sure to learn too much.

And Eldon's mining claim was staked in the stretch of river under Stubblefield's jurisdiction.

A mining claim was not an uncommon place for a person to live in those days on the Salmon River. I'd left the commune by that time, mid-1970s, and moved to a small unoccupied cabin next to Kate George, a woman in her late sixties. She explained Eldon's situation to me with her usual mastery of politics, history, and local gossip. The first miners came into Salmon River country about 1850, she said. People were discovering gold all over northern California, and the Salmon River was no exception. The first flood of miners came with the January thaw into what is now Cecilville. They established camps, but they quickly became snowbound—winter is just getting started in January that far up the South Fork. Some of them starved. The ancestors of Kate's departed husband Clarence "Pop" George came soon after, miners from Wales. Some of them married local Native women. "Those Indian women were all New River Shasta, and you don't find many of them these days," she said, with evident pride in Pop's roots.

"When I lived up at the Black Bear commune I heard that the property there was a patented mining claim. Is that different from other mining claims?" I asked her.

"Black Bear was a productive mine, and the mine owner had the claim made permanent. Most claims are year-to-year. It's all spelled out in the 1872 Mining Law," she said, in the gravelly voice of someone who's smoked too many cigarettes in their time.

"You mean the law is over a hundred years old? How come everybody doesn't just patent their claims and be done with it?"

"You'd have to prove there was a lot of gold on the claim, and nowadays the Forest Service makes it hard to do that. They'd fight you every step of the way. We got a little slack a few years ago with the Church-Johnson Act. It let miners convert their claims to private land status. My place here is Church-Johnson."

"Why didn't everybody do that? It would have solved the problem for good."

She shook her head. "Some of them didn't want their county taxes to go up. People can be pretty stupid." And she singled out two or three neighbors by name who she thought typified short-sighted stupidity.

She settled into her chair by wiggling her butt, as she often did when she was telling me her favorite stories, and continued: "Over the years some folks were pretty clever at trying to fool the Forest Service. There was a Native man named Orcutt up Methodist Creek who got harassed by them for starting a cabin on what was his family's land from way before there was a Forest Service. The ranger told him that a new permanent cabin wasn't allowed anymore on a claim, so Orcutt said he'd live in a tent. The ranger, whoever it was then, would come by now and then, even in the dead of winter, to make sure Orcutt hadn't built anything. What the ranger didn't know was that Orcutt had built a little cabin inside the tent. That whole Orcutt family is pretty smart."

"So what's our ranger gonna do to Eldon?"

"Eldon's claim has an existing cabin. It's not fancy, but it's a cabin. The way the Forest Service can challenge that is to have a mineral exam. They'll make Eldon prove that there's enough gold on the claim to justify his staying there. If he can't, they can start evictions. The standard in the law is that the claim has to have enough gold to support 'a prudent man.'"

"That's pretty vague, and it is a gold mine. Miners dug it all up around there years ago. Doesn't that prove something?" I protested.

Kate George (left) lived in Cecilville with Clarence "Pop" George about thirty-five years before we began the Black Bear Ranch commune. She was one of the first locals to befriend the hippies.
Contributed photo.

"Honey, they dug up a lot of ground around here in the old days, but Pop George always said only one Salmon River miner ever got rich that he knew of. It was that miner who moved to Etna and started the bank. Also, Eldon's a good talker, but I'm not sure he could find gold in a jewelry store. I feel sorry for his wife, Betty Ann. She's a friend of mine. Some of her neighbors are gonna have to help."

"I don't get it. How come they still have a hundred-year-old law?"

Kate said, "A hundred years ago they passed the law to help settle the West. Nowadays it mainly helps the big mining corporations like Kennecott. They keep any new law from happening. But you have to admit that it helps people on Salmon River. There's almost no regular private land. It's all federal land. Of course, the Forest Service keeps squeezing our miners with new regulations that they invent every year."

"Do you think they squeeze Kennecott?" I asked. "They get millions of dollars of minerals a year for free." Kate just shrugged.

We had about a week until the mineral exam at Eldon's claim, so a team quickly assembled. Jerry Cramer, a real miner who had befriended us at the commune years earlier, gave me a crash course on which spot on the claim was most likely to produce color. Color was what miners called gold, maybe because it flashed so bright when a miner swirled the sands in a gold pan. Jerry talked about the floods that followed the retreat of the last Ice Age and how that concentrated nuggets and even fine gold particles in certain places. Jerry was a heroic figure in all our eyes, but it took me a while to figure it out. We younger men used to posture as heroic figures by swagger and bombast, but Jerry Cramer needed none of that. He spoke in a quiet, almost feminine voice, but he operated massive pieces of machinery—giant Cat bulldozers and noisy rock separators—with more control than most of us have over a pencil on paper. He had been an early friend to us when we started the commune, a time when we had few friends among the river locals.

We became miners overnight. Little Jake had taken over a family claim upriver about the same time we'd started the commune, and he helped. He brought over a suction dredge, a machine that floated in the river on pontoons and pumped up the gravel like a noisy vacuum cleaner. The dredge was too heavy for even a man with powerful muscles like Little Jake to move; it took four of us to lower it on ropes into the steep river gorge at the Morehouse Creek claim. People brought wetsuits and pry bars, rock-pulling grip hoists, and gold pans. Within a day, we had an operation. By then Eldon had faded into the woodwork, but his wife, Betty Ann, was well-liked on the river and was also a good cook. It was summer, and she cooked berry pies, apple pies, quiches, soufflés, and other tasty cuisine for all visitors. The main miner turned out to be me, but it wasn't that bad on the hot days of a river summer. A compressor supplied air through a regulator when I was underwater, and I would lead the fat suction hose into the gravel, loosening it with the bar where needed. The rocks would flush out through a watery classifier called a sluice box. The sand and gravel shot right through, and the gold, which is much heavier, collected at the top riffles of the box. Not that there was that much gold. As I got deeper, it improved a little, but I still wasn't getting rich. I wondered if I was even paying for the gasoline that powered the noisy pump. It was exciting, though, when I saw a few flecks of gold just before they went up into the vacuum hose. My coaches would come every day with helpful tips. I learned that gold migrates down to bedrock and concentrates more in the inside than the outside bends of the river channel. It was just like Jerry Cramer, Brian Bundy, and the other established miners had told us. Experienced friends would make adjustments in the machinery, and they'd give encouragement. We'd also stay for dinner when Betty Ann invited us.

Finally, the day of the mineral exam came, and a crowd of locals showed up early. This time they brought food in pots and casseroles along with pies and cakes. Potluck is a highly honed tradition on Salmon River. Eventually, a contingent of Forest Service employees arrived, with others posted on the road. Neither Eldon nor the ranger came. But there was an air of celebration. Also a sense of peril. Besides the fact that a local home might get destroyed by the feds, no one, especially the feds, could forget that a mineral examiner was wounded by a sniper a year earlier during a similar exam in Denny. That was a town even more isolated than Forks of Salmon on the Trinity River side of the ridge. Relations there between miners and Forest Service were more akin to guerrilla war than to the carnival this day on the banks of the Salmon River. The chief examiner for our test was a man named Emmett Ball, who was well known for this sort of work. He was friendly and explained the ground rules: run the dredge for two hours, collect the gold for laboratory assay, and make a determination if the claim could return enough to support "a prudent man." It was easy, he said, and very objective.

I slipped into one of the wetsuits, Jake started the pump, and the test began. After thirty minutes, another neighbor with more mining experience took my place, and I moved over to the sun-warmed rocks where Emmett Ball was telling stories. Ball was not a young man, and he said that he was close to retirement. Maybe he said that to make himself less a target. Higher up the bank, children were playing, people were eating and drinking, and one woman was even giving haircuts to her neighbors. Ball said he'd been at the exam with the shooting, and another man was wounded, just a scratch on the neck. Ball said he thought the shot had been aimed at a rock as a warning, but that a ricochet fragment had hit the other examiner. He didn't seem to bear any grudge, but many of the other Forest Service employees there kept scanning the landscape for any sign of another sniper. Ball, himself, was a great storyteller. He talked about a miner, back in the Gold Rush, who had a novel trick to increase the value of a claim he was selling. He would carefully roll a cigarette with a generous pinch of gold dust. Then, as the swindler was swirling a sample in his gold pan, he'd let the ashes fall into the pan. The sample, of course, always looked great, and we all laughed that such a transparent ploy might have worked in the old days.

Finally, the two hours passed, and the riffles were scrupulously cleaned and weighed. Ball announced that the resulting gold would be sent to a laboratory for analysis and assay to calculate its value. "It looked pretty good to me," said Ball. "This claim is probably going to pass." And he passed us a signed receipt for the bottle of gold. His Forest Service colleagues continued scanning the surrounding bluffs for the imagined snipers. The locals gathered around the food, finished off the beer, and said ruder things about the district ranger than Eldon ever had. No snipers. A little bit of gold.

Over coffee the next morning, Kate George wanted a full report. I told about the crowd, the food, the nervous Forest Service employees. I told her who had run the suction dredge and even about the haircuts. She questioned me for details, especially about Emmett Ball. I asked why she hadn't come, and she said, "It's okay for you young people to scramble down the bluffs at Morehouse, but, if I'd gone down, you all would have had to carry me back up. I'm no kid any more. But it sounds like a great party anyway. But did you find any gold?"

"We found some, but I'm not sure how much. Emmett Ball said the labs would decide its value."

Dismay registered on her face, and she went to the stove for more coffee.

When she returned, I said, "Kate, can you keep a secret?"

"There's nobody on this river can keep a secret better than Kate George. Cough it up."

"This one's important. You promise?"

"It'll go with me to the grave," she said, with her hand on her heart and her eyes turned upward to the heavens.

I paused, then said, "While we were doing the exam, I saw someone drop something into the sluice in all the hubbub. I asked him afterward, and he said he'd decided to give the Forest Service a little extra gold. It was Little Jake. He did it while Emmett Ball was telling stories. That distracted everyone. Jake said he'd just dropped in the gold I'd found in the previous few days. It wasn't much, but it should be plenty. It had to be fifty dollars' worth, plus we found some during the test, maybe sixty dollars in all. That's thirty bucks an hour. A prudent man should be able to get by on that."

She clapped her hands and laughed out loud. "That is a hoot. I can see why you need to keep it secret. Who else knows?"

"Just you and me and Jake."

"Well, Betty Ann and Eldon are lucky to have so many friends. Since you young people came to the river and started the commune, there's been a lot more of that kind of spirit around here. It used to be that way during the depression when a lot of people came up here to stake claims and mine because they would have starved in the cities. There was no unemployment insurance then and no welfare. Neighbors on the river helped each other then, just like people did today."

———

A year went by after Emmett Ball's mineral exam at Morehouse Creek, then a year and a half, and Eldon and Betty Ann heard nothing more from the Forest Service. Denial is a useful human faculty, and we all employed it. A person could imagine they'd forgotten about Eldon's insult, and they'd forgotten about the whole mineral exam. The rest of us were happy to forget, too. But then the letter came. It was not the message we wanted to hear. In formal language, it said the mineral exam proved that the Morehouse Creek Mine could not support the famous "prudent man." In an attachment, it said there was less than five dollars' worth of gold found during the mineral exam.

I went to share the news with Kate. I was irate. "I know there was more. I know because I know how much Little Jake dropped in the sluice."

Kate shook her head and thought for a while. Finally, she said, "You were right, you and all your friends were right to try to help out Betty Ann and Eldon. It wasn't even wrong that Jake salted the top riffle. But you made a mistake. You tried swimming with the sharks."

"Sharks?"

"You tried cheating the biggest cheats of all. You and Jake were amateur cheats, and you went up against the pros, the US Forest Service. They've been cheating people around here all my life, and they've gotten pretty good at it."

I shook my head, confused. She got up to bring a second cup and said, "I still have your bottle of brandy. Want some in your coffee, Honey?"

———

An update: There are still dredgers on the Salmon River these days, but they are not a source of harmony for the locals. Betty Ann passed the claim with its cabin to a friend, but eventually the Forest Service forced them off. For the agency it was a template of how to kick lots of people off the river, but that campaign was still years away. That part is not a pretty story, but I'll get to it, if you're patient. A few years ago, an entrepreneur in Happy Camp on the Klamath River started staking all the nearby vacant claims. Next, he started advertising that the gold dredgers would be able to find riches, and he started selling memberships. He even sold his clients fancy dredges if they didn't have them. "A great vacation for the family and you can get rich," was the pitch. I never heard of anyone getting rich, except maybe the guy who owned the operation. The miner who started the bank in Etna would have been proud of this guy.

Then this same guy started staking all the open claims on Salmon River. The next few summers were contentious. A mile downriver from our place at Butler Creek he staked a flat where the Forest Service had forced off the previous miner and burned his cabin. The flat filled up with RVs and vans, each one pulling a trailer with a shiny new dredge. They installed a whole lineup of portable toilets, but nobody knew where these people drained their dishwater or how they could keep gasoline in the pumps from polluting the river. And even if one little dredge like mine, so many years earlier, might be relatively benign (and it probably wasn't), a dozen dredges in a half mile was an environmental disaster. The Forest Service, which had been so intent on removing miners' cabins earlier, said they couldn't do much. This was a legal use under the 1872 law. They removed miners when there was an illegal occupancy, and the RVs were just temporary, the Forest Service reps said.

This didn't sit well with the evicted old-time miners and their friends. Some started trying to harass the RV towns where they had sprung up. Some of the RVs left, but others made it known that they had guns and knew how to use them.

Things were even more tense with the local Native Americans. They'd been working hard for many years to protect the fish runs from destructive influences like too many dams creating toxic pollution on the Klamath and Shasta Rivers, too many steers in the creeks dumping manure into the Scott River, too much logging and road building dumping sediments everywhere.

Toz Soto is a fishery biologist for the Karuk Tribe; his father and mother were dredge miners on the Salmon River in the 1970s and '80s. Toz said there was catastrophic damage done by the original Gold Rush, with the huge movements of land into the river channels. "That still hasn't been repaired," he said, "and suction dredges make it worse. They stir up the cobble beds where the fish need to lay their eggs, and they release the trapped mercury the original miners used a hundred years earlier.

"Besides that," Toz said, "the word 'miners' means something different to the Native Americans around here than it does to other people. Miners represented genocide against the tribes, and they haven't forgotten. To call your business 'recreational miners' to the tribes is like calling yourself 'recreational Nazis' at a Jewish Community Center."

CHAPTER 6
The Company Loves Misery

The lead tree-planting auger on the crew below us revved up loud and then stopped. I was one of the mechanics, so I looked down over the bluff. When I looked, all the planters around me paused and looked.

Down below, looking like a scene in miniature, Edna Watson, who had started running auger only that morning, strode purposefully away from her tool. When she got to one of the other women planters, one who was stuffing twelve-inch seedling trees into Edna's freshly augered holes, Edna paused until the woman stood straight up. Then she punched her squarely in the nose.

Most of the planters near Edna, who had also been watching, swung back to work, maybe pretending they hadn't seen it. My own part of the crew on the bluff did the same. I watched Edna march back to the auger, still perched in its last tree hole, and start up the engine with an angry yank on the pull rope. She drilled the next twenty holes at a sprinter's pace, not in the usual oblong gait of most operators, who needed to drill three thousand holes a day and somehow live through it. I remembered that Edna had spent a little time at the commune when I lived there a few years earlier, but this was the mid-1970s. Edna often seemed like someone who could get really mad in those days. She even went off on me once, but no sucker punches. I rubbed my nose gratefully.

I swung back to my own work, carefully stuffing the delicate conifer seedlings into the ground. The work had its own rhythm: unravel the tree from the bundles of hundreds in bags around your waist; clear the hole to its bottom with the left hand; drop the tree in, a little too deep with the right. Then, as one hand started dumping the drilled-out dirt back in the little hole, tug lightly upward on the tree. That straightened the roots. The biggest sin for a tree planter was to leave a root that curved back up. Inspectors from the US Forest Service followed us and dug up a sampling, looking for these J-roots. Too many and our crews suffered cash penalties.

When the hole was filled, I'd tamp it expertly with my foot and, almost in the same motion, move three paces to the next hole. It would have been hot and dirty work if it were not so damn cold. The morning had started with a light snowfall, not quite enough to shut down the job. But snow didn't last long in the high desert country east of Oregon's Cascade Mountains. It didn't really thaw. It just sublimed away like little piles of moth balls in a closet.

It was a big reforestation crew. Some of us had earlier lived at the Black Bear commune and gotten small planting jobs then, a carryover of the planting job we'd done in Hoopa a few years earlier. Others were newer arrivals who'd moved to mining claims or small private places in what passed for towns along the river. There was even a handful of people who'd come to Black Bear after our first wave had mostly dispersed. Together we'd started a reforestation co-op and called it Ent Forestry. We'd borrowed the name Ent for our reforestation co-op from the fierce walking trees in the Hobbit stories by J. R. R. Tolkien. To enlarge the crew for our biggest jobs like this one, we'd even invited tree planters from a similar co-op just across the state line in Oregon. They called their outfit Green Side Up, which they said was the punch line to a joke, although I never heard the joke. The work was often a lesson in humility. Hardship sometimes breeds a sort of gallows humor, and one of the favorites among the GSU planters was their motto, "The company loves misery."

At lunch, a few of our crew members drifted down to join Edna's team. "Edna punched Rosa," they reported, "cuz she wouldn't stop hassling her about the depth of the holes. Edna said she was hitting rock at eight or nine inches and couldn't go deeper. When Rosa wouldn't slack off, Edna let her have it."

"What's Rosa say?" I asked.

"Dunno. She didn't eat with us."

"I don't think violence solves anything," one woman offered.

"You can say that," said another, "but I remember two days ago you were ready to paste her yourself. And Edna's only running auger because so many of the men are getting disabled." Both women swung around and frowned at me and another man who had been running auger when we started the job. "I say hooray for Edna," one of them concluded.

I personally never would have punched Rosa, but I did not say so aloud. It was not for some high-minded value. I just knew Rosa and figured she'd have knocked out all my teeth if I'd tried.

"Let's get back to work," the other woman said. "We don't want to get stuck up here in Oregon forever. It's time to start gardens back home."

We grabbed our tree bags and stumbled out into the huge clear-cut. One year before it had been a lodgepole pine forest, but now its trees were gone, off to paper and plywood mills in Bend and Klamath Falls.

That evening, while the cooks were finishing the last touches on dinner, I joined Bob-O Schultze, another commune veteran, over at the welding gear adding another layer of hard-face, an ultra-strong metal coating, onto the auger tips. "Show me how to do it," I said.

"I was wondering when you were going to ask," he said with a grin. "Just watch this." First he cleaned the worn surface with a spinning wire brush. Then he ignited a torch with the little characteristic pop that oxygen and acetylene always make when they're lit with a squeeze of the striker.

He motioned for me to pull down my goggles and pulled down his own. Expertly, he adjusted the controls so the flame went from a long red-orange tail, spouting thick black smoke, to a short two-part flame, white within blue. "Now steal just a little oxygen," he instructed, "to make it a reducing flame. See how it's a little like a tongue there, waiting to lick something."

"Only you could make welding sound sexy," I teased him.

"Try it and you'll like it," he said, and he passed me the torch. "Now get the tip hot first. Whoa, don't hold the torch in one place or you'll blow away the base metal."

Through the shaded goggles, in the dimming evening light, I watched the metal change color. First it reddened; then it became incandescent white. Finally, the surface began to shimmer like it was sweating. "Now start feeding the hard-face rod on and use the heat to draw it around."

I watched the light and sparks dancing off the tip as I worked, and I grew hypnotized by the play of color. When I was done, I shut down the torch and said proudly, "Whaddya think?"

"It's ugly," he said, "but it's a start. Try a couple more and then we can go eat." About eight thousand years ago, a geologic eye-blink, Mount Mazama in the southern Cascade Mountains had a violent explosion. When it subsided, the mountain was almost a mile shorter and is now the placid Crater Lake. The powdered volcano top blew east and blanketed much of that part of Oregon, including where we worked that season. We'd learned that this volcanic pumice would chew our augers to toothpicks in a week if we didn't keep adding metal. Bob-O started a second torch and began laying hard-face on the races that spiraled up the auger shafts.

The planters were quiet at dinner, speaking in hushed tones about their children back on Salmon River and whether they might do better in gold mining. Or cultivation, another planter would counsel. The laws against marijuana were still strictly enforced then, and what later became an industry was just getting a foothold.

It was snowing again in the morning, but heavily this time, which was good news. It meant the contract was shut down for the day, and we could rest. Smoke spilled from the chimneys of all five of the huge army-surplus tents that housed the crew, and snow had begun to pile on the trucks.

Many planters were gathered in the cook tent, sipping coffee, eating fresh-baked rolls, and playing cards when I entered. The cooks had turned in for a morning nap, but Barbara Short, a pretty young planter, was stirring a big steaming kettle on the stove. An acrid smell filled the tent. She was brewing ganja butter, a river favorite in those days. The recipe was simple: two pounds of butter and a pound of shake. Shake, the leafy waste product of serious marijuana growers, was worthless on the river. People might compost it or feed it to their pigs to see if it would stimulate appetite. But the oil in the butter extracted something from the leaf that made for a serviceable high, better than serviceable. Chill the kettle and skim the iridescent green fat off the top; you had ganja butter.

I'd heard that the planters from our sister co-op in Oregon had introduced the recipe. It could spike brownies or the cookies they called Ginger Mind-Snaps. One planter used it on his morning oatmeal and could still plant trees twice as fast as I could.

Bob-O entered, more morose than the others, who were enjoying a day off. He sat down next to me with his coffee. "Who tore a hole in the tent?" he asked. A gaping hole in the canvas was covered by a large sheet of clear plastic. The plastic had filled with snow melt until it hung in a forbidding, pendulous blob, barely clearing the heads of the poker players, who seemed not to notice it.

"Dul dropped a tree on it yesterday," the woman at the kettle answered. Dul was short for Abdul, the name he had adopted earlier in the spring. When people asked for an explanation, he said that he took an Arab name to come to terms with any Zionist tendencies that might have sprung from his own Jewishness. No one asked him why he had dropped a tree through the tent. But, on cutting jobs, few sawyers would work near him. I'm not sure he was really very Jewish.

"I heard about Edna sucker-punching Rosa," Bob-O said. "This crew is going nuts." The other planters pretended not to notice his outburst, just as they ignored the hole in the tent. One got up to dip his breakfast roll in the steaming kettle of ganja butter, a preview of tomorrow's cookies.

"We're all going nuts," Bob-O said, louder. "This is the worst fucking contract we ever took. We left $45,000 on the table. We're making about four dollars an hour and we've been making fifteen up until this job."

I banged him on the shoulder as hard as I could without getting hit back and then tugged him upright, through the canvas tent doorway and out into the deepening snow. "Listen to me," I ordered. "If you keep mouthing off like that, people won't stick with the contract."

"But I'm right. You know it."

"Of course, you're right. If you were wrong, it wouldn't be a problem. But some of those Oregon planters put up their homesteads as bond to

Ent Forestry, our community reforestation cooperative, would set up a portable city at jobs with large canvas tents for kitchens, dining rooms, and dorms. They were heated with woodstoves and comfy by the standards of that industry but Spartan by any other measure. Photo by Jeff Buchin.

get this contract. They did it as a favor to us. If people leave for home and we default, they'll lose their places."

"I offered to put up my place as bond," Bob-O defended.

"Right. You can really get a big bond for a mining claim on US Forest Service land called Starveout Mine."

Bob-O started to answer but then started laughing at the two of us standing in shirtsleeves in the lightly falling snow in a canvas shantytown, surrounded by rusting trucks, augers, and welding gear.

We started work rested the next morning, but by lunch the crews were sapped of energy. I'd run auger for three hours, but I realized that I was exhausted and bathed in a fine coating of motor oil from the chain drive of the auger. An auger was really a cross between a chain saw and a big, heavy drill, connected by an orange gearbox to form an awkward letter L. It was loud; we wore noise-canceling headphones. It was dirty. It would grab buried roots or rocks and jerk the operator off his or her feet. So I got White Water Wally to spell me. I fell into line next to Jerry-Joseph planting into the augered holes.

Jerry was not his real name, but he'd adopted it during the Vietnam War when he'd lived at the commune to avoid the draft. Lately he had switched to Joseph, which may or may not have been his real name. Nobody was sure. We'd call him Jerry still sometimes, and he'd insistently correct us that his name was Joseph. He'd go nuts, sometimes, if we forgot.

Up ahead, White Water Wally's auger grabbed a long root chunk left from the logging, swung it around, and slammed it into his forehead. He started to rub his head but stopped because his hands were already so dirty from the grease. "Jerry!" he yelled. "Am I bleeding?"

Jerry looked up at Wally. "Joseph," he corrected, with great patience.

CHAPTER 7

Playing with Fire

In early summer of 1977 we'd been thinning trees up in Montana for a couple of months. Only a fraction of the tree planters signed on for an Ent Forestry chain-saw job. At first glance it looked lucrative. So much for judging by appearances. And I take back whatever I may have said about tree planting being the hardest work in the world. Reforestation may have been the most miserable, but that thinning job in Montana was the hardest job we'd ever had. We came home not quite broken, but plenty sore and also in great shape. Tucked under my arms were muscles where there'd only been school books before.

As soon as we got home, three cutters from our Montana crew, Little Jake, Jeff Greeley, and Les Harling, talked their way into working as fallers for Rice Construction, a road builder. It paid big bucks. Montana had been small trees but even smaller bucks. Despite the risks in cutting big trees, Jake and the others all admired their inventiveness in passing themselves off as fallers in real timber, that is Big Trees. In the afternoons, I'd sit with Jake and speculate whether I should get on the job. He asked me why a veteran of the commune who had gone to court to stop logging was now thinking of becoming a logger. It was a good question, but I didn't have a good answer. Finally, he told me, "You will never find a logging job safer than this one. It's road building. We're just cutting enough trees to open the right-of-way. We already got all of the cutting jobs, but they have other jobs. And they seem to hire new guys every day because guys jump to better jobs on other outfits or cuz they get too drunk on payday to show up on Monday. It's this or nothing, Malcolm."

All weekend I deliberated, but Monday morning at 4:30 a.m. I was standing outside the Forks of Salmon General Store. I had a lunchbox and thermos clutched in one hand, a banjo canteen slung over my shoulder, and a hard hat stuffed under my arm. The scene, normally quiet and slow, was pandemonium in the earliest dawn light. Logger crew vans called crummies were everywhere, and their headlights punctuated the darkness. Men were yelling, and horns were honking. I found the foreman whom Little Jake had said he'd made arrangements with. The foreman shrugged and said he didn't need anyone. I walked away crestfallen and poured myself a cup of coffee to better ponder my fate. I'd barely taken the first sip or launched the first ponder when the foreman came over and yelled, "I can use you after all. C'mon. We can't wait forever."

In thirty minutes, in the growing light, we were on the job site. The loggers piled out like bears after hibernation. A tall, rubber-tired tractor called a skidder raced up to us in a cloud of dust, and a gangly young man caked in the red dust jumped down to the ground with a grin. The foreman grumbled, "Go work with him."

The skidder operator's smile grew even larger. He stalked over toward me, hand extended, and said, "Howdy, I'm Crazy Dave." I shook his gloved hand. Dave's craziest quirk turned out to be that he was always happy, always upbeat, even as the day grew hot, despite the dust and noise. He was especially happy that I'd come along because he was just learning to run skidder, and no one had trusted him enough to set his chokers, the long cable loops that dragged the logs behind his skidder. This was my assignment. He finally had his own choker setter.

He showed me how to drag the choker cables through the brush, how to wrap them around the logs where they'd been felled and bucked into shorter lengths by the fallers, and how to thread the even bigger cable out of the skidder's winch and attach it to the chokers. Then I'd scramble out of the way while Crazy Dave played in the winch and then lurched up the emerging roadbed to a log landing. Within a hundred feet his skidder with its clutch of logs would disappear in his own cloud of red dust.

The sun oozed over the ridge, and the dust thickened. Sometime in the morning Jake and Jeff exited quickly in the old Jeep pickup with

Les sprawled in the back, resting impatiently on a bed of dried horse manure that Jeff had collected for his garden. They explained that Les had dropped a tree on his leg, and they were going to take him to see a doctor in Hoopa. Then they disappeared into the dust. The romance of industrial logging was fast disappearing when Jerry Vessells showed up. Jerry was tall, with prominent features and long, stringy red hair. Like Crazy Dave, he smiled more than seemed appropriate to the situation. Jerry grabbed five chokers and headed down through thick brush, which seemed to part ahead of him like the Red Sea parted ahead of Moses. He was all arms and long legs. The shattered branches and ceanothus brush that tugged at me so much when I tried to drag down even one choker— the same gnarly landscape seemed to welcome Vessells like the dancers in the San Francisco Ballet welcomed Rudolf Nureyev. He was the master.

But even the presence of Vessells's wily artfulness and Crazy Dave's unsinkable cheerfulness couldn't distract me from the heat, which grew worse every day. After the first week, word came after quitting time that a faller on another crew had been killed. It wasn't even from dropping the tree. He'd already dropped it and was bucking it into log lengths when it suddenly shifted on the slope. He was no novice. People said he was a week from retirement. Next Monday morning hardly anybody on the crew showed up. With a full week of experience, I was practically the senior guy on the crew except for the boss's son, Crazy Dave, Vessells, and the foreman. But I stuck. In the steamy afternoons after work, I'd go to a swimming hole on the South Fork to wash off the red dust and relax. From there I'd head over to Creek Hanauer's place on Know-Nothing Creek to have a beer. Creek was, like me, a veteran of the Black Bear commune who'd moved down to Salmon River. He'd also been on that tree-thinning job in Montana. Sometimes I'd play a card game called Speed with his stepdaughter, Shasta. This was the same Shasta whom I'd talked to years earlier when I was dosed on some psychedelic in San Francisco and she was still *in utero* in her sleeping mother's belly. At this point Shasta had emerged as a nine-year-old card shark, but, if I ever won a hand, she'd go bring me another beer to dull my game. We were playing one afternoon when a Forest Service truck flew by up the river road at an unusually high speed. "Must be that lightning this afternoon started a fire," Creek said. "That was Jimmy Bennett and a couple other firefighters."

I'd never been up close on a forest fire before, and I saw a curl of smoke rising up river, then another across the river up where we'd been building road. I'd not drunk too much beer to drive, but plenty enough to reinforce my courage, so I jumped into my weathered Jeep pickup and chased after the firefighters. They'd stopped not far up the road, and Jimmy and two women on the crew were gearing up when I arrived. I grabbed a shovel from my truck and headed up to join them. One of the women was Liz Pullen, who earlier had also lived at Black Bear. As we raced uphill, the smoke thickened, and I said, "Liz, I never fought fire before. What do I do?"

She laughed and said, "You just follow me, Honey." So I did, much to the amusement of Liz and the others, and we held that blaze until a bigger crew arrived. But there had been many down strikes and many fires, more than the local crews could handle. The fires, all of them, were eventually called the Hog Fire, after Hog Range where one of the blazes began, not after the voracious appetite of the flames in a tinder-dry forest in mid-August.

After dark, Jimmy Bennett promoted me to real firefighter, much better than apprentice choker setter, although I did miss Crazy Dave and Jerry Vessells. Bennett sent me off immediately with a bulldozer operator named Andy McBroom, what they called a Cat skinner in the parlance of logging. Our job was to build fire line around another lightning fire not far from the Rice Construction road-building operation. And very early the next morning—sleep was quickly forgone in a big fire—Bennett assigned me as a swamper to two young timber fallers. My job was to handle their extra gear and maybe to keep them out of trouble. They were cousins, Dean McBroom and Andy, the Cat skinner from the night before. Even though they might have been better named McMischief than McBroom, they were expert fallers. They'd size up a huge snag near a fire line. It was often already on fire. With surgical precision, they'd remove the V-shaped undercut, no small task even with the massive chain saws. Then they'd begin the back cut, with a pause to drive nylon wedges so the tree couldn't settle back on the chain saw's cutting bar. Painstakingly, they'd continue feathering the back cut, maybe even tap the wedges deeper. These were not small trees. Suddenly, there was a shift and a crack like a gunshot. The faller would yank the saw and run like hell to get clear. Crash. Crunch. The ground would shake. Both cousins would laugh like crazy scientists in a movie. The fire lines were already long. They cut many trees that day.

I remember getting home to Kate George's from the fire lines that night around midnight. Kate was still awake, and Billy Harling, Les's brother, was there, the who later went into ruby mining in India. Billy pulled a bottle of good brandy from his bag and offered it as a cure for smoke inhalation. It may not be, but it was certainly good for relaxation. We sat there for an hour in the darkness, too tired to go to bed, emptying the bottle and waxing philosophic. And we watched the flames on the opposite ridge race toward Godfrey Ranch, where many friends lived. It was not the last time Godfrey would burn, that night in 1977, but I did not know that then.

The next morning I woke with a headache, as much from the smoke that then choked the canyons as from Billy Harling's brandy. My first stop was for coffee at the kitchen table at Kate's. Mid-cup, several Forest Service trucks pulled up on the county road by her house, and firefighters started piling out.

We wandered up and saw they had fusees, the phosphorous flares used by firefighters to start a back burn. "What in the world are you doing?" she yelled.

"Hiya, ma'am. We got orders to back burn above the road here," their crew boss said, big smile. Out-of-town crews had finally arrived, and their boss didn't know Kate George or her reputation.

"Doncha know that you're on the wrong side of the fire line?" she protested.

"No, no ma'am. We have orders. Don't worry about a thing."

"Well, you call back to get your orders straight, and while you do that I'm going to go down and get my rifle." She hustled back down to her cabin.

There was a rush of radio calls and other clamor. What I remember most is the sound of her chambering a round in her weathered carbine when she was halfway back up the path. By the time she got to the road, huffing and puffing, the last of their trucks were leaving, never to be seen again. If she hadn't stopped them, the Hog Fire would have grown far beyond the fifty thousand acres it eventually became.

On the third day of the Hog Fire, I again followed Little Jake's advice (and ignored Les Harling's broken leg) to pawn myself off as a faller to the Forest Service because the pay was so good. That's how I ended up that first time at Butler Creek, where I still live today. Joe Miller, who owned the place, ignoring the worst fears of his Butler tenant, had rented the entire space to fire crews as a base camp. From there, hundreds of young men marched up the steep Salmon River Trail, and Dave Atwood, the Forest Service packer, brought them provisions with his string of glistening black mules. Atwood loaded my saw and fuel on mules, but he told me to hold on to my hard hat. "It preserves your dental records. Makes it easier to notify your widow," he said without apparent humor.

Until then, the flat on that side of Butler Creek had been the tenant's private cannabis arboretum. Suddenly, it was a swirl of firefighting activity. I didn't get enough time for a good look-over, but, if I had, I might have seen the tenant grudgingly pulling his pot plants too young for market. As an economic aside, this premature harvest almost certainly disrupted his game plan: get a good crop and take the profits to buy Butler. There was no love lost between the tenant and Miller. Miller thought the tenant was scum, to use his word. Of course, he thought most of us were various kinds of nonvertebrate pond life. Maybe the tenant was a standout. Maybe not. The tenant, in his own right, could go on eloquently for ten minutes on how much he hated Miller. "When the motherfucker dies I'm going to dig up his grave and throw his body in the river," he'd tell me with much conviction. He'd say it every time Miller's name was mentioned. Still, if his marijuana harvest had gone as intended, the tenant would have set aside his anger and passed the dollars to Miller as a down payment. Similarly, Miller would have overlooked his disgust and accepted them. Escrow, they say, is thicker than water.

Without saw and fuel, the steep walk up to Butler Saddle was easy, maybe ninety minutes. I walked up there last year, almost four decades after lightning started the Hog Fire, and the whole scene came back to me. Dozens of crews, hundreds of firefighters, mostly from the deep South, were strung out along the seven-mile-long fire line. They build a fire line by removing everything that can burn right down to the dirt. They call it "getting down to mineral soil." This means trees, brush, down logs, leaf mold, roots, everything, so the fire can't creep across the barrier. Often the lines are two or three feet wide. This one was twenty feet wide. It was the interstate of hand-built fire lines. Nothing smaller had held, and the Forest Service was desperate as the fire approached and then passed the fifty-thousand-acre mark. As I crested the Butler Creek side at the saddle and looked over into the Lewis Creek drainage, everything was on fire as far as I could see, though I couldn't see far through the dense smoke. This middle stretch of the seven-mile line was already getting hammered by fire, and the ends weren't even built yet.

The southerners were spread ten or fifteen feet apart and were ready to respond if the Butler side of the line started burning. They seemed stunned by the steepness of the Salmon River Mountains but undaunted by the fires licking near their feet and overhead in the forest canopy. I spotted my saw and pack near a big stack of emergency rations and full canteens. This lull was my last chance to replace the chain-saw carburetor part I'd been stalling on since the Montana job, so I plopped down in the shade of the last remaining tree and began the disassembly. But then the noise began. Somewhere down in the smoky reaches of Lewis Creek it started like a cross between a strong wind and an approaching train. I looked at the southerners, and they seemed oblivious. The sound grew and grew until the ground was shaking. I scooped all the saw parts into my pack and got ready to run when I realized the southerners still had not moved. A few smoked cigarettes, which seemed superfluous. Then the closest tall trees, already burned up fifty feet high, but still green on top, carried the fire another twenty feet up into their crowns. I realized the trees were crowning from underneath, a layer at a time instead of all at once. Each pass of the flames—that was my railroad train noise—dried out the next layer up so it was ready to burn on the next pass. I finished the saw repair as quickly as possible, and then the noise rushed up at us again. The southerners leaned on their shovels. One took a long draft on his canteen. The ground shook again. They stood impassive in the thickening haze. The roar this pass was even louder. They did not move but watched the fire race toward them, a hot feeding frenzy of noise and flame that ate another twenty-foot layer of the crown. I imagined a Confederate line braving withering Northern fire at Antietam.

These southerners, the white ones, would confide in me later during breaks that they knew how to handle "coloreds back home," perhaps suggesting that they could have useful advice for us Californians, if we only had sense enough to ask. What about me encouraged such talk, I wondered. There were black men on the crew, but they didn't tell me how to handle white people. Racial tension notwithstanding, these firefighters from Georgia and Alabama and Mississippi, of every color, were made of something like granite. Something in me squirmed to admire them all. Smoke impairs your judgment, I said to myself.

A polite man with a southern accent I could barely understand approached me and explained that I should head up to Butler Mountain where I would tie in with an Alabama crew that needed a faller. I connected with them halfway up the slope from Butler Saddle. They had had no chain saws, and their progress was slow. The lead men had chopped some trees with Pulaskis, the fire tool that is part axe and part hoe. Or imagine a double-bladed axe, but turn one of the blades at right angles to the other. It's what you carry when you need both, but as soon as it hits a few rocks slicing roots, it stops being a very useful axe. Never underestimate it, though. A year earlier, a Forest Service crewman named Bruce Klein had missed a swing, sliced his boot, and settled the Pulaski deep into his own foot. "Lawton just watched me to see if I was gonna bleed to death," Bruce recalled, naming a Forest Service co-worker. I doubted that was true. Even without smoke, Bruce was a little delusional, but he may have lived through his own bad aim just to spite Ron Lawton, so I guess paranoia isn't all bad. Bruce had dropped a tree on his own Forest Service truck just a year earlier. Few of us would work very close to him.

Maybe Lawton was just weighing the odds. This was a year before the tree planter we called Abdul dropped the tree on our cook tent.

Anyway, the Alabamans were exhausted, and when they saw me show up with a saw, I was cheered like I was Eisenhower entering Paris. I walked with what I imagined my most heroic gait although my feet were still blistered from the bad boots of two days earlier. I soon got to prove my hero stuff. There were twenty of them, and they were tired of going slow. I started dropping medium-sized madrone and oak as fast as I could, maybe one every two or three minutes, and they would clear them off the fire line like a horde of ants and then scrape the line of every scrap of burnable fuel. We were ahead of the fire now. When I'd fall a particularly big tree, they'd send up a cheer while the dust cleared. When I'd run out of gas, they'd bump up my fuel and refill the saw while I guzzled down quart after quart of water. There were no mountains like this in Alabama, they confessed, and few trees of any size. "Sheet, when we get a fire back home, we just send out a tractor and plow around it. Never seen nothing like this." I nodded as sage a good-old-boy nod as I could manage. I didn't tell them it was my first fire in any terrain. When I cut trees, their crew could fly. That's all that mattered to them. Maybe Eisenhower confused Paris with Brussels. So what.

The day became a blur. During a fuel break, one of the southerners told me, "You sure do have some beautiful country here, if it all wasn't standing on its side." My blisters began to insist on attention. A large, leaning madrone barber-chaired with a snap like a rifle shot as I began the back cut. I remembered a tree like that had split as it fell for one of the Ent Forestry cutters the year before. The half that shot in the air had come so close to his head that it knocked off his tin hat with the force a bat hits a baseball. "That tree could smash your head like a ripe melon," said the Alabaman who had become my self-appointed adviser on racial matters.

Too close for me. I tried to concentrate more on the next trees. The blisters started singing to me, a little off-key. I daydreamed of Ruby the night before in fire camp. Ruby had come to Forks the year before in answer to Bob-O's personal ad in the *Mother Earth News* classified section. Bachelors had always complained about the dearth of eligible single women on the river. Bob-O was never one who complained when he could take action. I'd never thought of him as much of a writer before, but the letter was a work of art. He described Salmon River life, his cabin, the gold-mining operation, the goats and the dogs, his beautiful young daughter, the moon, and the stars. He even listed his astrological sign, although I doubt that he took those things seriously. A fisherman who hasn't caught anything for a while will try any bait. He didn't mention that he was a good fisherman.

I'm not sure how most personal ads do. Some of us kidded Bob-O, and he took the teasing well. That all ended when the magazine came out. First he got a few letters. Then he got a lot of letters. Then he was flooded with mail. He scrupulously answered every one, whether they stirred his interest or not. After the paper screen, he began inviting a few of his favorites one at a time to visit his cabin at the mining claim, the place the old Gold Rush miners had named Starveout. I don't think he mentioned that name in the want ad either. He scheduled their visits with the caution of an air traffic controller. Overlaps could have disastrous consequences.

Their visits became the stuff of legend that summer among all the other bachelors and bachelor wannabes who peopled the Beer Tree. The Beer Tree was a graceful spreading walnut tree that shaded a picnic table across the road from the Forks of Salmon General Store. The Forks store in those days sold a few groceries, candy, and ice cream for the kids, beef jerky, nugget jewelry, and ice-cold beer. This was before the days of boutique beers and Häagen-Dazs ice cream in country stores, but that didn't matter to the bachelors. They would sit together in the afternoon passing around cans of Hamm's and an occasional marijuana cigarette. They traded stories about Bob-O's quest with the disdain that only the truly jealous can manage.

Soon it escalated. No woman flatlander, the Beer Tree word for a tourist, could step out of her car without someone yelling across the road, "Hey, I'm Bob-O." Then another would yell, "No, I'm Bob-O." They'd dissolve into gales of laughter. It only fed their fervor when one of Bob-

O's visitors arrived at the Forks store a day early, picked up with a young miner from Sawyers Bar, and never made her appointment. Then Ruby arrived, and Bob-O ended his search; the rest of us would always call it "his long, painful search," with as much irony as the envious can summon. Ruby was tall, slender, and beautiful, with translucent skin. She had the figure of a young woman but also the beginnings of gray in her hair and the look of someone who had seen too much unpleasantness with her blue-gray eyes. Sometimes, when she talked to us, she seemed to be tugged by reminders of a past none of us knew.

Still, she thrived at Starveout and soon joined us on the big tree-planting contracts that Ent Forestry would take with the US Forest Service. I'm not sure if she was a hippie before she came to the river, but she would strip to the waist on a hot spring day of planting the same as the other women planters. We men on the crew liked it for the scenery, I guess, but we liked it more for the discomfort it caused among the most sanctimonious Forest Service inspectors. She and Bob-O did well for a while, but by the time the Hog Fire started, she was single again. She signed on to fight fire and worked well. Tree planting was so hard that every job ever after seemed easy in comparison. If she advanced her reputation as a worker every day on the fire lines, it was in the teeming fire camps every evening that she established that she was single and free. One night she picked up with a tall, lean young engine captain from Redding who had shiny ebony hair and deep Aztec cheekbones. I imagined Ruby in a scanty jaguar skin, draped asleep across his muscled lap, with snowcapped volcanoes in the background like the calendars in Mexican restaurants.

The next night I missed her choice. Normally, I would have found out the next day at the Beer Tree, but all the regulars were off on fire lines, and the picnic table was full of out-of-town firefighters who spilled over from the fire camp, with its no-beer rules. Last night she was with a contract timber faller. You could tell by the felt pad threaded on the suspender strap over his right shoulder. She led him out like a pony she'd bought at the auction. He looked dazed—the man who'd won the lottery, but it hadn't quite sunk in yet. As we passed, she looked right at me, gestured at my chest, and said, "You're next." Then she and the faller disappeared into the darkness.

I pondered her pronouncement from the night before as I cut the next several trees near Butler Mountain. It was getting late in the day. Ten minutes without blisters and a cold beer sounded as good right then as being next on Ruby's dance card. Finally, we caught up with the work of other crews. We had finished our section of line. We collapsed on the ground in the first real break of the day. In a few minutes, a division supe from Wyoming marched up and introduced himself with great importance to the Alabama crew boss and to me. We needed to get moving down the line before dark. It was still a long way to the river, and a new crew was coming in any minute to start a backfire that would secure the line. Then he headed back down the line, resonating with authority. Alabama and I exchanged glances and picked ourselves off the ground. "Okay, you slugs," he grumbled to the crew in his soft drawl. "That very distinguished gentleman has informed us that we need to start moving out right now unless we want to eat a bunch more smoke. Let's leave it for the night shift."

I shouldered my saw and fuel pack and limped off down slope. My blistered gait must have looked so pained that two Alabamans offered to carry my saw and my pack of gear for me. At first I said no, but then I agreed. They soon disappeared into the haze, and I wondered if I'd ever see my chain saw again. Eventually I caught up with the Wyoming division boss. He was stopping often to issue the burnout orders. Soon, a couple of fusees dropped out of his pack. These phosphorus torches were expensive, and he might need them later for the burnout, so I picked them up and tried to catch him. Before I got too close, a couple more dropped out, and I picked them up, too. Soon I had an armful. This guy was as stupid as he was pretentious. I'd almost caught him to return his lost fusees when one of the Alabamans ran up to me and said, "How come you're picking up all the torches? The burn-out crew is gonna need them." I gave him an of-course-I-knew-that nod, dropped the fusees into a big pile and limped faster than ever to the bottom of the steep, rocky line.

You can still see the vestiges of that line today if you look up to the left of Grant Creek from just downriver. It's harder to see now, because the trees are returning and the brush has grown back bigger than ever. You need to squint. Imagine smoke. Imagine that your feet have turned to hamburger. Our fire line would hold, although I didn't know it that evening. The Butler Creek drainage would go unburned for a few decades more. I was herded over to a bunch of fallers less counterfeit than me. In the dwindling light all of us walked around the bluffs to Butler Creek, where a van would carry us back to Forks of Salmon. Some of the fallers wore caulks, the nail-bottom boots that let loggers defy gravity in heavy brush. In the growing darkness, the nails in the soles of their boots struck little electric sparks on the paved road as they walked. The Salmon River at Grant Creek was so beautiful in that hazy twilight that it took my breath away. When we rounded the bluffs, I caught the first glimpse of Butler Creek, a much larger tributary than Grant Creek. The wooded cleft of the Butler canyon was so moving, even in the dwindling light, that I may have cried.

CHAPTER 8

Meet the Famous Flores Sisters

There's a whole other story from that summer of 1977 besides the Hog Fire. I guess I should tell it, even though it's got some secrets. Like many of the best stories in those days, it began with Kate George. She always could keep secrets better than me.

There was no way to approach Kate's house without rousing her dogs. Day or night. On the hottest days or in the clatter of the windiest rainstorm. A few of the dogs might sleep. But a few were always awake. This time the two littlest dogs led the charge up the path to the gate. They looked like dust mops with tiny rows of teeth as they bounced in my direction. All the rest followed, annoyed that their slumber had been bothered by an intruder. Even the old black dog, which looked from the distance like a bear and had a snarl that sounded more geologic than animal, even that old dog hobbled toward the gate behind the rest.

If you asked people why Kate had so many dogs, they'd just tell you that she was the Matriarch of the Salmon River, as though that were an explanation. A matriarch may be hard to define, but you know one when you meet one, and Kate definitely qualified. She had lots of grown children who were pillars of the community. Many of them worked in the timber industry. She'd arrived on the river in her early twenties in the mid-1930s. So she knew everybody's stories, the ones they wanted public and the other ones too. Most important to me, she had befriended us at the commune in those first few years when most locals avoided us. That said something good. And she was looking after me these days several years after I'd left the commune (even though I was supposed to be her young, able-bodied caregiver as she grew old). Everything said matriarch, so if that meant a lot of noisy dogs, so be it.

I waited at the gate. There was no hurry. I was home after five weeks off in tree-planting camps across southern Oregon, and my eyes drank in how much everything had grown while I was away. The rains of winter and spring had finally backed off, and the dry season was just beginning. Meteorologists might have known that a giant forest fire might begin in early August, but I was clueless. After the interlude of barking dogs, Kate yelled to me from the little greenhouse between her house and the ramshackle cabin where I lived when I wasn't off planting trees somewhere. The dogs, except for the mops, took Kate's yell as an excuse to drop their guard. Kate waved her arms for emphasis, so I slipped past the gate and threaded through the winding paths that led to the greenhouse.

Kate's yard was a warren of old, low fencing, raspberry patches, horse corrals, abandoned gold mining diggings, decaying Ford trucks, and patches of orchard and bogs, which seemed fed by some oozy spring or maybe a broken pipe. There was no short path anywhere. But it was where she had lived for a long time. I was a relative newcomer, living in the cabin where Doc Hartman, her recently deccased sweetheart, had lived before me.

"Welcome home, Honey," she greeted me, all smiles, and we hugged. I'd grown to miss her and the comforts of her hospitality in those months I'd spent in the muddy tree-planting camps. I was always struck that she was still a beautiful woman, even as she approached seventy years old. Old-timers told me she was famously beautiful when she first came to the river.

"Did you kids fill up every clear-cut in Oregon?" she teased.

"It seems like we did. I thought there was a lot of logging around here until I went to Oregon. They've logged everything."

"It makes work for you tree planters, Honey. Wouldn't you rather they do their logging away from here?"

"I don't expect that kind of talk from a woman like you, Kate. Your sons are mostly all loggers."

"They may be, but they hate logging on Salmon River, too. Look at Monte Creek. Look at the rape of the Little North Fork. Nobody wants that to happen to the river any more. But save your politics for coffee. I have a present here for you." She made a dramatic gesture to usher me into the tiny greenhouse.

It was steamy inside and crowded with two of us. I looked over the flats of seedlings: tomatoes, peppers, lots of flowers I didn't know. I glanced at her, waiting for an explanation.

She paused, then with great drama pointed to a dozen small pots in the corner.

"What are they? They look like marijuana."

"They are pot plants, sir, and good stuff. An old woman up by Sawyers Bar gave me the seed. It's from her nephew."

I glanced around nervously to see if anyone was watching. This was before the era when a doctor could write you a prescription to grow pot legally. Even when I lived up at the commune, where pot was prized, we didn't grow it. This was partly because of police scrutiny. Remember the time the sheriff came in, confiscated the tomato plants—they'd identified them as marijuana—and threw three hapless hippies into jail? Maybe we early communards also didn't grow it because, at that stage of the game, anyway, we weren't so great at growing anything. Mostly, it wasn't just illegal in those days. It was very illegal.

Kate poked me on the shoulder. "Stop being silly. These seedlings are for you. You don't make enough money planting trees to buy a decent truck let alone a place to live. C'mon. Let's go have a cuppa." And she headed out of the greenhouse back toward her kitchen.

I followed behind and pressed for explanations. "I don't have a place to grow it. You don't expect to grow it here in the garden, do you?"

"I know the perfect place," she said. "But first, coffee. You've just gotten home. I saw a lot of your planters back on the river yesterday." Just then, a wind came up, and the sky darkened noticeably. Late spring is like that on the river. Weather systems shift through the canyons like attitudes in a person with a mood disorder. Sun, then bluster. A few minutes of rain and then sun again.

I seated myself at her table. She always made me feel so welcome that I could almost call it "our table."

I tried to explain my delay: "I had to stop at the Piss Fir station in Ashland yesterday to sign off on the contract and get the exhaust pipe patched on the green crummy."

Piss Fir was the pejorative locals used for Forest Service employees, and a crummy was logging talk for a crew truck. I'm not sure where either term originated, but a piss fir in woods slang was a white fir, a high elevation tree without much value at the mill, and the interior of a crew truck was often kind of, I don't know, crummy.

The dogs had stirred restively as we'd passed into the house, and then slumped back into the slumber of the warmth of late springtime. Not far below, the South Fork Salmon rushed, gorged with snowmelt, and its noisy gush filled the air and mixed with the calls of a dozen songbirds. A shiny, black horsefly buzzed the dogs, but they ignored it.

Kate's house was a work in progress spread over several decades. Lots of river houses seemed that way. The kitchen was an early chapter. Its ceiling was low, and the floor was uneven and spongy. A few of the back rooms were much more recent, with right angles, plumb walls, and standard windows. Kate incorporated them all without apparent bias.

At the table, she spooned instant coffee into the mugs and, as she usually did, filled them with water so full the cups brimmed, quivering over the top. She laid a cup at my spot and slid an open can of milk my direction. I worked to sip off enough of the steaming coffee to add the condensed milk. Finally, I said, "I'm not sure I need more money to get a place. I'll just find a mining claim and fix up the cabin. That's what everybody else on the river does."

"The Forest Service doesn't want people around here. They want everybody to live in cities where they can be controlled. They'll kick people off the claims one of these days, just like they're trying to do with Eldon and Betty Ann."

"You always say that, Kate," I argued. "They've tried to close the claims before, and they can never pull it off. They get a little bad publicity, and they run for cover. The claims are safe. Besides, more than half the people in Forks of Salmon live on claims. No claims, no town. They couldn't do that."

"They'll try it, and they'll do it. You'll see. They don't care about people. People are a bother for them. People see what they're doing, and they don't want that. And they'll figure out how. They broke 'Pop' George, and I never thought they could. They're hard to stop."

"Pop" George was her first husband. She always described him as a man of mythic capability. I'd never heard her say anything to suggest that he had any failings. He'd been a gold miner and a packer most of his life farther up the South Fork. Before there were many roads in the area everything was transported by packers on strings of big horses and giant mules. It was an Olympian occupation, and only a few families still have the skills. I waited for an explanation, but none was forthcoming. How could a government agency harm a man who could load ten or twenty obstinate mules and get them to march in a line along narrow mountain trails?

"They can't do it," I said, with little conviction.

She just shook her head. I pooh-poohed her again and said, "Why would a federal agency want to do that?"

She replied, "You hippies are such bad criminals. What's the First Law of Crime?"

I shrugged.

"The First Law of Crime," she said triumphantly, "is No Witnesses. The Forest Service doesn't like all these people around here seeing what they're doing to the place."

I tried to discount her warning.

———

By noon, I headed up to the county road where I'd parked the battered Ent crummy. There was only one road along the South Fork of the Salmon River. Everybody passed Kate's house, and most of them honked hellos. As I walked up to the crummy, Bob-O pulled up in his own truck and sat there for a few seconds in laundered, well-scrubbed, if threadbare, comfort. Bob-O, like me, had lived for years at the Black Bear commune before he moved down to a mining claim on the river, and he was one of the mainstays of the Ent Forestry co-op. Many of the people at the commune in my era were college educated, even with graduate degrees. A few others had had real jobs before they arrived at Black Bear Ranch. Bob-O, for instance, had been a diesel mechanic for Caterpillar. In some ways he still had blue-collar values, but they were covered by a solid veneer of hippie-dom. He sported a fringe of a beard and long hair, but his clothing was a hybrid, more northwest logger than Haight-Ashbury. Some of the no-college crowd seemed privately cowed by their own lack of higher education, as if it were a personal deficit. They imagined that they would be smarter if they'd gone to college, and that everybody could tell that they hadn't but that they were too polite to say anything. Bob-O had figured out just how much smarts college really conferred on people. He could see early on that they were skilled at the commune's frequent public arguments, but they came to him when they couldn't get a piece of machinery to run. Bob-O's style of public argument was demonstrative and loud.

Like me, Bob-O was just back from tree planting, and he said, "Welcome home, boychik. I was worried you'd gotten stuck in Oregon. Where you headed now?"

"To the Ent Shed. I've got the last of the gear to unload."

"By yourself? Those tents are heavy."

"Little Jake said he'd come help me."

Bob-O cleared his throat in disapproval and said, "Jake's best at helping himself."

"I know some people criticize him, but . . ."

"Some people? Everybody!"

"He seems to do okay with women around here. How does he manage that?" As soon as it popped out of my mouth, I remembered that an ex-girlfriend of Bob-O's had picked up last year with Little Jake.

"You know how he does it? I'll tell you how. He's got a big cock. That's how." And Bob-O glared defiantly.

I tried not to glance down below my own waistband, but I must have. Bob-O smiled and said, "Don't worry. You're okay. I'm okay. But he's big."

"Bob-O, are you saying that, in this respect, women are as shallow as men? What about all that 'Size doesn't matter' stuff?"

Bob-O prided himself on saying things outrageous and politically incorrect, but suddenly he paused. "I gotta go. Make him work hard unloading those tents." He bounded back into his truck and fired over the engine.

"And how come they call him Little Jake?" I yelled, but by then he was already driving away, downriver toward Forks of Salmon.

————

We called our two buildings the Ent Shed. They were built when the tree-planting business got too big for someone's living room and a corner of someone else's garage. One building was tall, sided with corrugated metal and wide sliding garage doors. It stored all the equipment—the mountain of huge army surplus tents with their plywood floors, heat stoves, and plumbing, plus the tree bags, augers, and hoe-dads that are a tree planter's tools of trade. Behind it was a generous wood-frame building under a large canyon live oak. It was sided in rough-cut lumber, and we liked to call it the Ent World Headquarters. It was there that the Ent Board, elected by their fellow workers, set policy, and a few of us pieced together bids for the contracts. If our bids won, we could find seasonal work for sixty-five or seventy people in the local towns.

Little Jake was already there when I drove up in the lumbering crew truck. Jake wasn't tall, but his arms and chest were massive. Since I was a kid, I'd wanted to be strong like that. Comic books I used to read had ads about how to look strong. My pop, a newspaper printer in the days when printers still used lead type, had hard-muscled arms from toting the trays of lead around the print shop. Even at the end of a grueling tree-planting season, when I was as buffed out as I would ever be, my arms still didn't look like the arms in the comic books. Or my pop's arms. But it was time to unload from the last long job, and Little Jake had come to help. By the time I arrived, he was already dumping garbage into barrels in the back of his truck for a shuttle to the town dump. The Ent Shed was always a transitional zone of storage, an interplay between valuable tools and junk. Jake waved briefly and kept filling the garbage barrels to make room for the tools I was delivering.

I backed in close to his truck—the loading space was not generous—and started working without formality. The last tree planting of the season usually came in late May or early June. The truck I was driving had been to four or five separate jobs since January, ferrying crews, tools, and other equipment. It had not been cleaned thoroughly in that time, and that was part of our job. The tools were easy. Mostly they were bags that held the trees and hoedads. A hoedad is a device that looks as odd as its name. It's swung like an axe and has a curved handle like an old-time carpenter's adze. Its flattened steel blade is attached to the handle by an offset collar, not balanced the way you'd expect. It looks like it was invented in a Roadrunner cartoon. Most new planters thought it was given to them by mistake on their first day, but soon they realized that it was ideally adapted to the grueling conditions of reforestation. Much of the tree planting was on steep ground—very, very steep ground. So besides slicing open holes for the baby trees, the hoedads provided a movable handhold when the clear-cut logging operation on steep ground had left little else. Many planters had a favorite hoedad, which they marked accordingly, and even a favorite tree bag.

Jake connected a hose, and we began rinsing off the tools. Most were caked in a layer of mud and the fine silvery vermiculite crystals that were a leftover of the slurry dips used to keep the tree roots moist. The glistening particles of vermiculite flew everywhere, and some even glistened in Jake's whiskers and long hair. A few bags had clotted remnants of forgotten seedlings, long past their prime, and we dumped them into the garbage. Next, we tackled the interior of the truck, with its two rows of seats. Mud and vermiculite were smeared everywhere, and we swept it out as best we could. Cleaning under the seats was the worst and comparable to what I imagine it would be to exhume a grave. The most common detritus consisted of half-eaten lunches, forgotten months earlier by some exhausted planters at the end of their shift. In the farthest recess, I found a box labeled "Four Dozen Condoms." I showed it to Jake and said, "At least somebody was having fun in tree camp."

John Gibbons took a few years off from his career as a wildland firefighter to plant trees with Ent Forestry, our local co-op. In his right hand is a hoedad, the main planting tool, and in his left is a two-year-old Douglas fir seedling. John could plant 600 to 700 per day. Photo by Jeff Buchin.

"I'm not so sure," he answered in his deep, droll voice, as he studied the find. "You notice that the box hasn't been opened."

Jake, in fact, was college educated, but he had successfully avoided any job that required his degree. He'd explained to me once that the current phase of his life should be physical work. Many of the Ents hated tree planting because the conditions were so miserable and the work so demanding. But Jake loved it. Sometimes, when it wasn't planting season, he'd hire on a logging operation as a choker setter or on a thinning crew as a chain-saw operator. He could talk about getting slapped in the face by a branch like it was an unexpected kiss. I'm not sure what he studied in college, but he must have done well in poetry.

The only heavy item in the truck was one of the big tents that Ent used for kitchens and dormitories out on its far-flung jobs. It was all the two of us could do to roll it out of the truck bed and into the shed. Two guys my size might not have managed it, but Jake was more powerful than most of us, and even then I saw the veins bulge in his arms and on his forehead as we pressed against the tent, a huge beached whale of dead brown canvas.

Finally, we were done, and both of us plopped down on the tailgate. Jake reached for his pack and produced two cups and a well-used thermos. To call it well-used would be to call the city of Beirut slightly scratched after the Lebanese Civil War. We all had the same brand of stainless steel thermoses in those days, but they were all easy to tell apart because of the different traumas they had survived. Jake's was the easiest. It had been run over by a bulldozer on a logging job and crunched to half its former size. "It still works?" I asked.

"Works fine. Still keeps stuff hot all day. Course, it only holds half as much." He began pouring steaming coffee for each of us, and I served up a bag of fresh-baked cookies.

"Cookies courtesy of Kate George," I said.

"Hers are the best. She must be happy to have you home. She told me she misses your company when you're off planting."

"She had a little present when I got home. She started me a bunch of pot plants in her little greenhouse while we were planting. Who would believe? She's almost seventy."

Jake pursed his lips and smiled. Finally, he said, "Kate's a smart woman."

"Whaddya mean? I don't know the first thing about growing pot."

"It's no harder than tomatoes. I grow a little pot. It's not rocket science. A guy can't live on tree planters' wages."

I was surprised by his candor and said, "I didn't know that. And that's just what Kate said about tree planters' wages. But the feds and the county seem so intent on busting people. Doncha worry about that?"

Jake smiled thoughtfully and finally said, "The business part of cultivation depends totally on law enforcement. Without it, what would pot be worth? About the same as blackberry canes." He gestured at an invasive thicket of brambles spreading a few feet past the Ent Shed. "Government has always intervened to prop up agricultural prices. They pay a farmer thousands of dollars not to grow soybeans or alfalfa as price supports. They'd do that with pot, but it'd be a political embarrassment. 'Jake, here's ten grand not to grow cannabis this year.' It's better for them just to grab some plants and make a big show in the media. They inflate their street value and apply for a bigger enforcement grant for the next department budget. It's a win-win."

"Not for the people who get busted," I said.

"Who gets busted, around here, anyway? Nobody. It's all a well-lubricated system of government price supports. I just do my little part."

"That's all fine," I said, "but I don't like the effect it has on tree planters. People get stoned, and they don't plant as fast as they could otherwise. Take DJ Hartley for instance. Sometimes he gets stoned while we're planting."

"I see your point, since we all get paid by the hour and not by the tree," Little Jake agreed. He paused, then added, "On that last full day at Ashland, what did you plant? How many for the day?"

"Maybe five-fifty, six hundred. It was rocky ground." I may have exaggerated here but who wants to admit you didn't even get to five hundred trees in a day, no matter how rocky the ground?

"Six hundred," Jake repeated, with a grin. "You know how many DJ planted that day? DJ planted nine-fifty. I asked him because he was covering so much ground. What do you say to that?"

I had no answer. I grabbed another cookie, chewed it for a while, and admired its crunch. Finally, I said, "You guys who started the co-op started a pretty good outfit. Was it hard at the beginning?"

"It didn't start out as a co-op," Jake said. "A half dozen of us took one contract from the Forest Service to replant some new clear-cuts up near Cecilville. We bought some tools, and we bought one of those big tents from an army surplus outfit. At the end of the job we divided up the money, and John Albion wanted us to cut up the tent into six equal pieces. Just like the one we just moved. You know how much canvas it takes to make a tent that big. "After we got a few more jobs, other people joined. At some point we invited in women, and that was great for the business."

I winked knowingly, but Jake said, "More than romance. Women turn out to be great planters. The strongest men can plant more in an hour than the best women planters, but, at the end of the day, the women will have planted more. Not sure how. But it's true. It is a good local business."

"But nobody makes that much money," I said. "Maybe tree-planting season is too short. And maybe that's why some people grow a little pot on the side." Jake nodded in agreement.

"Also, you must end up with some great stuff to smoke," I said.

"Malcolm," he said, "I never smoke anymore. I only smoke when I want to be stupid." With that he gathered the cups and the crumpled thermos, threw the pack in his truck, and started to leave.

"Thanks for the help on the unloading," I said.

"Thanks to you, for yours." Then he started his truck, backed up onto the Salmon River Road, and headed home.

———

The next morning Kate drew me a detailed map of where I could plant her horticultural gifts. It met the requirements: difficult to find and a good water supply. I found the old path on a little flat dissected by gullies in previous floods, regrown with brambles, ferns, and woody brush. Soon the trail veered up a steep bank, the remains of a hydraulic gold-mining operation that had washed away the mountainside a century earlier. I carried a hundred-foot coil of black plastic pipe and a Pulaski, that firefighting tool also favored by many horticulturists. In places the trail disappeared, and I bushwhacked for a dozen yards before I found it again. In others, it was so skinny that I found myself staring straight down at the flat far below. Finally, I reached the top, an even smaller bench flat, and found the spring shown on Kate's hand-drawn map. I

anchored one end of the pipe into the spring and unrolled the other end
toward a clearing in the small pines and madrones that grew there. When
the pipe ran out, I scratched a shallow ditch further, and the water flowed
freely. Kate had said the spring never went dry, and I could see why she
had picked this spot.

Within two weeks, safely past the last frost, I shoveled in horse manure
from Kate's corrals and then transplanted out her perky little starts on
either side of the meandering ditch. I could see that the plants would get
enough water but not too much. They would not need much tending,
which was good because, if I used the path too often, I might crush the
foliage. That would be like posting a sign that said: *Dope Patch Ahead—
Rip-offs Invited*. It was also good because it was a summer less lazy than
most on Salmon River. For starters, a handful of Ent tree planters, me
included, headed off to that six-week tree-thinning job in Montana near
the Canadian border. It was one of those surefire, big money operations
where you end up losing your shirt. I still tell that story sometimes.

I felt I'd earned some sloth after Montana, but I talked myself into
that logging job with Crazy Dave, the first one I'd ever had. I'd always
avoided logging because it was environmentally a disaster and because it
was so dangerous. But loggers were a likable lot; I didn't expect that. Just
a few weeks into my career as a logger was when the Hog Fire started.
A few of the afternoons after logging, and even sometimes during the
fire, I'd steal up to the patch. I'd check the watering and add manure.
Each time I was stunned by how much the plants had grown, even when
the Salmon River canyons were choked with smoke from the wildfires.
Friends taught me how to tell female plants from male, a critical skill
for growing the prized sinsemilla seedless pot. I was never sure I had it
down, but, if they said a plant was male, I'd dutifully pull and toss it. It
had to do with identifying tiny luminescent pistils, or was it stamens?
In the end, anyway, I had seven certified big momma plants, and they
flourished. If any male plants survived, then all the females would be full
of seed, and the smoke was expected to be much less potent. This was the
wisdom of veteran growers, and I did not test it.

When the smoke finally died down from the fires, there was time to
relax. Locals gathered at the swimming hole closest to the Ent Shed on

the hot afternoons and lingered in the slow-moving water, washing away a hard season's sweat and grit. We'd earned it. Finally, life returned to the pace that made river life so livable. It also gave me time to start paying some attention to the patch. Miraculously, the water system had managed to deliver all summer without a hitch. Eventually, I was advised that it was time to begin the harvest.

The plants by then were huge, ten feet high and six feet wide. I cut down the first and realized that one single plant would be all I could manage down the steep brushy trail. I paused at the Salmon River Road before crossing, listening for approaching traffic. Predictably, there was none. I leaned the first plant against the wall in the snug kitchenette of Doc's former cabin and opened the windows so it would dry. Its sweetness filled the little cabin and the surrounding yard. The next day I loaded down another and the next day a third. That day I wondered if someone else had been up the trail because the brush looked broken. At the patch, I saw a track from a smaller boot than mine and looked for any sign of theft. For safety, I cut and packed two more, and by then Doc's little kitchen was packed, so I left the remaining two plants to fatten up at the spring.

There seemed to be some variation in the plants, so I named each of them with Spanish names and started to remove the floral buds as they dried. Painstakingly, I packed the buds into large Ziploc bags and labeled them Maria Flores, Anjelica Flores, Rosario Flores, and so on. I thought of them as the Famous Flores Sisters and handled their sticky bounty for a couple hours every day, until their resin made it too hard to handle them. I didn't know anything about selling so much marijuana, but how hard could it be? Lots of my neighbors managed it just fine, and they could give me tips. The Famous Flores Sisters were producing lots of bulging Ziploc bags. There would be a lot of money. Certainly, a down payment on land. Maybe more.

It was then that I heard the radio program. Radio was always dicey in the Salmon River canyons. The best reception was at night on powerful AM stations like KGO out of San Francisco, a long day's drive away. Daytime reception was not so good, usually not good at all. It was an evening talk show with a wide range of extreme political points of view, which made it a lot like the demographic profile of the river community. I remember looking at the Salmon River election results in 1980 and the results were 40 percent for American Independent, a very conservative and libertarian party, the same for Peace and Freedom, a very left progressive party. The remaining 20 percent was divided equally between the Democrats and the Republicans.

KGO also had news blasts every half hour, and they were a kick. All of us particularly liked the traffic reports. There's something profoundly satisfying, when you live on a one-lane, barely paved mountain road where cars rarely drive, about hearing that traffic's backed up for eight miles in the morning commute because of a big rig jackknifed in the Caldecott Tunnel. It's an especially rewarding cultural experience.

But the news on the radio was more unsettling this morning. The announcer described how two drug enforcement officers were killed in a bungled raid on a set-up marijuana buy in an East Bay motel. The broadcaster said the shooting had started between two heavily armed officers from different agencies who didn't know each other and who started shooting when they saw each other. The actual dealer and a buyer, who was really a cop, listened to the gunfire in the motel room but didn't know what was going on. It was just a standard broadcast of a drug bust turned deadly sour, but then the announcer said that the dealer was a man named Lawrence Feinstein and that he would be charged with drug dealing and with felony murder. That's what they charge when someone is killed in the commission of a felony, even if the defendant never pulled a trigger.

But I knew the guy. I knew the hapless dealer in the motel room. It was Larry, the F. Larry had been in my Boy Scout troop when I was eleven years old. Jeez. Larry, the F, who knew more dirty jokes than anybody else in the troop and was a pretty cool guy. I didn't always get all of his jokes, but I could always tell when it was time to laugh. I tried to imagine his sinking feeling as he heard the gunshots outside the room, and he realized that the buyer was really a cop. I spent the next couple of days thinking about poor Larry stuffed in some jail on murder charges and then thinking about the big hedge of weed drying in my little cabin. I imagined myself in his spot. Dreams of land purchases suddenly got cloudy. I got more and more depressed. Those dreams were replaced some nights with dreams of getting chased by the police. In one I was trying to sneak through a parking lot heavily patrolled by police cars. I was hauling one of the huge plants on my shoulder and tried to look inconspicuous, standard dream fare. In the back of one of the police cars I saw two of the beautiful Flores sisters except they had turned into real-life curvaceous Latinas in bright-colored dance-hall dresses, no longer bags voluptuously bulging with golden, almost purple, crystal-coated marijuana buds. They saw me through the window of the dream-world squad car and pouted. After that, everything seemed to change.

Aimlessly, I pruned my way through the huge shrubs, bagging the sticky flowers in big Ziplocs and shoving the leaf—what locals called shake—into garbage bags. Kate never asked me about the whole process, but she may have noticed the smell of the smoke when I'd burn the stems in my little stove to start the evening fire.

One evening, Al Adato showed up with a bottle of wine; he was to help with the trim work. Al had been a successful businessman in the Bay Area, but he'd walked away from that in the fall to come fishing. He had bold, dark Sephardic features and a massive physique. A hug from Al, and he loved to hug, was a hug from the friendliest bear you ever met. Fishing was good in those days, and he'd stayed. The same social skills and brains that made him good in business got him invited to work as a fishing guide with a lodge down in Somes Bar. It was an invite never offered to flatlanders or newcomers, but it was offered to Al. And he was good at it. A natural. Strong, smart, charming, and he could think like a fish. Al was a natural at most everything he tried. Charming people came to Al as easy as catching fish. Maybe he *was* part bear.

"I heard you pull up a while ago," I said. "Were you over there charming Kate? She loves you."

"She didn't love me today," he grumbled. "Kate heard I was fooling around with Ariel up the South Fork, and she got very uptight about it."

That surprised me. Ariel was a pretty single mom who granted her favors among the river men as she chose. "Why did that bother Kate?" I asked. "She likes Ariel. She adores you."

Al shook his head as he opened the wine and poured out two glasses. "She told me that I was being unfaithful to Kelsey." Kelsey was Al's sweetie back in the Bay Area, but I knew their arrangement.

"That's not the kind of thing that would bother Kelsey. I wonder what's bugging Kate?"

"Dunno," he said with a shrug, but his attention shifted to my harvest that, by then, filled every corner of the little cabin, and he nodded approvingly. "You've got a real down payment here, my friend. Good work." One of Al's businesses had been real estate.

"I'm not gonna sell it, Al."

His dark eyebrows rose in wonder, and I explained to him about Larry, the F. I left out the dream with the Flores sisters in the police car. Generously, he did not ask if I'd lost my nerve, although clearly I had. Finally, Al asked, "So what you gonna do? That's more than you're gonna smoke." He knew I hardly smoked at all.

"I'm going to give it away, that's what. You said you were headed back to the Bay Area on Wednesday. You can give it away to our friends down there. They all have to pay too much for pot."

Al assumed a Santa Claus posture with one of the two duffle bags of the trimmed Flores Sisters slung over his shoulder. He said, "Ho, ho, ho," with conviction. If Santa Claus could have had a black beard and a big Sephardic nose, Al would be perfect for the job. "But who should I give it to?" he asked.

I named a few names and said he could figure out the rest. He said it would not be a problem.

"But what about you, Al?" I asked. "What do you want for yourself?" He looked over the piles of Ziplocs and the plants that were still untrimmed. Finally, he said, "I just want this," and he snipped the largest flower off the top of lthe argest plant. It was fat and resinous, too long for the biggest Ziploc bag, and he smiled like a connoisseur picking a fine wine. "Dealer's choice," he murmured to himself. Then he turned to me and said, "Of course, size doesn't matter."

CHAPTER 9

Winter Sun

It was nearly winter solstice of 1978, and everybody was ready to give me advice. Kate George had watched the arrangement evolve, and she had the sagest advice.

Eight of us—mostly veteran expatriates from the Black Bear commune—had thrown a down payment together to buy an eighty-eight-acre parcel of land downriver on the main stem Salmon River at Butler Creek. A few days before winter solstice, I told Kate that I was going to move downriver for at least a while to figure out which house site on this new land was best and also to make sure the place didn't get vandalized or even torched in the transition of ownership. She may have had reservations about me entering another collective real estate venture after the Black Bear commune, but she did not voice them. "The most important thing," she said, "is winter sun. Everything else is nice. The most important is winter sun." She gave me that intense stare that we reserve for the dull and the profoundly stupid. She added, "Winter sun." I considered reminding Kate why I'd left the commune and how a new venture would be different, but did not. Black Bear was still full of people. I was just ready for other arrangements.

Joe Miller, the retired Los Angeles businessman who sold us the Butler Creek place, also had advice, and he was even more outspoken. Kate George had warned me that Miller was uptight about hippies and just about everybody else—white and Native alike—who was there when he first arrived from Southern California. But he always seemed evenhanded and cards-face-up with us. I don't know what thawed his bigotry. His initial contacts with our group were Efrem Korngold and Masabi Guerra. Even back then, those two could project charm and smarts enough to wither any stereotype. Maybe that was it.

Miller also hated his tenant, a Vietnam vet who was then renting the tiny cabin at Butler; he was glad that tenant was not the buyer. The bad feeling was pretty reciprocal.

"You're nuts to get into this deal," Miller confided one day after signing a set of real estate papers in his shaky hand. I'd heard that before and waited for details. "Eight partners. That's too many. It'll be trouble. Nobody will ever agree."

I thought to myself that I could never afford the $100,000 price tag on my own. Most of us were making less than five grand a year at the time as tree planters. One hundred thousand was as out of reach as a billion. It was partners or nothing. "We already have a lot of experience with each other," I told Miller. "We know how to work things out." He nodded, not especially in agreement. "Are you trying to talk me out of the deal?" I finally asked.

"Look here, Terence. The doctors tell me I'm dying. I want to finish the deal. But I've got so little time that I don't want to hide anything. Too many partners." He shook his head again and handed me the papers with a trembling hand. The deal was closed, and that was the last time I saw him.

There were no partners with me when I arrived at the sole, weathered little cabin at Butler at midday on winter solstice 1978. It was boarded up and padlocked, but Masabi had given me the key. The sun, which blisters the Salmon River so intensely every summer, was now a distant winter star barely peeking over Butler Saddle to the south. I'd only been there once before, two summers earlier when the flat was an impromptu firefighter base camp during the Hog Fire. I glanced at the meadow where they'd tied my chain saw, my fuel can, and my pack on a shiny black mule to be packed up the fire line on the ridge. But in winter the sun retreated behind that ridge for most of the day. In the places where the sun didn't shine, which seemed to be most places, the hoarfrost grew deeper every day. "Winter sun," Kate George's caveat, rang through my brain. I could see now why it was important. The cracked cast-iron woodstove in the cabin was full of partly burned wood, blackened beer cans, and ash. I cleaned it out, started a fire with soft rotted wood stacked nearby, and set out to find more. The small shed out north of the house had a few pieces. Curiously, one corner of its roof was shot full of bullet holes. The bed of an old red Chevy pickup was overturned to the west, and it harbored a few more pieces of wood. It was also full of bullet holes. Beyond it was the ruin of a birdhouse in the grass. Full of holes.

The cabin was Spartan, but I'd gotten used to bare-bones when I'd lived at the commune. That wasn't the reason I'd left there after four years and ended up living on the river. I learned a huge amount there. More than anything I learned what I needed to learn. That was a long list. Lots of people left Black Bear about the same time that I did, but the population was large then. The place got very polarized that last year, and people got very abrasive with one another. Kate George said it was a collision between the Be-ers and the Do-ers. She categorized me as a Do-er, and she liked that. Many people had similar interpretations. Certainly, I'd tired of the friction. But later on, most of the people I argued with back then became my closest friends, and a few became partners in this Butler Creek venture.

Masabi was still living in Berkeley, but he'd told me to be wary of the ex-tenant, who was the author of all the bullet holes. In Vietnam, the tenant boasted, he'd been part of Project Phoenix. I remembered that this was an American army campaign in South Vietnam to assassinate Vietnamese suspected of supporting the Viet Cong. In those days America was full of vets returned from Asia. Most were happy to be home, happy the war was over on any terms, and happy to stay stoned. Some were haunted by particular demons.

The only visitor that first day was a handsome and affable Karuk man who lived nearby and had seen the smoke churning out of our chimney. He offered a handshake and welcomed me to the neighborhood. Then he said, "My pot's growing over there (and he pointed up the mountain to nowhere in particular). Where's your patch?"

I said I didn't have a patch. He gave me the smile you give someone who has, of course, lied to you, and thereby passed an intelligence test. He asked me how the place was doing, and I said it was okay, but that the departed tenant was a little scary.

My visitor nodded and said with a smile, "That guy's scared of me." I tried to look pleased at this news.

The tenant had moved downriver only a few miles with his wife, a pretty mouse of a woman. I remained wary. Even before I saw the riddled birdhouses, I'd heard of his reputation. Story was if you even stopped to piss near Butler Flat, the tenant started shooting. Not many stopped.

The water worked in the sink, and I scrubbed out a dirty cup to try a sample. Finally, an auspicious sign. The water tasted good, and there was so much of it. The river and the creek had made a hushed, slurring background noise in the summer a year and a half earlier during the Hog Fire. Both river and creek were running much fuller now with December runoff, and they roared insistently, even with the doors and windows closed. I had lived in the desert before coming to Salmon River country, and streams that ran year-round still amazed me as much as snow.

A shaky ladder in the entryway went up through an open trapdoor into the attic. I dragged my bedroll up there. It would stay warmer there after the fire burned out. I arranged kindling so it would be dry in the morning, found the coffeepot in my gear, and went to bed.

In the morning I brewed coffee on the gas stove and eventually headed out on my quest: to locate winter sun. It was not early when I finally stepped outside the cabin, but the sun was still behind the ridge when I emerged onto the porch. The air was crisp, and there was a blanket of frost everywhere. A Cat road, a dirt track built by a bulldozer, headed across the meadow toward the source of the creek, and I headed up it. The sites where three creek cabins were later built were then still heavily wooded with fir, madrone, and tanoak. The ground there was frozen hard and thick with frost. At one point the road forked, and, after much chilly deliberation, I took the right fork, up the stream. Soon it ended where it overlooked a loud, breathtaking waterfall that dropped in stages, maybe ten feet, then another ten, then twenty more into a huge jumble of logs and boulders. I backtracked from the falls and tried the left fork.

It looped through the woods, and I noted its condition. Dirt roads didn't last long through the wet winters, but this one was still in good shape. Eventually the road broke back into the meadow above the cabin. I realized that the sun was shining on the cabin, and I hastened down to bask in its distant warmth. As I walked down, I spotted two small clearings on either side of the upper part of the meadow. Down at the cabin, the frost had melted and was dripping voluminously off the roof. Suddenly everything that had been hard and frost white was soft, wet, and even green. I began to understand why Kate George had attached such importance to winter sun. I returned to explore the two small clearings above the cabin, and by then the sun had overtopped the ridge at Butler Saddle enough to pour into them, too. They had become soft, green, and beautifully drippy. I circled back around the loop to see where else the sun had hit. It filled the treetops in one place on the back road, but most of the others still sat in frozen shade. Just across the creek, the sun was hitting the ground, but on my side it was just brushing the highest treetops. Light breezes stirred their leaves as the air warmed slightly, and frost sprinkled down from them, a cross between fine snow and a shower of diamonds. When it hit the ground, it did not melt. I saw another small clearing, just above the fork in the road, and it seemed tucked so close into the toe of the ridge that I named it Ice-Box Flat in my mind. My mission was complete; I had tracked winter sun and found a little. I could return with honor to the warmth of Kate George's hearth.

Both chimneys were smoking thin silver streams when I got back upriver to Kate's place, and my heart jumped. One fire was warming the house, and she was cooking on the other on a big, iron wood range that was older than she was. She had begun to teach me the subtle complexities of the woodstove that winter, and I was impressed. This lever damped the chimney; that one circulated heat around the oven. Fir burned hot and quick, but oak burned even hotter, once kindled well, and made a bed of coals that took less tending. If needed, you could make the thick stove top so hot it glowed cherry red and you could remove a ring so a pan got the direct blast of the flames. The left side was hottest, and the right was cooler, with an infinite gradient in between. If it got too hot, Kate would just pull a ring, grab the ever-present steam kettle, and pour a little water on the flames. On top of all that, it had a pipe coil in its fire-box that heated water for showers and washing. We abandoned a whole range of possibilities when we settled for gas stoves.

Kate's house that day had an unfamiliar smell, kind of musky, when I walked in. Kate barely looked up, but she stirred a huge kettle on the stove. "Hi, Honey," she said. "Sam slaughtered a beef today, so I had to make neat's-foot oil from the hooves. Did you ever make it?" I wasn't sure what neat's-foot oil was, but, from its smell, I hoped it wasn't something you eat. "I'm not sure," I said. "What is it?"

She chuckled and said, "I noticed the leather on your boots is cracked. You can use it on them. It's better than bear fat. I expected you'd get back tonight. Can you smell the apple pie in the oven?"

I sniffed deeply. Neat's-foot turns out to be an archaic reference to cows' feet, and the smell of them boiling dominated the room. Behind it I sensed a trace of cinnamon and nutmeg. "Smells great," I lied. She made the best pies, and although I'd tried many times under her instruction, I could never match them. Maybe she was leaving out some key step or ingredient. (I learned later that bear fat had other uses besides as boot grease, but she didn't share that at the time.)

"Haul this kettle outside," she commanded, "so the broth can gel in the cold. The oil will be easy to spoon off the top in the morning. Then go wash up. Supper's almost ready."

By the time I returned, the table was set with meat loaf, green beans with bacon, mashed potatoes, and a steaming pitcher of gravy. "It's beautiful," I said. No fib this time. "When are the other ten people coming?"

She laughed and made a mock curtsy for the compliment. "Dig in," she said, "and then I want to hear all about your new commune."

"It's not a commune, I don't think," I said between mouthfuls. "It's mostly Black Bear veterans, but there's nothing like living with sixty hippies to dispel any romantic illusions." It was safe talking this way to Kate. When we had first come into the country ten years earlier, nobody in Siskiyou County had ever seen a hippie up close, and what they read in the papers triggered their deepest fears. Most people shunned us, but Kate was one of the few who welcomed us with open arms. She said she was tired of the things river people talked about—bulldozers and poker—and longed for people trying out some new ideas, regardless of how weird they looked.

Kate had told me her story many times, but piecemeal. She herself had come to the river in the early 1930s, in effect running away from home. She'd grown up in an upper-crust East Coast family with a tyrant of a father. Kate had been forced to drop out of Barnard College to get a job when her father lost everything in the Depression. "He still tried to boss me then, even when I was making the only money in the family," she recalled. "He ordered me how to vote in the 1932 election—for Hoover. I voted for FDR and every Communist and Negro I could find on the ballot just to spite him."

Finally, Kate decided to go out West to the wilds of northern California, where she had an aunt who was married to a gold miner on the Salmon River. It was wilder in those days; many of the river trails had just barely been replaced by roads. The miner was in his mid-forties and was the descendant of miners from Wales who came to the South Fork Salmon River in 1850. Kate's aunt was quite a bit older than the miner, but Kate insisted her aunt had lied about her age and was crazy, besides. One night the miner woke to find his wife—the aunt—standing over him with a butcher knife in her hand; that's when they had her shipped back to the relatives. Kate explained, with a girlish flourish, "After that it was just the two of us there. He was a beautiful man. We went up to a cabin in Cecilville and fell in love. That's when we made Claire."

Claire was the first of their children, followed by five sons, most of whom still lived on the river. Some old-timer skeptics on the river hinted that the aunt had gotten unhinged by the arrival of her nubile Ivy League niece, but I preferred Kate's version. Kate outlived "Pop" George and had become a schoolteacher after his death. Later she picked up with another miner named Doc Hartman. There was some dispute whether Doc was really a doctor. He claimed he was a dentist, and his claim was mostly taken at face value. He had worked for several years on the teeth of his neighbors and their horses. He worked in trade for fish or nuggets, or for free, and people were willing to overlook that there was no framed certificate on his office wall, or no office for that matter. It was quicker than a trip out over two snowy mountain passes to Yreka, and the price was right. Doc had also welcomed the hippies at the Black Bear commune and would ride his horse up the back trail for frequent visits, bringing along other river people who became our friends. But Doc died, too, of esophageal cancer.

After he was gone, Kate slipped into frequent bouts of depression. When I moved into Doc's little cabin, next door to her, and became her de facto houseguest, her relatives were almost relieved. They would have been completely relieved if I were not an expatriate from the hippie commune, but Kate was happy with my company, and they had long ago stopped trying to talk sense to her. One day she got a letter from an old friend, also in her late sixties, in which the friend gushed with excitement that she'd heard a rumor that Kate had found a new young lover. I liked being part of a scandal. Kate showed me the letter, shook her head, and said, "Can you believe that woman?" She never made the time though, it turned out, to tell the woman that the scandalous rumor was false.

One night Kate had announced, "You know, I'm kind of a hippie. Did I tell you what happened up in the wilderness? We were at some lake, maybe Water Dog Lake, me and a lot of my kids and grandkids. There were some hippies camped across the lake, and they started skinny dipping. My family went nuts, and they started hooting and hollering and making this huge racket. They were being so stupid that I stripped off all my clothes but my underpants and swam over to the hippies to apologize for my family's bad manners. That shut my kids up. Anyway, I figure that makes me a hippie, too."

It was always hard to tell whether I was caring for Kate or she was looking after me. I helped with the firewood and gardening and invited a stream of people through her dining room who talked about things more interesting than poker. She would give me useful advice when I asked (or when I should have asked) about everything from stone masonry to how to best manage an affair of the heart. She was always ready to appraise the occasional woman who would come to keep me company at Doc's little cabin. (She never approved of any of them, by the way, until she met Sue, but she told me that Sue was probably too smart to have anything to do with me. But that came later.)

That evening when I returned from that first exploration of Butler, Kate was anxious to hear the report. I started with a rush of details. The soil. The water. The vegetation. I spilled out plans I was already hatching. I asked her about the ruins of a tall chimney along the creek by a row of ancient walnut trees. She said the Grant family had built a two-story hotel building there as a way station on the Salmon River Trail, but, when the road was built a few years later between Forks of Salmon and Somes Bar, no one needed a way station. "They still had dances there. I used to play piano," she boasted. "There was an old miner who'd bring his accordion all the way down twenty-five miles from Cecilville in a wheel barrow. The whole building was undermined in the '64 flood, and that chimney's all that's left," she said, and then slyly added, "What about sun?"

I was prepared, and I gave her the whole report: which sites were good and which bad.

"So what are you going to do with this information now that you have it?" she said.

"I'll share it with the other partners, I guess, so nobody has any inside information on the good sites and nobody gets stuck with something they don't want."

Kate stared at me for a moment, perplexed. I'd given up anticipating what she would say about anything. A few months earlier she asked me who I was going to vote for in the election for Siskiyou County sheriff. "I don't know, Kate. Who do you think?"

"Well, there's two main guys running. The incumbent is a drunk and never does anything. The undersheriff is also running. He's a real go-getter, and he's brought lots of grants into the department and started lots of new programs."

"So it's the undersheriff," I ventured.

"No. No. No. Why would you want someone like that for sheriff? Of course, you vote for the drunk." She shook her head with frustration at my inability to figure out even the simplest things.

But for this conversation, the focus was winter sun. "So you know which are the best sites and you're going to tell everybody, right?"

I nodded nervously. She shook her head and broke into a huge grin. She said, "I guess the world would be a better place if everybody was hippies. Me, I'm ready for pie. How about you?" The apple pie was, as always, delicious. Halfway through she said, "Notice anything special about the pie?"

"Yeah. It's great."

"No. Something different," she pressed.

"More cinnamon. No, I give up." Please don't tell me about bear fat, I prayed to myself.

"It's got no bottom crust. Only a top crust," she announced proudly.

"Of course it's got a bottom crust," I protested. "Wait, you're right. But you can't make pie that way. People would complain."

"The bottom crust just gets gooey. Besides, every pie I've ever made for you had only a top crust. You just never noticed." She clasped her hands on the table in front of her and grinned with pride.

I finished the pie and had seconds. After pie, I found a bottle of brandy in my pack and poured us each a small glass. She started telling stories about the lifting rock, which still sits in her front yard. I'd seen it there, a large flattened boulder of granodiorite with a smooth surface and a greenish-gray tint. Only a few miners, in the days when boulder moving was a miner's main activity, had ever managed to lift it even a few inches clear of the ground. Clarence George, her deceased husband, had been one of them. She called him Poppa or Pop, and she missed him very much. Then she pumped me for stories from the commune. I started talking about Zoë Leader, my partner from commune days, and wondered if I'd ever find anyone I loved as much as her. Kate and I grew more and more comfortable in each other's company as the evening unwound. It was a sweet and rare rapport for two people thirty years apart in age. Finally she sighed, looked deep into my eyes and said, "If I was just fifteen years younger."

I, too, sighed, and in a dreamy voice said, "Or if I was just fifteen years older."

"No, Honey," she corrected. "If I was fifteen years younger."

CHAPTER 10
Water and Love

Some stories seem to converge in the way tributary streams join to form a river. So this is the story of a great engineering project that wrapped itself around my favorite love story. Engineering feats require attention and maintenance to serve you well. So do romances, of course. The engineering part—let's start with that. It wrapped itself around my favorite stream and began in the summer of 1981. I wasn't sure if we could pull it off. "We" were the eight families who had, two and a half years earlier, bought the land at Butler Creek and then spent most of a year deciding how best to use it. And then we spent another year convincing the Siskiyou County Planning Department and other agencies to give us permission for our plan. There was permitting with the county and the US Forest Service, consultation with state Fish and Wildlife and the National Resource Conservation Service, reports from an archaeologist and a botanist, tests for water quality and water percolation. It was all to build eight house sites on nearly ninety acres of land. But we wanted to keep it as one piece of land instead of sawing it up into parcels, partly because of the topography and partly, perhaps, because of a romantic notion that people lived better in cooperation than divided by individualism. It was a notion that had survived, against all odds, the years that many of us had spent at the Black Bear commune several miles upriver in the same Salmon River watershed. We used to joke that it was one to five years at the commune, ideological indeterminate sentencing. Notice that we wanted eight separate houses. I guess we wanted a little privacy as much we wanted cooperation.

The project we faced now was constructing a water system that would serve these eight as-yet-unbuilt houses. We already had a patchwork of half-assed systems. One worked in the summer and another in the winter, but neither provided enough flow for even the two or three house sites that were already halfway occupied. The solution was to build a dam way up the creek—not a storage reservoir but a diversion that would let us capture some water. It needed to work in the polite flows of summer and also survive the rampaging runoff of the winter rainy season. We'd carefully surveyed the creek. We showed the state and federal agencies that we would take only a small fraction of the flow at the driest time of year. Because two large waterfalls permanently blocked the upstream passage of salmon and steelhead, the agencies gave us the go-ahead. Bob Banning, a veteran irrigation vendor in Scott Valley, took our surveys and recommended sizes and amounts of pipe, starting with a half mile of six-inch PVC pipe above ground in the gorge, then dropping to four-inch and three-inch on the flat as it would run underground to the different house sites. This is a lot of pipe. One twenty-foot piece of Schedule 40, six-inch PVC pipe weighs 65 pounds. Empty. Fill it with water and you add another 250 pounds.

The diversion dam was the first step. There were the remains of an earlier dam way up the creek, but it was smashed by the 1964 flood when wild flows sent hundreds of trees down the channel and hammered the dam apart down to its concrete footings. To avoid a repeat of that, Tommy Soto suggested that we build an adaptation of the old diversion dam that was built up Know-Nothing Creek. That dam was built of logs, not concrete, but it had an additional feature. Besides the logs that crossed the creek perpendicular to flow, it had other logs—poles really and not even very big ones—parallel to flow that shielded the perpendicular ones. Tommy called it an apron, and it had survived in Know-Nothing Creek through that flood and many other high-water events. Tommy, another commune veteran then in his "gold miner" incarnation, may be the most inventive person I ever met. Not the most diplomatic. The most inventive.

You want an example? The inventiveness of gold miners is a storied source of pride on Salmon River. There were always stories

Butler Dam Crew 1981. We rebuilt the small diversion dam on Butler Creek with a new feature so it could better withstand high-water flows. We added an "apron" of Douglas fir poles. After we finished the dam in a rainstorm in November, my partner Susan (holding the rear of the righthand log) invited the crew to our impromptu wedding. After all, we had some champagne. Photo by Jeff Buchin.

about this or that miner who might construct a rock classifier out of scrap from a wrecked pickup, some rusty bedsprings, and three fifty-five-gallon drums. There was no choice. Salmon River is remote, and few miners made much money. Years ago, decades ago, when we still lived at the commune, I was traveling up the North Fork Road with Tommy. It was a hot summer day, and our old truck's radiator had pinhole leaks. We'd refilled it twice at creek crossings already when we reached Sawyers Bar, so Tommy stopped at the house of Sheldon Wilson, a rare friend in Sawyers Bar in those days. Wilson was off logging, so Soto slipped into his henhouse and came back with three fresh eggs. He broke and dumped them into the radiator. "Whaddya doing," I protested. "That'll stop up everything."

He ignored me and, one by one, I watched the leaks seal themselves as the raw egg cooked and blocked the holes. We made it over the mountain. And years later the apron worked on the diversion dam.

I worked with Catherine Thompson Guerra, one of the Butler owners and a Black Bear veteran before that, to build a trail from the flat up the gorge to the dam site. Bill Minehan, a young gold miner from the North Fork, brought up a bag of dynamite to chip away a minimal path around a rock face at Sue Point. We named it Sue Point after Sue, my sweetheart and bride-to-be, slipped off right there walking back alone from a cement pour one afternoon. It was a long fall—nearly thirty feet—and she had only a tangle of blackberry vines, a rotten log, and rock cobble to cushion her landing. She lived to tell about it, more than a little scratched and dazed for the next few days. (Sue is the star in the love story part of this tale. Add to the list of life's close calls.)

The engineering part I wasn't sure about was whether we had the technical know-how to build a dam in the middle of a fast-running creek, and we probably wouldn't have if it hadn't been for Vinnie Rinaldi. Vinnie was also a Butler partner in those days and a veteran both of San Francisco's Diggers in the 1960s and of building projects all over the world since then. The pour itself was a simple project for him, and an old bridge builder further up the Salmon River said diverting a creek's flow was easy—build a temporary dam upstream with rock and plastic sheeting and carry the water past the cement pour in a string of fat wooden boxes called flumes. What oozed past the temp dam could be pumped with a large portable pump.

The next obstacle was logistics. It was, after all, a half mile up the gorge. Portable pumps are not really that portable. And what about cement, plywood forms, the logs and poles for the apron, a cement mixer, and an electrical generator to power hand tools and the mixer? The solution for that came from Ethan Guerra, a son of one of the Butler families. Ethan was gifted physically and mentally and was making his living those days as a hooker for a large helicopter logging outfit. The job title was perhaps intentionally provocative, but it meant he was the guy who attached sawed-down trees to a long cable line from the giant harvest helicopters as the copters churned in the sky above him. It was a task that required all his gifts. Plus, did I say that he was fearless? He arranged with his employer to fly up all our tools and supplies in a series of short ferries and, while he was at it, positioned giant bundles of six-inch pipe at points along the gorge. We wouldn't install the pipeline until the following year.

Through the withering summer weather we worked on the frames and the cement pours. Into the fall we backfilled the cement work with rock, installed and buried the pole apron, and built a cement penstock. I won't explain a penstock, but I wanted to use the word because I designed and framed it and it worked. I will take you up to show it off whenever you want. By fall, Vinnie had returned home to San Francisco, and the project was winding down. As we put on the finishing touches, the winter rains began. Finally, as the creek was rising in late November, we were done and invited over a crowd of friends for the finishing touches. All day we worked moving the giant flume boxes up onto the bank. There were places in the channel where we went knee deep and even waist deep into the water. It was no longer the cool, bracing water of summer. It was swift and icy. The skies opened up and poured rain as we started packing out the equipment. Hand tools went into backpacks. There were no helicopters that day for the big items like the generator, portable so-called, so it went out on a pole sling. The porters were burly tree-planter friends like Little Jake from upriver and Robert Hirning from the reforestation co-op just over the state line in Oregon. It wasn't just guy muscle. Many of the women tree planters were as tough as the men, and they did their share and more of the heavy lifting. Each would grab an end and carefully head down the trail. As they rounded Sue Point, each grabbed the safety rope we'd installed since Sue's plunge.

Finally, by dark, we were done, and everyone gathered at our cabin, which in those days was still quite small. Sue quickly started the fire blazing in the woodstove, and the crew was soon slipping off their clothes, wringing them out, and hanging them on hooks to dry, at least a little, while several of us made some food. Most of the crowd had spent months every spring in the teeming tree-planting camps all over northern California and southern Oregon, and no one was a stickler on mainstream standards of privacy. Sue and I loaned people dry, warm clothes, and they settled in while supper was served up. The room was soon comfortable and steamy. A hubbub, but a quiet one, filled the room, and a gaslight hissed brightly over the kitchen sink. A kettle of sausage soup simmered on the cookstove, and a teapot steamed on the woodstove. Suddenly Sue said, "Is anyone here a Universal Life Church minister?" People looked perplexed.

Now our story gets to the romance part. Sue and I had already lived in the little cabin for a year and a half. Before that we'd lived at the teacherage, an even smaller apartment upriver that the country school provided for the teacher. That teacher was Sue. I was in love. Sue was smart, enthusiastic, and beautiful. The Forks of Salmon School had a good staff, and Sue was a great addition. She had taught in the roughest schools in Chicago and then in the newest experimental public schools in San Jose's Silicon Valley. She didn't just teach reading, writing, and arithmetic. She taught in a way that helped students understand where they lived on the river and what their responsibilities were to the greater community.

And she had an incandescent young son named Slate. He liked to announce in those days, with the self-assurance of a nine-year-old who'd barely escaped from San Jose, that he knew from the time he was born that the river was where he belonged. Slate was a bonus in the whole deal.

I'd been single quite a while before I was smitten by Sue. Like many bachelors, I was good at fooling around, but lousy at sticking around. I still remember when I first met Sue. It was at a community building project, kind of a barn raising, but maybe for a chicken coop, not a whole barn. She was statuesque, athletic, and beautiful. But the world was full of pretty girls. What made Sue stand out was her enthusiasm. She loved the idea of people working together. "Let's get started," was probably her motto. Hard not to fall for someone like that.

In those days I was still living next door to Kate George. She'd met my girlfriends/visitors before and would dismiss them with short critiques. But she loved Sue. Sue was different. I told you about Kate's warning. "Sue's great," she said, and I nodded in agreement, "But she's too smart to settle down with you." History has shown that Sue is plenty smart about many things, but she's stuck around with me for nearly forty years and counting.

Sue Terence says an early sign that we were right for each other was that we both ran the same model of Stihl chain saw. This was handy during an Ent Forestry brushing job when Sue pulled the carburetor off one saw to keep the other operable. Photo by Jeff Buchin.

Sue had just quit teaching school in the San Jose area and was looking for a change. I coaxed her to apply for a vacancy at the little two-teacher school, which may not have been the kind of change she intended. But she applied and got hired. A perk of the job was free rent at the teacherage, which was an add-on apartment to an earlier school building. Over the years the schoolroom part had been converted into a hall for meetings and dances, but the teacherage was retained for new hires. My normal practice at this point in meeting a woman was to play it cool. Take my time. But not this time. I helped Sue move in and then stayed the night. And the night after. And never left until we moved together to the little cabin at Butler Creek a year later.

Sue loved it on Salmon River. She loved the school kids and their families. She loved the local bands and the dances that happened next door. She loved the river and the mountains. She loved that we made our living planting trees, which even many of the regular tree planters weren't too crazy about. More than anything, she loved me. Irresistible.

There were times, of course, when I'd be really dumb. After years as a shallow bachelor I could act pretty egregious, which is another word for dumb, but it sounds smarter. So Sue would tell me and teach me how to act better. I've always thought that any guy who picks up with a woman who's a pushover, afraid to stand up for herself, that guy is crazy. She taught me other stuff, too, but this isn't that kind of story.

So back to the room full of people, the dam-repair crowd, standing around in borrowed clothes while their wet clothes dried around the wood-stove. None of them answered Sue's question. So she asked again, in her best schoolmarm voice, "Is anyone here a Universal Life Church minister?"

The Universal Life Church was a real thing, at least as real as any church, but it was an invention in the late 1960s of an affable redneck in Modesto. We met him once on that trip when a handful of us were raising money from rock stars to buy Black Bear Ranch and start the commune. The money-hustle was in Hollywood, and the side trip to Modesto was just a kick. We were traveling in the old Coors Beer truck in that stretch, and Kirby Hensley, the church founder, was sitting in the shade sipping beer with friends when we pulled up. If they were disappointed when the truck turned out to be full of hippies and not beer, they did not show it. Instead, they welcomed us with smiles and handshakes. Maybe Modesto is that kind of town. They asked if we wanted to be ordained in their church. It was as simple as that. No money exchanged. They'd write our name in a book and hand us each a little card that made us a minister. More handshakes. More smiles. Then they asked if we had any friends who wanted to be ordained. We reeled off about fifty names of friends back in Haight-Ashbury and they wrote them as fast as they could in the book. Hensley himself counted out fifty blank minister cards and passed them to us so we could let our friends know the good news. That's what it took to be a Universal Life Church minister, and that's why it wasn't so unlikely that one of the folks in the room might just be a minister. (They still exist, although Kirby Hensley is no longer around. Look them up online.)

Nobody in the cabin volunteered that they were a minister, so Sue blurted, "Malcolm and I want to get married, and we have a license, and we have some champagne, so this is a perfect time. Except we need a minister." Sue was well known for radical ideas, and the suggestion of a wedding, however impromptu, struck the crowd as radical. Marriage had fallen out of fashion in the 1960s, as least among hippies. Nuclear families had descended into practically the same disrepute as nuclear war. So Sue's statement hit the crowd as though she'd suggested that we go down the block near some imaginary University of California campus and throw bricks through the front window of the Bank of America. People perked up at the idea, as much for its novelty as anything else.

Little Jake said, "I think Gail's a Universal Life minister." Gail Ericson tried to shush him up, but Jake was not easily silenced. "Can't anybody be a minister if you say you are? But Gail's official, if that's the right word." Jake grinned at Gail's discomfort.

Gail, of course, had lived at the Black Bear the same years I had, but she was one of the few people at the commune whom I'd known before we all moved up there. I was near the end of my years as a newspaper reporter in Los Angeles and had met Michael Tierra, an anarchistic musician and performance artist. He was doing something or other in New York City, and he met Gail there. She traveled with him back to Los Angeles just as he was starting a rock band with some other people I knew. About the same time, they asked me to become their business manager. So, in a way, Gail and I had this commonality, kind of like the band hangers-on they called groupies in those days, but with more privileges and way more responsibilities. I won't tell the whole story of the band, but I will say that we were fairly successful—a recording contract and club and concert dates all over the country. This is synonymous with saying that our lives became very crazy. Gail was always saying she wanted to leave and take Michael with her to some place less nuts than LA.

I remember I promised her a Rolls Royce if she stuck around. In those days you could promise a lot. I'm not sure what Michael had promised to get her to come to the West Coast, but she must have been a lot more malleable back in those days. And she had toughened only a little, a year later, when we reconnected at that Willard Street Victorian in Haight-Ashbury. No one would call her gullible anymore on that crowded night in our Butler Creek cabin years later, standing around in damp clothes, when Sue was looking for a minister. Nor was Gail romantic.

She pouted and said, "Will it take very long?"

Everybody else in the room, this crowd of bedraggled tree planters who'd helped us finish Stage One of the epic water project, shook their heads "No" in unison. They probably wanted to see a wedding, however unexpected and out of fashion. Certainly, they wanted Sue to pop open the champagne. One of many things I've always admired about Sue is her impulsiveness. Since that first year together in that crowded teacher's apartment across from the tiny Forks School, our relationship had only flourished. After that, we'd moved down to the Butler Creek cabin and, by then, we were even more in love. We had planned to get married. It takes two people, two enthusiastic people even, to get a license. And we had one from the Humboldt County Courthouse. In my commune years I'd been ambivalent about marriage, but that suspicion was the conventional wisdom then. If this was a big current in the mainstream of 1960s culture, it was especially true on a commune where everything was shared, from food and housing to child rearing to our sex lives. Who needed marriage? Weren't we all married? There were still couples at the commune, but few of those survived commune life. Some of that had changed as we left the echo chamber of the commune and joined river life. Many of the families there were large and cohesive, if not in lockstep harmony. Sue, who had never lived at the commune, had decided the moment was right, an impromptu event, a surprise, for an unplanned dinner party. A few of our guests tested their clothes for dryness and then settled back to enjoy an unexpected party.

And so we were married. Gail rose to the occasion. She made a show of pronouncing us wed. Ceremoniously, she signed the license. People cheered. They were, as much as anything, happy to be done with that stage of the water line project. They were also overjoyed to be out of icy clothes and soaked work boots. A wedding was frosting on the cake, although I can't remember that we had a cake. A scene came into my mind of a movie I'd seen in Los Angeles years earlier. It was titled *Battle of Algiers* and was about Algeria's bloody revolution against French colonialism. It was a great film, and my favorite scene was the wedding of a very young Muslim couple in an old quarter of the city. The Islamic wedding itself would have been forbidden and the guests jailed if the French had known. The camera pulled back for a view outside the building. On the doorstep stood an armed lookout. On the rooftop stood four more armed sentries. We had no armed guards there that evening at Butler Creek, but we felt a little like revolutionaries and a lot like the beginnings of a family.

When the champagne was gone along with most everything else edible in the house, our guests again checked their clothing for dryness, put them on, and drifted off into the evening. Water and love. We had it all.

CHAPTER 11

Storming Oz

There were times on Salmon River when it would have been better to have a telephone, but there was no telephone at Butler Creek in the late 1980s. Kenoli Oleari had sent us a letter from Berkeley that we needed to be down in San Francisco in eight days. We had a very important meeting scheduled with the regional forester, the head of the US Forest Service for all of California. It was our chance to make our case about the agency's use of herbicides in the forest around us.

As it was, the mail finally arrived a week later, so we had to rush the four hundred miles south to make the meeting at all. A handful of us in the car navigated beautiful winding roads for hours along the Salmon, the Klamath, and the Trinity Rivers until we finally could speed up along the interstate. The terrain then shifted from steep mountains to the great alluvial terraces of the Central Valley. The forests of conifers, oak, and madrone gave way to rice fields, all flooded and divided by geometric dikes. Long-legged birds stood knee deep in the water, searching for frogs and other edibles. Twice we saw fast, small aircraft spraying the rice, and we could smell the faintly metallic chemicals from a long distance away.

It was so late when we finally came to Kenoli's house in Berkeley that he already was gone. His housemates said he was on the radio on KGO, a twenty-four-hour news and talk station. We all huddled around the radio to listen to him talk. He was midway through a brief explanation of why phenoxy chemicals were especially dangerous to humans. The dangers included increased risk of cancer and Parkinson's disease.

With Kenoli at the radio station was a woman named Harriet Bein-field. Both of them had lived at the commune in the years I'd been there, but both now lived in the Bay Area. Harriet had been trained as an acu-puncturist and herbalist with Chinese medicine, and she spoke about health problems that were linked to herbicides.

She said that people became aware of the problems through the work of Mavis McCovey, the well-known Karuk medicine woman in the little town of Orleans on the Klamath River. Mavis spotted clusters of birth defects among Orleans women in numbers much greater than would have been predicted from the small size of the community. And the timing correlated with the heaviest use of herbicides around Orle-ans in the tree plantations that had replaced the huge clear-cut logging blocks.

I'd heard of McCovey's studies, but I didn't know she was a medicine woman. I only knew her as a nurse in the Tribal Health Clinic. And I didn't have a clue what phenoxy meant.

We nodded approvingly that our city cousins could come across so smart on the radio and told them both so when they returned to Berke-ley an hour later. "You better be ready to sound smart yourself," Harriet cautioned. "We'll be talking to the regional forester tomorrow, and I've invited the press. Torches and pitchforks community organizing may work in Salmon River, but it won't play as well here." She looked around the room and said, "I thought you were going to bring some loggers with you. You're all just hippies."

"We didn't have much time," I said. "Anyway, who's talking?"

"Granted," she said with a sheepish grin. "But that's what makes this such a good organizing issue. It's not just tree huggers bashing loggers. Nobody, including loggers, wants their kids poisoned. When I was up there for that demonstration, there were timber wives lined up yelling at the Forest Service. They were louder than the hippies."

"I get that part of it, and I know people hate the herbicides," I coun-tered, "but it ducks the real issue for me, which is that they're logging too fast and in places where they should never build roads."

Kenoli cleared his throat and said, "There is a connection you know." We all turned to face him. Everybody enjoyed Kenoli in his professor incarnation.

"The Forest Service is required by law to only log at the rate that the forest is producing new wood," he explained. "They can only cut a million board feet if the remaining trees and the replacement trees grow a million board feet. You know, a board foot, twelve inches by twelve inches by an inch deep."

"Yeah, we know. Get to the point," I coaxed. Kenoli's explanations were convincing, but they required patience, and I'd just spent eight hours on the road.

"This concept is called sustained yield, and they have a complex computer model to show how fast the forest is growing. The plantations that replace clear-cuts are part of it. And when they use herbicides to reduce competition from grass, brush, and nontimber species, they calculate that the plantation trees grow quicker, so that justifies more logging in the big old-growth trees. They can claim it's agriculture, but it's really mining. Old-growth mining."

"And if a few moms in Orleans have problems with their pregnancies, the Forest Service claims it's anecdotal evidence," Harriet chimed in. "That's brilliant, Kenoli."

Kenoli took a mock bow, and then Harriet carried around slices of fresh pizza to each of us. The one vegetarian brushed the pepperoni over to the next piece before she took her slice. I had to admit that "brilliant" was a good word for his analysis. Kenoli followed by handing everyone a bottle of beer. More brilliance.

———

The next morning we continued the trek to Forest Service headquarters. It was located in those days in a towering federal office building deep in the San Francisco financial district. Well-dressed men and women stared at us as we walked in a brave clump through the sea of our more fashionable peers. We had tried to dress up for the day. When I'd worked for the *LA Times*, I'd had a closet of Brooks Brothers clothes—suits, ties, wingtip shoes. But they were long gone. Some of us had borrowed

Protest standoff over herbicides. US Forest law enforcement muscle rallied to greet locals when they protested widespread use of herbicides in the forest. Mavis McCovey, a nurse in Orleans and a Karuk medicine woman, spotted troubling patterns of birth anomalies that corresponded to the use of the sprays, but the Bureau of Indian Affairs sent her out of the state when investigators from Sacramento came to check her claims. Photo by Jeff Buchin.

clothes for the day. Mine was an old suit that I'd found in a thrift store. I think it had belonged to somebody four inches shorter than me and many inches wider.

In the lobby, a courteous guard in a gray uniform gave us directions, and Harriet motioned us over to two reporters and a television crewman who were seated on a long marble bench. If the guard saw the rendezvous, he pretended not to. We all slipped into the nearest of the elevators with ornate Victorian doors and left the lobby behind.

The umpteenth floor where we spilled out for the meeting was different from what I expected. Instead of a rarefied world of long mahogany conference tables, it was a warren of hallways and cubicles. People moved about quickly and barely looked up at our ragtag passage. After several wrong turns, we were face to face with someone who claimed to be the

receptionist of the regional forester, the highest-ranking officer for all
the national forests in California. Harriet stepped forward as our spokes-
person and announced that we were here for the meeting. Unfazed, the
secretary said the regional forester wasn't in the office today, but we could
leave a letter.

Kenoli stepped to Harriet's side, and, almost in unison, they
announced that we knew he was there, and we would stay until he met
with us. The cameraman shouldered his camera and began filming. The
secretary first curled her lip in defiance and then shrugged and excused
herself. We did not see her again.

Ten minutes passed, and an older, immaculately dressed woman
walked into the room. She said that the regional forester was looking
forward to the meeting, but that he needed to finish another meeting
first, and we would have a short wait. We broke into smiles. She gestured at the couches that ringed the room, smiled, and left. Nearly a
half hour later she returned and told us that the meeting was scheduled
to be with only two people, and the rest would have to wait. We said
nothing, and she led Kenoli and Harriet to a gleaming door of blond,
densely grained pine. As soon as they entered, the rest of us streamed in.
She made no effort to stop us until the cameraman approached her. He
hesitated, and she relaxed. He slipped sideways past her in a move that
seemed as practiced as any basketball feint and joined us in the regional
forester's office.

The man himself was not whom I expected. The Forest Service bigwigs we knew in the mountains were forceful men, and big. This man—
his name was Zane Grey Smith—was slight, wearing an expensive suit
with broad padded shoulders. He had carefully coifed, thick gray hair.
He walked around the room shaking each hand, even the cameraman's,
and asked the secretary if she could find more chairs. He did not seem
upset to have a crowd of protesters in his inner office.

In a few minutes, all of us were seated except the cameraman, who
prowled restlessly in the background. Earlier in the year, his channel had
run a tell-all documentary on the findings of Mavis McCovey, so they
had a commitment to the issue.

The regional forester slipped off his jacket and rolled his chair from behind a large desk so we were all in a large circle. He settled into the chair, made sure we were comfortable, and began to speak. "I've heard from your district ranger and your forest supervisor about your important work over the last two years, and I want to tell you that the United States Department of Agriculture and particularly we in the United States Forest Service are grateful for the kind of work community people like you are doing on the ground."

It was not the message we expected, and we glanced at each other nervously. He continued, "You know that we have worked extensively to meet the timber needs of the country in compliance with the National Forest Management Act and at the same time collaborated extensively and continuously with the Environmental Protection Agency to protect the public from unnecessary exposure to dangerous chemicals. Besides that, we operate under extremely rigorous NEPA regulations and cooperate with state and local agencies. That said, what can I do to help you today?"

His opener seemed better than what I expected—far better, really. He didn't even downgrade the National Environmental Protection Act. Usually Forest Service bigwigs would mention its requirements in whiny voices, as in, "The NEPA is killing us." I glanced around to gauge the others. Kenoli was rolling his eyes. Another man from Berkeley made the universal gesture in his lap of someone playing with himself. Harriet saw him and nodded in agreement. The regional forester could not see the lewd mocking gesture, but he saw Harriet nodding approvingly and paused for effect. Then he pointed to Harriet and said, "Tell me, what I can do to help you?"

"That's simple," she answered with a sweetheart smile. "Stop the herbicide spray program, starting with the Klamath and the Six Rivers National Forests." She smiled again for emphasis.

"I wish it were that simple," he said. He picked up a steno notebook off his desk and began to write. "But the law mandates a multiple-use approach to forest management. And timber harvest is one of those uses. We can't just manage for you hikers and campers, as much as we'd like to."

"We don't represent recreational users," Harriet countered. "We're speaking for the people who live in and near the national forest, the ones who drink the water, the ones who suffer the birth defects like the clusters they've found in the community of Orleans." The regional forester wrote himself another note.

"And that's only part of it," Kenoli said. "The whole spray policy comes on the heels of forty years of too much logging."

The regional forester nodded, wrote another note, and said, "Nobody is more conscious than the United States Forest Service of the mistakes we have made in the past. There was a time when they logged like there would never be an end of timber. They even built roads right up stream channels to drag out the logs. Thank God, that's all behind us now. Our foresters have a level of university training that they never dreamed of in the past, and we have learned a lot from our own mistakes." He made another note in the steno pad.

For another ten minutes we listed the herbicide horror stories—the birth defects, the grisly results of spraying chemicals from Agent Orange that showed up after the Vietnam War, the toxicity studies with fish—and the nontoxic alternatives. He took many notes and interrupted a few more times to agree with us. Finally, he said, "I have to tell you that I left another meeting to join you, but I really have to get back. Do any of the rest of you have anything else?" And he smiled across us like the pope might force a smile to a clutch of visiting Mormons.

Ann Pullen, an antiherbicide activist who lived up at Godfrey Ranch on the ridge above Forks of Salmon, spoke in a small, girlish voice. It was not the voice I expected from her. She was slight and pretty, but she was tough. She was the lead singer in a band, and I'd seen her yell a drunk logger off the stage one night in the late hours of a dance at the Forks of Salmon town hall. She thanked the regional forester for his support and asked him, in thin, shy speech, "Could you please drop units thirteen-B and fourteen from the spray plan on the Salmon River district?"

"What is it about them?" the regional forester asked, with the biggest smile so far.

"They're located on either side of the spring where we get our drinking water, and I'm just praying they don't get sprayed."

He made one more note in his book and then began shaking hands with every one of us again, even the television cameraman.

In a blur we were out of the office, out of the reception room, out of the elevator, and downstairs in the federal building lobby. The guard who had welcomed us was gone, and his replacement eyed us suspiciously.

———

The walk from my cabin at Butler Creek to the mailbox is a short one, just a few hundred yards of gravel driveway, but sometimes the trip took a long time. The biggest obstacle was the Salmon River. I didn't have to ford the river or anything. I just had to keep from getting distracted by the sweep of it. Where we lived at Butler Creek, the river made a huge bend and then continued another seven or eight curvy miles farther downstream, where it joined the much larger Klamath River.

Some days I'd just stare at the flow of the water. Other days there were rafters beginning their trips or juvenile salmon and steelhead popping out of the water in great numbers, chasing insects that strayed too close to the water's surface. The worst distraction was when I looked up at the ridges. I could spend a long time doing that. There could be long fingers of fog topping Orleans Mountain to the west or Portuguese Peak to the east. I might study the pattern of the patches of treetops, conifers here, hardwoods there, and wonder about the fire history and if the Natives who lived here before me started some of them intentionally to promote healthy acorns or supple basket materials. A large bird might catch my eye, and I'd need to wait until it was close. Was it a turkey vulture, an osprey, a bald eagle?

And there was always the mail, which I'd pick through on the uphill walk back to the cabin. This day it was mostly woodstove fire starter, but there was a fat envelope from the US Forest Service. I tore it open and read as I walked. When I entered the house, my relaxed mood was gone.

"Anything good?" Sue asked as she reached for the pile.

"Ask if there's anything bad. We got the new revised spray plan and they haven't made any changes. It's still a huge number of acres."

"You expected miracles just because we know how to drive to San Francisco? This campaign has been going on for years. Let me see the letter." She tugged the bundle of pages out of my hand and began leafing through it systematically. She stopped at a complex table of specific units to be sprayed and pored over each line.

"I see they dropped the units up by Godfrey Ranch, the ones that Ann begged for." Sue's face broke into a huge grin.

"What's the message of that?" I asked. "Somebody in the delegation gets her way, and everyone else gets sprayed?"

"I guess you could read it that way," Sue said. "But I think the message is clear, and I like it. The lesson is: 'If you don't want to get sprayed, don't just sit there. You better be an activist!'" She pumped the air with a power-to-the-people gesture of her fist, some artifact of peace marches in her past.

———

Gail had argued about everything I said the whole drive to Yreka, and now that we were waiting in the Forest Service building she was even worse.

"They said it's just a routine audit. Nothing more. Why are you so worried?" I said.

"Routine audit? If it's so routine, how come we got the notice four days after Petey's crew stopped tree planting and drove three miles to disrupt an herbicide spray operation. If that's not bad enough, somebody had welded the steel gate shut overnight, and the piss firs had to wait three hours for another welder to open it."

Piss firs was the slur everybody used for Forest Service employees and to hear Gail use it, even in a whisper, in the headquarters of the Klamath National Forest made me realize how angry she was. (She probably used it a lot when she still lived at the commune.)

"I know who welded it. It was a logger, not some tree planter," I defended.

"At least the logger had more sense than our hippie tree planters. He did it in the dark. Our crew got in a tug-of-war with the head inspector over the main hose they use to mix the herbicides." Her whisper was turning to a subvocal growl. She slapped her forehead and stared down at the floor. She would not speak further.

We were rescued when the receptionist came into the room and said, "Mr. Davies is ready to see you now."

Gil Davies was the contracting officer for the Klamath and was prosecutor, judge, and, in some cases, executioner for tree-planting outfits like ours. We had passed him our payroll sheets thirty minutes earlier, and we waited like sheep in the lobby. Years later, Davies published a scholarly and articulate history book. I doubt that our meeting that day appears in any of his chapters.

"Have a seat," he said, with a gesture and the familiar smile of Forest Service executives.

"So how's it look?" Gail asked. She was the bookkeeper for Ent Forestry, our plucky reforestation cooperative. I'd been dragged along because Gail refused to go by herself.

"It looks very good," Davies said. "I see you are exceeding the wage standards mandated by the Davis-Bacon Act. Very commendable. I can see you have a successful little business out there on the river. Very commendable."

Gail relaxed slightly and said, "So it's all okay?"

"It's all fine. It's all fine. I told you in the letter that this was just a routine audit requested by the Labor Board."

Gail started to rise out of her seat when Davies cleared his throat and said, "There's just one thing. You have many employees exceeding eight-hour days and forty-hour weeks, but you haven't paid them overtime."

"But our wage exceeds the minimum by more than time-and-a-half," Gail said.

"And we are all owners of the company, not regular employees," I added.

Davies's smile grew, and he spoke directly to Gail, who had slumped back into her chair. "That sounds good to me, and it sounds good to you, but we both have to follow the rules set by the Labor Board. Here's what you have to do. You'll need to pay all that overtime plus a 25 percent noncompliance penalty, and you'll have to process the checks through the Labor Board—I guess that's us in this case—so we can confirm the law is being observed."

"But we paid more than overtime. We already paid out all the earnings from the contract," Gail said.

"I know you were trying to do the right thing, but we all have to answer to the Labor Board," Davies answered.

"This doesn't sound so routine to me," I broke in.

"Now relax there, buster. Your number just came up. It was totally random and totally routine. Every year they check a certain number of contractors."

I strained to believe him. Perhaps it showed on my face.

"Let me do something else for you." He picked up the phone and quickly dialed. "Let me talk to Eddie." He paused. Then, "Hey, Eddie. This is Davies over at the Klamath. I have a couple of small-business people here and I'd like you to look over their books. They had a little compliance issue here with the Labor Board, and we need to make sure they're straight with you over at IRS."

He paused, said thanks, and scrawled out a nearby Yreka address on a sheet of paper. "You need to go see Eddie over on Miner Street. He wants to look over your books, too. And remember. Don't worry about a thing. It's totally routine."

CHAPTER 12

Born at Butler Creek

The first thing that Erica Kate ever saw at Butler was that kerosene lamp in the corner of the room. It was still dark outside, an uncharacteristically chill morning in late July when she was born. It was not just any summer day; it was July 26, 1983. Four time zones east, people in Cuba were already awake and celebrating *veintiséis de julio*. It's still the biggest holiday of the year for them. It commemorates the storming of the Cuban army barracks at Moncada in 1953.

All this geopolitics was lost on Erica Kate when she got her first look at Butler. She had spent most of the previous nine months absorbed in the usual gestational activities: intense cell division, differentiation and rearrangement of new organs, practice stretches of new limbs, exploring and then filling every recess of her mother's growing belly.

Butler Creek, where her mother and I lived, is part of a large flat in the Salmon River frame of reference, where the terrain mostly is steep. There were once many such flats up and down the river, but most were washed away by miners during the Gold Rush. The only evidence of this pillage of industrial-level, intentional erosion were vast fields of moss-covered boulder piles with a scattering of stunted brush and conifers. But the flats at Butler Creek delivered insufficient gold to warrant mining, so they are still there. The space supports vigorous stands of tanoak trees, *Lithocarpus densiflorus* to botanists, and, lately, the incursion of taller young conifers, mostly Douglas fir, *Pseudotsuga menziesii*. The tanoaks were a bountiful source of acorns for the tribal people who lived there a century ago. The flat rests at the outside bend of the Salmon River in the biggest sweep of its whole run from the snowy high country to where it spills into the Klamath River. At this confluence with Butler Creek, the Salmon River makes a long, tight detour around a shoulder of Portuguese Peak. Viewed from above by helicopter or on a map, the river describes a tight curve. It is much like the curve that Erica Kate described in her mom's belly.

Sue, her mother, grew large and radiant, as pregnant women often do, when Erica Kate swelled inside her. Sue was still teaching less than a month before the birth. Perhaps her role in the little country school ten miles upriver gave her confidence that this was a good place to raise a child. They were not an easy ten miles. Every bridge and culvert along the road had been scoured out by high water in the '64 flood two decades earlier. The stretch from Morehouse Creek to Butler Creek was the deepest run of the gorge where the road creeps around the bluffs on narrow, fragile ledges of decomposed granite. Geologists call some rock "incompetent," and there was much incompetent rock in this stretch.

It was late summer when I first set foot on Butler in 1977 during the Hog Fire, and this stretch of road was punctuated again and again by falling material, burning brush, dislodged rock, even whole, massive blackened tree trunks, which would slide down through the gulches, giving no warning, with the momentum of a runaway train. For a time, only fire crews were allowed to pass on that stretch of road. The crews would race through the smoky gauntlet in convoys every hour or so. The lead vehicle was a huge dump truck with a hydraulic blade that would sweep the road of boulders and burning debris. We all knew that the blade would be zero protection in the worst case. People too often criticize denial as a human failing. We might argue that denial and forgetfulness are among the most important human faculties. Certainly, they do us little more harm than our vaunted intelligence. Examples are available on request.

By springtime, Sue was already quite large with Erica Kate growing quickly in her uterus. On the warmest days, Sue would sunbathe upriver with her friends and looked to the world like a Minoan fertility goddess, with her full, perfect breasts and large, sun-browned belly. But not every day that spring was warm. Some weeks it would rain without cease. The runoff would trigger rockslides small and large. One night, on the bluffs upriver between Grant and Butler Creeks, the entire cliff above the road went incompetent all at once. It fell so hard and so loud that Sue and I awoke in our bed nearly a half-mile downriver. We listened for more and heard only the roar of the river and the driving rain. When it got light, Sue needed to head up the road to Forks of Salmon Elementary School. At the bluffs, her path was blocked by the biggest slide either of us had ever seen. Slides that blocked the road were not uncommon. Sometimes the biggest ones took the road crew a whole day to clear. But this one had plugged the road and nearly plugged the Salmon River where it rushed through the gorge 250 feet below. More than that, it was not the usual jumble of rocks, crushed trees, and debris. The rocks were the size of living rooms. I remember they were kind of the shape of living rooms, too. Salmon River people develop a wide repertoire of coping skills for the unexpected. The ordinary river way of dealing with a slide even a fraction of this size was to give up and go home. And that is what we did. I remember it as a pleasant day.

The next day the foreman from the road crew scrambled over the jumble on a scary little trail scratched over and between the huge boulders, and walked to our house to report. We poured him coffee, and he said this slide would not be cleared as quickly as most. The boulders were too large for their biggest equipment to budge, but they couldn't dynamite because none of them had confidence that they wouldn't just blow away the whole ledge and have no road at all. Sue poured him more coffee and offered him a fresh cinnamon roll. He accepted and said a crew of blasting experts was headed out from Yreka, but they had prior assignments and might not come all week. Sue liked the news and offered him lunch. He remembered that his crew was waiting on the other side of the jumble, thanked her, and headed off into the rain. We had another pleasant day at home.

The next morning, Creek Hanauer, the school bus driver, knocked on the door and said he was parked on the upriver side of the slide and was ready to ferry Sue up to school. "Forget it, Creek," I said. "That slide's too dangerous, and Sue's about to have a baby."

Creek said, "They improved the trail yesterday so Lillian Bennett could get across when she and Barb Bennett did the mail run." Lillian Bennett wasn't pregnant, but she was sixty-five years old, so I knew my argument was weakened. Sue was already putting on boots and raingear. I watched her wobble fearlessly behind Creek over the outsized rock pile. They looked like two mountain goats of different shapes.

By Friday the experts began swarming the slide, then drilling, and finally shooting off one small charge. I clambered over their handiwork afterward to make sure Sue could negotiate the new version of the trail. The blast had done little, but it had left the air with the faint smell of cordite or nitroglycerine, a brown twine-looking explosive, which smelled to me like vomit.

The road crew specialists returned with their expertise, their drills, and their coffee breaks on Monday. All week long they whittled at the pile. The sun finally came out. They had little incentive to hurry and much reason to be cautious. Every morning Sue picked her way over the changing jumble, and every afternoon she negotiated the new path. The stink of the explosive grew. Some days the path seemed to hang directly over the river, just below the huge rapids that kayakers and rafters call "Freight Train." Erica Kate continued to grow, oblivious to the hazards that her mother was braving. Every day, Sue seemed bigger and a little more wobbly. Finally, two weeks after they fell, the rocks were gone.

Don't think, by the way, that Erica Kate's first sight was a kerosene lamp because we didn't have any electricity. We had electricity. Plenty of electricity. Well, not plenty, but enough to run a few lights. Did I say that we had indoor plumbing? This was not that stable in Palestine I remembered from Christmas pageants. It was one of the biggest cabins on the river. Actually, it was still a construction site, but within a year it would be a cabin, a big cabin. The winter before, Sue and I had started to feel cramped in the little cabin I'd found on that first winter solstice visit. We made several alternative plans. Then Sue pulled out her teacher retirement funds, and we built them all: the downstairs porch, the second floor, the living room, and the upstairs porch.

A year earlier two old guys from upriver had helped me install the first round of electrical wiring. It's deceptive to describe them as old guys. One was Ed Matthewson, and he'd worked in high-voltage electricity in factories before he retired to the river. Everybody called him Fast Eddy, and the name described him well. The other was Dick Haley, who'd come from Maine to mine gold. I'm not sure if Haley ever found much gold, but he did manage to dynamite under his own house to build a cellar. Where he came from, he explained, every house had a cellar. His wife thought he was crazy to want to blast right under the house, so he waited until she was across the river picking up mail. One dynamited rock flew up through the floor and through the roof, but he'd patched them both by my next visit. "You can hardly tell where it went through the roof," he boasted in his New England twang, "and I put that throw rug over the place in the floor so you can't even tell it at all." His wife watched us both like we'd strayed from the mental ward at some hospital's outpatient clinic.

In their first round of wiring, Haley and Fast Eddy got us electricity at Butler by hooking up to the battery of our car, a strategy that worked perfectly nearly always, except the occasional morning when we'd used too many lights and we couldn't start the car. Some of the tree planters from our co-op helped me frame out all the additions after spring planting was over, and Haley and Fast Eddy laid out another round of wiring. This time I read up on electrical installations before they came because their wild-eyed enthusiasm, if it didn't undermine my confidence, at least cried out for oversight. So we had electricity.

The kerosene lamp was so the baby would be greeted by gentler light. The thinking then was that babies liked to be born into a warm room with gentle light. The warm room part was a little harder because we hadn't gotten yet to the windows part of the remodel and that July night was uncharacteristically cold. Liz Pullen helped me staple plastic over the holes we'd left for windows, and we started a fire in the stove until the downstairs was warm as toast.

I keep calling the baby Erica Kate, but we didn't even know yet that the baby was a girl. At four months, Sue and I had driven down to the

UC hospital in San Francisco for amniocentesis. Since Sue was almost forty years old, the test was recommended as a diagnostic for Down's syndrome, spina bifida, and other developmental disorders that occur more frequently among babies born to older mothers. I remembered that I'd been surveying timber way down in Panther Creek in the weeks before conception and gotten exposed to herbicides once and gotten twenty-five yellow jacket stings another time. When the doctor said the baby had all its marbles, I was relieved. The doctor said the testing also revealed gender, and we said we didn't want to know.

I was busy that spring and early summer before the birth. The house doubled in size in a construction trick that fooled even me. It took only a busy week to frame and solid sheet the shell, but a shell, it turns out, is not a house any more than it is a snail. But I was working every day installing windows, banisters, partitions, ceilings, interior walls, sometimes moving quickly, sometimes at snail's pace. I spent a day erecting a huge antenna with help from Bob-O so I could beam a CB radio signal up to Geba Greenberg at Godfrey Ranch. Bob-O said that antenna could easily bounce a signal across country, but that it was more difficult to reach Godfrey, which was on a ridge an hour and a half farther up the watershed.

Geba was the most experienced of the local midwives, seasoned by some training and many births at the commune and on the river. I had seen several births myself back in the years when I'd lived at Black Bear Ranch. Mostly, they seemed long affairs with little sleep and much drama. Sometimes the mom and the birth crew seemed well prepared; other times not. One woman decided that no preparation was needed because someone told her that Native women of old paused in their buffalo skinning, delivered the baby and went back to skinning. So one summer morning, when contractions began, this woman moved up to the knoll where there was a little shade and a good view of the Trinity Alps. But the baby did not come quickly. Maybe the era of those quick and easy Sioux births was gone like the buffalo. Some people gathered and gave advice. I don't remember that Geba was around. The sun rose higher in the sky, the shade slipped away, and it grew very hot. The mother-to-be grew very tired and began to cry in surrender. Alan Hoffman, the fiery anarchist leader who had come to the mountains from the Lower East Side of Manhattan, told people to get tarps and blankets to restore shade and some kind of more comfortable bed. Then he started coaching the woman in her breathing. Gradually she regained her strength and her confidence. What seemed like days later, probably a few hours, a healthy baby was born. No more buffalo skins were tanned that day.

Most commune births, in those years before I met Sue and we moved to Butler Creek, seemed to be all-night affairs. The midwives would confer in quiet voices and look up things in the books they had collected. The rest of us would stand around and wring our hands like a particularly stupid Greek chorus. I remember one long overnight picking up one of the midwives' medical books and reading in the flickering light three vivid chapters about birth anomalies. Babies could be born without all their parts, even without brains. The books said there could be a mole pregnancy, which sounded like there was just a big brain-like cluster of tissue. They could be born with the life-supporting umbilical cord tied in a knot, which could cause death or disability. The midwives kept checking the fetal heartbeat. Were they worried about a knot? Babies could be upside down or backward in the womb, which might require instruments or skills none of us had. Each outcome was described in great detail, mostly with vocabulary I didn't understand and illustrated with drastic med school photographs that I could not get out of my mind. At the worst of this show of horrors, a woman interrupted me. "Check out the baby," she said. There it was. Whole baby. Slimy and alive. Drawing its first breaths. Squawking its first complaints.

The midwives grew more and more expert, and the moms grew better and better prepared. But Black Bear births mostly continued to be long, and the sense of drama never left. One autumn morning in 1969 my commune neighbor Kathleen Nolan went into labor with her fourth child. Kathleen was a highly organized woman, some would say obsessive. In her cabin at the junction of Black Bear and Argus Creeks, she had made lists of objects and procedures all week in case the midwives forgot anything. Sheets and blankets had been wrapped and taped in paper,

Gate Cabin. There were two small, ramshackle cabins at the gate when we came to the commune. We remodeled them so that they were habitable, and several families moved in. Kathleen Nolan delivered a baby in one, and Zoë Leader and I shared the other with a family of four. That may seem crowded, but when deep snow fell, the company and the sheer body heat was welcome. Watercolor by Elsa Marley.

then baked in an oven so they would be sterile. They sat in neat stacks near her bed, the paper faintly browned, like great, underdone cookies. Pots were collected to boil water. Boiling water seemed to be a key ingredient. She had me check the makeshift water system twice in advance to make sure it would work. We even sterilized string and a Swiss army knife so she could cut and tie off the umbilical cord after the birth. Kerosene was stockpiled, and lamp wicks were trimmed. She ordered me to stack lots of dry stove wood, and she cleaned the entire cabin twice. It was the cleanest it had ever been.

So that morning Kathleen waddled over to my cabin, which was next door, and asked me to fetch the midwives. I ran the mile to where one of them lived and burst breathlessly through the cabin door. "Kathy's having the baby," I gulped. There were a few women there, including the midwife. They looked up at me with patronizing smiles and told me to sit down. "She's-having-a-baby-and-she-told-me-to-tell-you-that-you-should-come," I managed. More smiles. "How far apart are her contractions?" one of them asked. I really didn't know so I said, "Ten minutes!" All of them feigned urgency and said they would be right there. As I exited, I saw one of them headed to the stove to get another cup of tea. I raced back to the cabin.

Kathleen had the stove roaring and kettles approaching a boil when I returned. I scrubbed my hands and followed orders to change the bed linen. If the contractions had been faint and well-spaced when I left, they were now intense and almost continuous. For some of them, Kathleen cried out streams of profanity. At some point, a great fount of body fluid came pouring out of her. Kathleen took this all in stride, rolled on her side, and asked me to use a new round of the baked bed linen. I was washing my hands so often I expected the skin would slip away in the boiled water. "What next?" I asked.

"Check the list," she said.

"Which step are we at?" I asked, scanning the twenty-one steps of delivery she had painstakingly written the night before. "Baby crowning," she yelled. I think this was step 19 or 20. "What about all those other steps?" I asked prayerfully. My eyes settled on step 7: Make herbal tea. That was something I knew how to do. "Baby crowning?" I asked, hoping for one of those easier steps like step 3: Stockpile firewood.

"Just watch as the baby crowns, and let me know so I don't push too hard and tear," she explained, and then loosed another string of expletives. I had avoided the actual anatomy of birth until then and realized that the top of the head was actually showing. "The head is showing a little," I said, and added, "The midwives aren't here yet," so Kathleen might decide to show a little restraint. She weathered the next contraction with as little pushing as possible, but much more head appeared. "Get the receiving blanket," she ordered. I was going to correct her because that was step 16, and we were much further along. But dutifully I sifted into the stack of hermetically sealed linens. "Quick," she barked, and I raced over to be there for the arrival of a long, sleek new human being. Guiltily,

I looked around for the midwives, but they were still a few minutes away. Kathleen looked at her newborn and announced that his name would be Emmett Paul.

————

And then I heard a birth story from Ida Lake. Ida was ninety-two when she came upriver to visit us at Butler Creek, where she'd lived as a child. She was part of the Grant family who had homesteaded the place where we now lived. Some of the Grants—her parents and brothers—are buried in the Grant cemetery over past our garden. She said Erica would be the first baby born at the Grant side of the creek since her little sister Melissa in '96—1896. Ida Lake said that her mother, Ellen Grant, who was from the Konimihu Tribe, had been a midwife, and Ida had been her apprentice. Ida told the story of the time when she was taken to the cabin of a woman who had already been in labor several days. It was almost dark. When she arrived, the father, a miner, ran off into the forest. He had gone crazy after all those days. So there was Ida, alone, with this woman screaming, writhing in pain and exhaustion, thinking she was dying. The baby was breech, which means buttocks or feet first. Ida told us she looked around the cabin and in the last light spotted a candle and a pot of bear grease. She slathered her hands in the bear grease like her mother had taught her, reached in and turned the baby around. It was a short delivery after that. The mom and the baby both lived. But Ida said she gave up midwifery forever after that. I tried to imagine that I'd be the resourceful midwife with a candle and a jar of bear grease, but privately I worried that I'd be the addled husband, running off into the forest.

I had been, until Sue became pregnant, an unlikely dad, even in my own mind. Kids were great, but that seemed true regardless of whether they were mine or not. Life in Forks gave a person as much access to kids as they could want. Sometimes people would urge me to have kids, and I would smile in agreement, but not really know what I would do or feel differently if one of the swarm of cool kids in my life was formally mine. Judy Beaver from Black Bear and Ramona George, Kate George's daughter-law, from Cecilville both already had what seemed large numbers of kids, and both of them seemed especially determined to let me

Kathleen Nolan delivered her son, Emmett Paul, in the cabin next to mine one autumn day at the commune. The midwives arrived after the birth, so her entire support staff was me. Photo by Jeff Buchin.

know that I was failing in my biological obligation and missing one of life's great pleasures not to have a child myself. I dismissed them politely like I once did a junkie intellectual in San Francisco who tried to explain to me why I should sample heroin addiction. Not my cup of tea. I was already in my mid-forties. Having kids was for, umm, kids. My reservations evaporated immediately when Sue became pregnant. Suddenly it seemed the best idea in the world.

But all of these stories—the scary and the sublime—became less abstract when it was my baby and my wife having the baby. True, Geba was even more experienced as a midwife by 1983, and the due date was mid-July when the roads were most passable, but she lived about ninety minutes upriver on roads that started out rough and then got worse. Our link to her was the CB radio, which usually worked great. But we had a backup plan. It was one of the other midwives who had started her craft at the commune, a woman named Yeshi Neumann. Yeshi had become a registered nurse and then formally trained as a midwife. She worked, in those days, at a hospital in Oakland. Yeshi had arranged to spend her vacation at Butler Creek with a week allotted either side of the due date. I could relax. But the due date passed with no new baby. I mentioned this to Yeshi, and she shrugged and told me only 5 percent of all women actually deliver on their due date. Two more days passed, and Yeshi came by to check Sue. Big smiles all around. No problems, Yeshi assured me.

"No problems?" I said. "You leave in four days and Geba lives up the worst road in the western hemisphere. If you're gone, who's going to be in charge of the birth?"

Yeshi smiled at me with that rich, indulgent smile I'd seen in midwives before. "Don't look at me that way," I said. "How could I be a midwife?"

"First of all, I don't have to return to work for a few more days. Also, you delivered Emmett Paul at Black Bear," she said, "and I'll give you some stuff to read." I must have looked unsatisfied. "And I'll make you a list," she offered.

Geba and Yeshi were graduates of the school of life at Black Bear, Yeshi always said. She had been a medieval history student in college and had studied the medieval heretics. They were women who felt they could know God without going through the male priesthood. They were mostly healers. Much later the connection was made that these women were midwives. In Yeshi's telling of Exodus, Pharaoh ordered the Egyptian midwives to kill the firstborn, but the midwives said, "Oh, Jewish women give birth so quickly, we could never get there in time." Yeshi found great strength in the subversive roots of her craft.

Yeshi flashed me another of those knowing midwife smiles. "We did quite a few births at Black Bear in those years 1970–74." She reeled off names of the moms and the babies. "The first birth I attended at Black Bear was Morningstar and Kishwuf. Then Neenya and Robadoo. Milagra and Senta. Geba was at those births. I was new. Melissa and Rio, Jo and Turtle, Catherine and Fanshen, Autumn Joy and Mila. All of them. Toz and Liz, Jesse and Allen, Gabriel and Suzanne, Mahaj and Toby, Karuna and Geba. Some of those births I came back for like Meredith and Tesilya. I missed when Geba had Allegra." Yeshi would pause now and then

Geba Greenberg was one of the midwives who attended the birth of our daughter Erica Kate at Butler Creek. She came to the commune near its start and stayed there much longer than most of us. Photo by Hank Lebo.

as she reeled off the names, maybe remembering the circumstance of the different births.

Part of the Black Bear commune ethic was that we needed to rebuild a better world by taking responsibility for all its parts—food, shelter, delivering babies. When Yeshi left Black Bear in 1974, she entered nursing school, the only legal route to midwifery. The schooling, with its hierarchical deference to doctors, was a challenge after commune life, but Yeshi stuck it out.

In the medical model and at San Francisco General Hospital where Yeshi did her training, the view was that childbirth was a pathological process, like some kind of disease that required an intervention. Despite the barriers, Yeshi had gotten her license and begun work at a hospital in the East Bay. She told stories of having seven different women in labor at once. One would be from Cambodia and one from Russia, one from Mexico, one from Nigeria. That's what County Hospital in Oakland is like. She worked with high-risk pregnancies, diabetes, twins, high blood pressure. Yeshi knew that the women who spoke little or no English were the ones who most needed to have midwives by their side.

Yeshi's birth stories always filled me with wonder and confidence. The dates of her vacation did not. I kept testing the CB radio, and Bob-O, who lived even farther upriver, told me to relax. "What if the signal doesn't get up there?" I asked anxiously.

"The way I rigged your radio they can hear you in Tennessee, Malcolm," Bob-O countered. "Don't worry about reaching Geba. You should worry about getting busted by the Federal Communications Commission."

The next day those particular worries evaporated. Sue went into labor, and Yeshi was still around. Suddenly the focus shifted from carpentry and CB radios, from gardens and long, rutted country roads to the serious main event. For many of the prefaces, the pollination, of course, and some of the ancillary technology like running vehicles, men are useful, but when delivery actually begins, the world shifts mostly to the work of women.

Sue's labor started in late afternoon. There had been a few light contractions earlier. She'd dreaded having a due date in July because it was normally so hot by then, but she spent the day lounging in a bed we'd set up in the newly built screen porch. She wandered into the garden and stopped for a long time at each of her favorite plants—gladiolas and lilies, foxgloves in tall columns laced with bolted lettuce plants, grapes, and peaches that were still ripening.

Sue told me the story of the birth of my stepson, Slate, thirteen years earlier. He was born in some old Chicago public hospital that served poor people. Women in labor got whatever doc was on duty. And it was fast—three and a half hours total. Sue could hear a woman screaming down the hall, and the nurses and doctor left her alone in the room. Sue had been to Lamaze classes that coached women before their labor in techniques to manage the pain. Sue was managing her breathing and was trying to push with each contraction when a woman doctor from India came in, unsmiling and unfriendly, but Sue focused on the red spot on her forehead. The baby, at ten and a half pounds, swam out in a big explosive wave of blood and fluid. The Indian doctor was bathed in the splash. She spun around and stormed out in anger.

The nurses whisked Slate away over Sue's protests. Then they started lobbying her about bottle feeding, how much healthier it was. There were fifteen mothers there then, and the nurses talked every one of them except Sue into bottle feeding. She stood her ground. If you knew Sue, you'd expect that.

It was a cool night for July at Butler Creek, thirteen-plus years after Slate's birth, when Sue went into labor with Erica Kate. There was a swirl of people in the house, as often happened at river births. Liz Pullen, who later became a nurse, took responsibility for big brother Slate, so he wouldn't be neglected if things got hectic. Bob-O's son Allen, who was then only a young boy, was peeking down from a stairwell through a gap in an unfinished wall. Geba had arrived. Judy Beaver, who was learning midwifery then, was there.

Sue started having back pains, but squatting or dropping into crawling position gave relief. She asked Yeshi if it was okay to give birth on her side. Things went very, very slowly, and past midnight the midwives decided the baby was facing backwards, head down, but faced backward. It was slowing the baby's descent. We heard Geba and Yeshi talking about whether Sue should go to town. Even without labor pains, the drive to the closest urban hospital took two hours. Sue says that somehow the grueling prospect of a town trip made the physical act happen; the baby turned around inside her. Yeshi felt the baby turn. She said, "Hold back a little now on pushing so you don't tear."

When Erica Kate was finally born, Sue remembers an enormous rush of gratefulness. We had a baby. It was over. We didn't have to go to town. She remembers the most delicious part was when they put the newborn on her belly. Erica Kate stretched out on Sue and turned her head to stare at the kerosene lamp, which was the only light in the room. It makes sense, huh? From in-the-belly to on-the-belly so the connection with the mother isn't lost. Erica Kate weighed nine and a half pounds, an alert, healthy baby. The next few days were all just a blur. Sue exalted in the wonderful feeling of curling up with her baby, a luxury they hadn't allowed at the Chicago hospital with Slate.

I remember that Erica Kate was born a different color than I'd seen before except in big Chinook salmon, a shiny, silvery color. I looked to Yeshi to make sure it was okay, and she said, "What a perfect baby." Of course, part of Yeshi's bedside vocabulary is that nearly everything is perfect. "That was a perfect contraction," she would say. "That's perfect breathing." When Sue hobbled outside to pee in the darkness between contractions, it was a perfect time to pee. So it made sense that when Sue had a baby the color of a big fish, that was a perfect color. Later, Petey told us he'd gone out to pee under the same fir tree, and there was a short, fat Butler Creek rattlesnake coiled there, maybe waiting in the darkness to greet the newborn. Ten years later, Erica's tenth birthday actually, I came home and found another fat rattlesnake in the same place. Maybe the snakes like parties as much as we do.

Those first few days after the birth were a reverie for me, too. I do remember that we toted Erica Kate out to the cardiology doctors in Arcata because her heartbeat at birth was a little fast, what the midwives called tachycardia. The doc in Arcata measured her, weighed her, listened to her insides, noted that she was ninety-fifth percentile for size, and concluded that she was a "perfect" baby.

In the hot afternoons, Sue would need naps, so I'd take Erica Kate out for long walks around Butler Flat. Those walks linger in my mind as the happiest I have ever been. We'd have long conversations together—the baby and me. I'd tell her about all the plants and trees and then have to make her responses since she didn't know how to talk yet. That seemed to satisfy her just fine, especially since neither of us resorted to baby talk. Her favorite trees, we both agreed, were the vine maples as the road entered the woods along Butler creek. She liked the way the maple leaves filtered and mottled the sunlight.

These dialogues may have seemed one-sided, but Erica Kate held her own and always prompted me, like she does still, for more stories. She'd

My wife, Sue Terence, took our daughter, Erica Kate, down to a beach along the Salmon River in the late spring before she was one year old. Sue is an ardent environmentalist, and Erica Kate grew up with the same passions. Photo by Jeff Buchin.

coo enthusiastically as I spoke both of our parts, and she'd fuss whenever I stopped. Within days I'd exhausted poems and little songs with all the species names I knew and even a few I made up. Then there were songs about birds and fingers and the little girl who lived at Butler Creek and was a friend with all the animals. At first Erica Kate spoke in a glossolalian babble, but conversationally, not like a crazed religious zealot. Soon she switched to real speech, and Sue used to speculate that Erica Kate started talking so young just so she could get a word in edgewise.

Midsummer might be an uncomfortable time to be pregnant at Butler because of the weather, but it's a great time to be an infant. Erica Kate spent her first weeks in our huge garden,

Erica Kate Terence in August 1983. That was a good time to fill a wheelbarrow with garden produce and our month-old daughter. It was a picture that decorated a hundred refrigerators. Photo by Peg Laird.

exploding with flowers and ripe fruit. Everybody was busy with harvest. The genre of baby pictures had never impressed me. Most babies' photos, no matter how beautiful, looked a lot like Winston Churchill, and Erica Kate fit in with the rest. I thought about photographing her with a cigar, but ruled it out. Or maybe Sue ruled it out. Then I started dreaming up a garden photo. In the middle of that, a neighbor's guest showed up. Turned out she was a food stylist, a job category none of us had ever heard of until that opportune moment. She heard our photo idea and hauled her cameras out of a van. We piled an assortment of apples, plums, summer squash, tomatoes, four kinds of peppers, lettuce, garlic braids, and six kinds of flowers grown for drying all into a wheel barrow. The food stylist smiled politely and unpacked it all. Then she lined the wheelbarrow with baby blankets and started meticulously polishing, arranging, and rearranging every object. The last object in was Erica Kate, who was fascinated by her new vegetable playroom. I'm not sure the photographer polished Erica Kate, but I'm sure she was tempted. She shot dozens of photos as Erica Kate gazed over her new surroundings. The afternoon passed, and we whiled away an hour baby watching as Rainbird sprinklers described great arcs farther out in the garden and swallows wheeled in their paths chasing insects we could not see. The river beyond purred in a late summer languor. I felt deliriously, ambitiously lazy and fulfilled.

Life, we see, is filled with adventures, and the birth of our children is one of the best. And it had all worked out so well. Bob-O knew his stuff, and Geba's CB radio worked. Yeshi's vacation was scheduled just right so I wasn't reduced to a crazy man, running off into the forest. Sue and Erica Kate managed her uterine roll at the right moment, and the baby-with-vegetables photo ended up on one magazine cover, one school nutrition poster, and at least a hundred refrigerators. I was as happy as I have ever been. It was all, as I came to say, a perfect birth.

CHAPTER 13

Coyote's Aunt

One day I decided that I'd imitate an old-school anthropologist and interview Violet Super, the old Karuk Tribe woman who had lived across the creek back in the early 1980s. I actually knew one real anthropologist, a man named John Salter, who was an on-again, off-again resident at the commune in the years I lived there and a good friend. John had taped lots of Native elders on the river, and he was my role model. John was the genuine article, PhD and all. More important, his work was respected by the Karuk Tribe. From time to time the tribe would hire him to write an academic paper that they would use to bolster a legislative campaign or a lawsuit.

Butler Creek had been a Karuk village site before the miners came, and it always made me aware that I was as much a guest on the river as I was a property owner. But I wanted details, and Violet Super seemed like someone who might talk to me.

Most Natives I knew on the river were friendly, but few were quick to tell stories. Why should they trust a white guy? The local history was replete with genocide, and even my own family had a history of genocide—as a target.

My mom told me the story many times of her parents, growing up in a Jewish village on the Russian-Polish border. There were frequent murderous attacks by what she called Cossacks, on horseback. Children and young women were buried to save their lives, she said, and her parents immigrated to America around 1912. My mom was born in Chicago just a few years later. After World War II, the Chicago relatives contacted the Red Cross to locate the family members who had stayed in the Old Country. Word came back that none of them survived, and even the town did not exist anymore. Many of the hippies at the commune in the years I lived there and after were Jews, not particularly observant, but certainly aware of the Holocaust. When we met Willis and Florence Conrad and their Karuk friends, none of us talked about this, but it may have made us all—hippies and Natives alike—more open to one another than white people and Native Americans usually were in those days.

So I put new batteries in the tape recorder and headed downriver to Orleans, where Violet had moved as she grew older. A silent Native woman led me into the back room of the crowded cabin. Aunt Vi sat there, on the edge of her bed, in a faded blue housecoat and slippers. She turned at the sound of our entry, like an owl hearing the skittering of a mouse through the leaves. I knew she had become blind over the years, but even the gaze of unseeing eyes shrunk me into some smaller, more edible mammal. The caretaker escort turned and left, and I fumbled an introduction. "I'm Malcolm, Sue Terence's husband from Butler Creek, and I want to ask you some questions because you used to live at Butler when I first moved there, and you know its history better than anybody."

A frown crossed her face, and she said, "I never seen you before in my life."

I tried to sputter explanations, "Sue and I used to . . . I know your relatives and . . . ," but she broke into a bird-like cackle. "Don' worry. I remember you and Sue. You live over there cross the creek at the Grants' place. Reason I never seen you before was cuz I was blind. But doctor fixed it."

"How come you didn't fix it years ago?" I asked, still puzzled by an eighty-five-year-old Karuk woman's idea of a joke.

"I met people who were doctors. Somebody from down Redding moved up here, was gonna be a doctor. He doctored me when my eye was aching. So he told me to have surgery, 'If you don't, you're gonna go blind.' Well, them days there was no way for us Indians to go to doctors. We didn't have no income." She said the word "income" with contempt.

"You know, Indian doctors used to get trained around Butler Creek," she continued. I held up a tape recorder asking permission wordlessly. White academics—anthropologists, linguists—have interviewed and taped old Native women since the 1920s and before, and she nodded assent without breaking stride. "People that gonna be medicine woman. Doctor. They go under the water. Yeah. Under the rocks there's still water under there, not moving fast. I guess there's a rock in there that looks like a person. So she's doctoring this rock. I guess she's learning to be a doctor. So they go under there, and then they come wading out. When they get through, they doctor. I never seen it. There haven't been that kind of doctor anymore."

Butler Creek originates in the high country and drops fast. I remembered my first icy dip there on a summer day. The water is barely warmer than snowmelt all year around, and my toes curled as she spoke. I tried to imagine old-time medicine women practicing their healing arts on that granite cadaver in a stream of ice water and could not.

Aunt Vi had lived across Butler Creek from my cabin when I first moved there. She had a trailer then near a handful of relatives who themselves lived in trailers and very small houses. They called her Auntie, raising the possibility that she was their aunt, although I wasn't sure. "Auntie" can also be an honorific, a name of respect. When her husband died, she moved to the more comfortable setting downriver in Orleans, and that was where I found her. I wanted details about Butler Creek, so I swallowed my reserve and plowed ahead.

"So you were born at Butler?" I asked and moved the tape machine closer.

"I was born and raised right there. It was December 3, 1917. At the upper end, yeah. Right at the edge of the creek. They were camping there, my parents, while they were building the house. And then later on they made it into a chicken house. My husband always teased me: 'You was born in a chicken house.'" She laughed and repositioned herself on the edge of the bed, possibly to be closer to the tape recorder.

"But when we were camping there, there was no chicken house," she continued. "The old Grant couple was over there on other side of the creek—on your side—and we used to go visit them old Grant people. She used to give us vegetables. They had a nice garden. We weren't allowed to plant anything on our side because Aunt Effie, my mother's sister, she just didn't want us to be there. Didn't want our house built there. So Anderson Grant, the white guy on your side of the creek, tell her, 'That's my property there. This line.' So we told her that and she didn't say no more." Aunt Vi began a long recitation of aunts, uncles, cousins, and more. I knew the Natives who lived there now, but she did not make it down to their generation. "So I'm the only one left in that whole outfit."

"Who was Butler?" I asked, forgetting the present-day relatives and hungry for more stories. I remembered from old maps I'd seen that a man named Butler had moved there in the second half of the nineteenth century and had lived across the creek from where I lived. "Who was the person they named the creek after?"

"Butler," she nodded. "He was a white man. He was married to somebody down in Weitchpec. A Yurok person. Some reason he committed suicide. And this wife of his wasn't gonna live there so she made a curse on that ranch. Whoever live there go crazy. And I guess we're all crazy." She laughed again, this time like a flock of ravens. She glanced over at me, maybe to see if I agreed about her sanity, and I laughed louder to show I got her joke.

She rolled on. "So that Yurok lady told my grandmother, Susan Charles, to go up there and stay at Butler's to take care of the place. We're originally from Ikes Creek downriver." I told Vi that I'd seen the name Butler Suzy penciled into an old map and asked if that was her grandmother. She just shrugged. What people wrote on maps was not her concern.

"Leland knows a lot of those old names," she responded, although I did not know who Leland was. "One of those old guys was my mother's father. These people saw in a book (that) Mary Johnny's father was one of those guys from Ikes Creek." I knew that Ikes was a creek along the Klamath River just downriver from Somes Bar where Natives many years earlier, when I still lived at the commune, had taken me night fishing with headlamps for lamprey eels. The taste of fried eels the next morning, in all their smoky brown succulence, played out on the back of my tongue.

"His last name was Charles," she continued, ignoring that I had already lost track of her familial narrative. "My mother's maiden name was Charles, so that was my grandmother's husband. Anyway, that's how my family ended up there. They say the curse don't work anymore when that person died. So I don't know. Them Weitchpecs are not very . . . they're friendly, but then they can get mean, too. My grandma Susan died in 1920—Butler Flat was in her name for a number of years. That's why Aunt Effie thought it was hers. She keeps saying it's her place. She wouldn't even let us kids eat fruit off that place. She'd shoot over our heads. But us kids would go back and do the same thing the next day. We'd jump behind stumps when she come out. Well, I found out nobody had this place after Aunt Susie died, so I took it up. An allotment." The allotment system was a method of claiming land and taking title subject to restrictions of tribal trust regulations.

I leafed through my notes trying to remember if Susan was Susie and if she was a grandmother or an aunt. Maybe Grandma was another honorific. Even though everybody called Violet Super "Auntie Vi," I doubted they could all really be nephews and nieces. While I paused, Vi wound up a small Elvis Presley music box. She smiled with pride when the doll Elvis sang "Hound Dog" and wiggled lewdly on its small pedestal.

She set Elvis aside and launched another story. "I got the name Super from Leonard Super, my only husband. My husband before that only lasted three years." She moved her hand in the air in a back-and-forth erasing gesture and scrunched up her already wrinkled face.

"I moved back up to Butler cuz that first husband and I were living up Klamath River next to his mom. And she's always trying to boss us around. I said he was a momma's boy; whatever she says, well, that goes. One day his car being worked on and he goes to the mailbox quite a ways. He left about four o'clock, and he didn't get back until nine o'clock. The door flew open, and there those two guys were trying to hold each other up, so drunk." She shook her head in disgust. "It made me so mad I told Jeanerette's dad, 'Come down and knock this guy down.'

So he got dressed and came down. My husband went right over there in front of the steps waiting to get knocked down. So Jeanerette's dad just hit him once, and down he went. Then I went over there and kicked him in the ribs and opened the door and pushed him out till he got out on the steps. I told him, 'Don't ever come back here again. I'm not gonna live like that.'" She looked up at me to see if I was registering enough disgust, but then her mouth broke into a small grin.

I checked the tape recorder and ventured another question. "Before the white people came were there people living at Butler?" I asked.

"Yeah, before the miners, that whole flat, both sides the creek, was Indians living all over. So was Oak Bottom downriver. You know where the Forest Service is; that was all full of Indians. There's a lot of crazy stories about them white people then. I don't like white people." She flashed me the sly smile of a woman sharing a secret. "I don't like white people because, when they first came in the country, they were real mean. One of them tried to rape an Indian, and she just got a dead hold of his pecker and she just twisted it and did everything she could and he almost died. He was in bed for a week. Nobody tried that for a while." She took another break of laughter.

"Course, some of the white men were good. They get on the Indian side. Trying to protect them. That's how come the Indians married the white men from way back. The white men were good to them. They helped them.

"But I know one outfit, the miners, when they came in there, there was an old lady sitting by her house and she won't leave her house. They just piped her out of there with all the water. Just down there where the gold go. Right down the sluice box. That's why we say they were mean. By time I was born it was getting calm, not like it was a long time ago."

"What did the old-time Natives call Butler?" I asked.

"The Indian name was *Ah-rin-chka*. They call mountain, I forget." Her eyes, both the one that could now see and the other, clenched closed as she searched for the memory. "*Tuu-Iish-ip* is a mountain. *Tuu-Iish-ip*."

The Karuk speech rolled out of her mouth triumphantly. I asked her the name of the place where her cabin was now.

"All these places had Indian names," she said. "You know why town of Orleans is such a big flat valley when everything else is so steep. Because Coyote went up into Oregon to get these beads they call money, Indians, they call it money. They use it for money. So went up and when he got back, he was so happy to get back to *Ip-sith-komen—Ip-sipt-kom* is land; he was kicking all over making a big flat. *Uva-Shu-Sha-Neen.* They call this ranch *Ivshshaneen.* That's Coyote talk. We say *If-thif-thanay* and Coyote say *ii-shiv-shaneen.*

"So Coyote has a language that's a little bit different?"

"Coyote was always doing something," she announced with evident pride. "Always making trouble. He always got away, though." Always getting away might be a value especially prized by someone who's made it for eighty-five years.

I puzzled for a while on what to ask next, and she reached again to wind the Elvis Presley music box.

CHAPTER 14

Sorting Forest from the Trees

They all looked up only briefly when I entered the meeting in one of the aging Forest Service structures. The timber planning officer, whom I called the TPO, was there. "He was our boss's boss's boss." Two of the foresters who worked for him were seated around the table. The geologist and the wildlife biologist were there. One man from firefighting I'd never met before had come from another district. The US Forest Service district ranger, the guy who had hired me, was heading the meeting.

The TPO glanced at me and then made a private what's-he-doing-here gesture to the ranger, and the ranger made some gesture back. These were the highest-ranking people in the district, and there were no other lowly timber cruisers, let alone one like me who had been hired only a month earlier.

"Do you all know Terence?" the ranger asked. "I wanted him to take notes at this meeting."

Most of them I already knew. They all nodded hellos, but the TPO shifted restlessly in his seat. One of the foresters rolled out a stack of large topographic maps, and they all started circling the wide tables that nearly filled the cheaply paneled room.

"Up here above Ti Bar around Ten Bear Mountain," one of the foresters suggested, and they all shifted their attention to the large blue-line map he was unfurling on top of the others.

"What's this over here?" asked the fireman, pointing at a large shaded patch on the map. He was stout and grizzled, a visitor from Oak Knoll, another district farther up the Klamath River. Unlike the others, he was wearing only his uniform shirt. It was stuffed into logger's jeans, chopped high at the ankles and held aloft by thick red suspenders. His boots were worn and oil stained, frosted with a layer of reddish dust.

"That's the Hell's Sale," the TPO answered archly. His pants and shirt were pressed, a rarity at the station. He barely glanced at the fireman, as though too long a look might soil his own shoes.

"And this?" the fireman pressed on.

"That's Hell's Sale, too," the TPO answered, trying to disguise the impatience in his voice.

The fireman's eyes widened, and he whistled. "I thought we had some big sales up in Oak Knoll, but this puppy takes the cake."

"What about this area, here?" the new voice ventured. It was the youngest forester poking a region on the same map. "I don't see sale boundaries here. Can we build a new sale here?"

"We could, but it's in the new Wilderness boundaries," the TPO said. "Finding space for the next few sales is going to be hard. Environmentalists are acting like they own the National Forest, and ignoring all the work we've done to replant after we log. In 70 years, 120 years at the longest, those plantations will be large enough to log again." When he mentioned environmentalists, I shrunk into a corner and worked intently at note taking.

"Don't count on that projection," the fireman said. "You've all seen the difference between the way the old growth burns and a plantation burns. Each year we lose new plantations, and the fire moves through the old growth not doing much damage, just here and there."

"Not much damage," countered the TPO, inhaling between each word. "How can you say that after the Hog Fire? It covered 55,000 acres." I remembered the Hog Fire in 1977, seven years earlier. It was my first time on fire lines, and I wondered what the fireman was talking about. There was a world of damage.

As though answering my unspoken question, the fireman said: "Most of those 55,000 acres, the fire didn't do much harm. If anything, it did some good. We've been putting out fires around here for seventy-five years. Some of us are starting to think we should be letting them wander around and cook out the low brush and blowdown trees. Fire like that, it helps the forest. People say the Indians used to burn like that near their villages."

"They'd do it again, if we let them," the TPO interrupted, shaking his head.

"Might not be the worst thing to try," the fireman continued. "But here's my point. Most parts of the fire were overall pretty harmless, but there were a few places where the fire was a big mess. Sometimes it would blow up on south-facing slopes or on recent clear-cuts because they had so much leftover fuel. But the absolute worst was the plantations. Every time one of those caught fire, they'd go off like a bomb and sometimes they'd spread ugly into any upslope old growth."

"It's even-aged management," one of the young foresters ventured. "Those plantations are perfect ladder fuels into the taller timber." The TPO glared at him.

"I think only one or two plantations made it through," the fireman said, scratching his head through a mop of thinning gray hair. "Now we've salvage-logged the whole burn and replanted it into huge plantations. Just a matter of time until we have another August lightning storm like the Hog Fire, and we'll have another big fire. Only it could be even bigger. With a bigger fire after that. And we're talking about a hundred-plus-year rotation. Every one of those plantations and every future plantation will get hit by fire. Not one of them will make it a full rotation."

The room fell silent at this heresy. Everyone gazed at the floor. But the TPO, who was actually a very smart man, took command. "We're making a case here out of anecdotal evidence. The latest sustained yield models from Redding support the rotation, and they show that high rainfall areas like our district can shorten the time span down to seventy-five to ninety years," he said, and he jutted his jaw defiantly. Being smart, I've learned, is not a defense against being wrong.

The ranger spoke to refocus the room. "I agree with both of you," he said. The ranger had just returned from a Forest Service personnel management workshop. Maybe that I-agree-with-both-of-you gambit was a trick he'd learned there.

"The rainfall is a big difference," the ranger continued. "We get a lot more down here, and the Redding model has more validity here than up in Oak Knoll. That same rainfall is the reason that the region expects us to put up 44 million board feet a year. And our job today is to find where we're going to find that volume over the next few years."

I'd just finished enlarging my cabin at Butler Creek until it seemed huge, milled our own trees, and nailed up lumber with abandon. We had used maybe 25,000 board feet. I started to do the mental math, but their conversation continued, so I returned to my note taking.

"We need to be looking at areas where there has already been some earlier harvest and find our volume there," the TPO suggested. He swept his hand across a map of the entire ranger district, slowing and hovering wherever there were clusters of existing logging roads. In one of the sweeps, his hand moved carelessly across my home at Butler Creek and floated, like a great bird of prey, into the wooded highlands that drained into the river just north of where Butler Creek entered the Salmon River.

The geologist, who'd not spoken, shifted over to examine the area. He started to speak, caught himself, then spoke anyway. "There's no shortage of roads there," he blurted. "That's the Monte Creek road system. Problem is that nearly every road is all blocked by massive landslides. It's all decomposed granite there. That whole system is the worst mistake the Forest Service ever made around here. I've seen the aerial photos from before those roads went in. A sophomore geology student could have predicted those slides. It was as bad as the roads up at the Little North Fork."

He paused to catch his breath and plopped down in a chair. Little North Fork had just been logged when I first came into the country many years earlier. Hardened loggers called it "The Rape of the Little North Fork." I'd never heard it mentioned before at this station, but it was well known upriver.

The geologist jumped up from his chair and launched himself again. "What I don't know is why we have to be in such a damned hurry to offer up timber volume if there's nowhere safe enough to cut. Don't we have some other responsibilities but stapling up our red clear-cut boundary markers and punching in new roads? I want to . . ."

The ranger stepped aggressively toward the geologist. "We're all getting carried away here," he began, in a voice louder than he probably intended. "Here's what's true. We are all hired to develop a logging plan that meets the law." He paused, caught his breath. "And meets the targets set by Congress and the regional office," he pronounced, pleased with his uncharacteristic assertiveness. "That is our job. If we aren't ready to do that job, we should find another place to work. Or maybe another kind of work." Another pause. Everyone stared at the geologist, who stepped back from the ranger.

————

"I can't believe you got to sit in on a meeting like that," my wife, Sue, told me that evening over a glass of beer. "Did they ever calm down enough to line out any new timber sales?"

"They found a few," I said, "but I'm not sure you could call the tone calm. It stayed edgy all day. They even lined out another sale up there in the Monte Creek road system." I gestured out the window in the general direction of the ridge that divided the Butler Creek and Monte Creek watersheds.

Sue rolled her eyes and asked if I wanted a second beer. When she returned from the fridge, she said, "It's amazing they're trying to launch another sale up there, of all places. The first one was a disaster. The people who planned it should be in federal prison. Every time they try to start another sale up there, it collapses of its own dead weight." Then she turned back to me. "And you got to sit in on the meeting."

"Why do you think the ranger brought me in to the meeting?" I said. "The timber planning officer didn't seem to like me there at all."

"I'm still trying to figure that out," she said. "At first I thought they were just trying to get your mind off antiherbicide organizing by hiring you. Maybe it's more. Maybe that ranger really thinks you'll fall in love with timber sales. I want to see the notes you took."

"I entered them into a Forest Service computer. I'll get a copy tomorrow."

"Good luck on that one," she said and shook her head. I finished the beer in one swallow.

CHAPTER 15

Blue Paint Rule Book

One of those mornings, in the three or four years I worked there, the TPO stopped us before we headed off into the woods. We tried to load the pale green Forest Service truck quickly when he headed our way and get out of the station parking lot, but he waved us over. He smiled broadly as he waited for us, all the more unsettling because he rarely smiled in my direction.

"Where you headed today?" he asked, although he must have known. The answer, which we didn't need to say, was that we were going out to do detailed measurement of a sampling of the trees growing on a prospective timber sales. That's what timber cruisers like us did. We packed vests full of specialized survey equipment because our information was used by logging companies to make bids on the upcoming sale. Precise measurement was needed because millions of dollars were at stake.

"We're marking a few more units up at Ram-Exit," my work partner, Von Tunstall, answered.

"How's it going up there?" the TPO asked. Maybe he knew that too.

"Going great," I said, feigning enthusiasm that he knew was false. "We're finding little pockets of old growth all over the place up there." Our job was on the proposed timber sale along the ridges just north of Butler Creek, where I lived. The area was very steep and already a checkerboard of clear-cut logging blocks and a collapsed road system.

"I hear you're having trouble with yellow jackets," he said.

We only grimaced and shrugged. His smile grew. "And I hear you're having some questions about how to mark the stream protection buffers up there. What's so hard?"

Von started a sentence about the twenty-five-foot setback and then swallowed it, mid-breath.

The TPO's smile grew ominously. "What can be so hard about a twenty-five-foot spec? Twenty-five feet isn't that hard. You men measure stuff all day long. I even have a little trick for you. If you have one foot in the stream and you can reach the tree with your spray can, then it's in the protected buffer zone. Paint it."

He made an exaggerated gesture of spelling the letters S-A-V-E. "Otherwise it's outside. It can be logged."

Neither of us responded to him, and his smile faded. "It's important to protect those watercourses. Very important." The sound of the word "important" was like a trigger to him that he had more important things to do than harass the hippies the ranger had hired for his marking crew. He wheeled and strode importantly back to the station.

Von and I glanced at each other and climbed into the truck.

Five minutes out of the station, I bubbled over, "I cannot believe that jerk. Only a twenty-five-foot buffer in timber that big and on terrain that steep? It should be fifty feet, a hundred feet. And now he wants us to shrink it to a six-foot buffer."

Von had just graduated in forestry at Humboldt State, and he just grinned at my venting. "Doesn't matter if it was five hundred feet. The boss would still say you could only protect trees you can reach with one foot in the water. I wonder who told him that we were, uh, enhancing the buffer zones. What I don't get about you, Terence, is how you could hate logging so much and still take a job setting up timber sales. Or why they would hire you, for that matter? Doesn't matter what we spray blue, probably. Some timber faller is gonna pretend he didn't see it and cut it down."

"Or he'll accidentally drop a tree into the buffer trees and damage them so bad that the inspector lets him cut them," I chimed in. "It drives me nuts." I didn't explain why I'd taken the job. It reminded me of a joke that ends with the punch line, "But don't tell my mom. She thinks I play piano in a whorehouse." I tried to remember the start of the joke, but just then Von ordered me out of the truck to lock in the four-wheel-drive hubs.

The road up into Ram-Exit, as the proposed timber sale was named, was deeply rutted, overgrown, and washed out, but we were now at the shoofly. This stretch was even steeper and more rutted than the road we'd just left. I think maybe the word "shoofly" means a road that connects places that were not originally linked that way. I'm not sure this road even deserved to be called a road. The Forest Service had first opened the area for logging in the late 1960s. It covered the next few watersheds in a downriver direction from Butler Creek, but that logging happened over a decade before I moved to Butler from farther upriver.

The original road plan intersected several steep, active landslides, but standards weren't so strict back then, and they'd already cut all the easy timber on flatter ground. And there isn't that much flat ground to begin with in Salmon River country.

It was not unusual for landslides to start moving fast a few years after a logging sale. We'd seen plenty of evidence when we were surveying older clear-cut plantations in the spring. From the road, they looked like even-aged Gardens of Eden, but when we walked into the thickets, fifteen feet high, the picture changed. Gullies dissected the old plantations, and jumbles of wrecked, decaying older trees, the detritus of the logging years earlier, were hidden everywhere. Sometimes an old skid road would end abruptly at a cliff. A whole bluff would have collapsed into the creek during a wet winter and eroded into the river.

But the road on this timber sale was a different story. The slides didn't wait. The main rock type seemed to be decomposed granite, and slides pooched out the road system while the loggers were still up there with all their equipment. There was no way out with all their Cats and the yarders with the giant towers. That's why they punched the shoofly down the spine of the ridge. It had never been much of an engineering marvel, even when it was new. Now, years later, the shoofly was almost impossible to navigate, even in our four-wheel-drive truck.

Von struggled to control the steering wheel as we slowly powered up the ridge. Finally, we hit an intact vestige of the old road system and turned left. He stopped to catch his breath and asked me to unlock the hubs on the front wheels. Along the road, off to the horizon, was a huge clear-cut. In the distance was Orleans Mountain. Its peak was the head of the Butler Creek drainage and the tallest mountain around. It was still barely logged on our side, but we couldn't see down to my cabin or even into the mouth of Butler Creek from this part of the road.

Across the river was Wooley Creek, still heavily wooded with old growth because it had been included in the most recent expansion of the Wilderness boundaries. Boss's boss's boss loved to rant about the wilderness. "What a goddamn waste of timber," he'd say. "Let those senators build a house out of spotted owls."

Von drove slowly along the road, a flat ribbon carved into the steepest terrain. Once around the bend, he pointed. "That must be Unit 42b. It's the only trees left; must be it." The small grove was easy to spot. The trees were 150 feet tall, and a few were even taller. Near the periphery, a few trees had blown down.

"Check out the windfall," I said. "That seems to happen after you log."

"Looks like it happened big-time," Von said. A huge sugar pine was down, and its top crossed the road. That's *Pinus lambertiana* to all you Latin-speaking botanists.

"We could cut our way through," I suggested. "I brought a saw."

"What's the point?" Von asked. "We're there. Anyway, those piss-fir saws would take all day." He cleared his throat. "Those agency saws." We clambered out of the truck and slipped on our vests full of instruments and blue spray paint. We would carefully measure and evaluate a sampling of the trees in Unit 42b so the loggers would know how much to bid for it when it went to auction. I thought the stand, with its majestic old-growth conifers, didn't look bad despite the scattered blowdown trees around the edges.

Von scrambled up the steep road bank and into the unit. He stopped in front of another giant sugar pine, this one still standing. Its long branches had the sweeping curve of the roof of a Chinese temple. He whistled and said, "Some mill could make a shitload of expensive molding out of this honker."

Sugar pine. I dutifully wrote an "11," the species code, into my log book. I started to unhook my diameter tape, the first step in our measurements.

"Save your energy," Von said. He pulled out a spray can and painted in tall blue letters the word "SAVE" into the ruffled red bark. Then he scrambled up around the high side and painted it again.

CHAPTER 16

Drift Smoke and Blackberries

The smell of smoke still gets me. Not smoke from a woodstove or a campfire. That smells like comfort and coffee in the morning. It's drift smoke that stirs me up. It's smoke from a fire in the forest. Memories tattooed into the brain by adrenaline seem to be the strongest.

We had been grabbed off the timber sale prep crew for the fire. You never knew whether it was a little spot fire or the start of something big. Either way we were buzzed. It was a change. The extra money for over-time and for hazard pay was also good. If we were a little scared, we didn't admit it even to ourselves.

This time, one late summer afternoon in 1985, we went way back into the mountains behind Orleans on roads I'd never been on before. Our trucks were parked on the road at the top of the steep unit, all turned around for a quick exit if needed. That was the standard prac-tice in the woods. I could tell that a cable yarder had sat there during the logging operations. The clear-cut was maybe a twenty-acre hole in the surrounding old-growth forest. It must have been planted with replacement conifers after the logging, but they were fast disappear-ing in thickets of hardwood bush, arrayed that afternoon like stacks of kindling. The timber companies and the agencies that govern pub-lic land were always ready to portray large-scale industrial logging as some kind of farming. They called logging the old growth "harvest-ing," as though it were potatoes. The US Forest Service, which admin-istered all that land, was even nestled into the federal Department of

Agriculture. It would have been better administered by the Bureau of Mines. They were mining old-growth forests. I'm not the only one who thought that way. Kenoli used to argue that during the days of the herbicide wars. I admit that I was working for them setting up the next round of timber sales, but that didn't make me love it.

Take a deep breath. We're about to head down into a smoky place.

It was a little burn right then, near the bottom of a logging unit, maybe started by the lightning bust overnight. "Doesn't look too bad from here," I suggested to one of the veteran firemen on the crew. He looked me over and said, "You got plans somewhere else for the afternoon?" The other firemen all started laughing at my naïveté. One of them handed me a wildfire tool called a McLeod. It's a beefy cross between a rake and a hoe. The second crewman, a tall, muscled woman in standard issue yellow shirt and green pants, gave me a sack lunch and a banjo canteen. That's a canteen that's round, maybe twelve inches in diameter and two inches thick, with a sturdy carrying strap. That was the standard of the industry in those days. She looked down at the fire and passed me a second lunch and a second canteen.

Willis Conrad, a Karuk man, was crew boss, and I'd known him since he befriended us hippies in the early days of the Black Bear commune. Willis led us down the flank of the clear-cut so we could approach the fire from the side. So far we saw no flames, only a growing column of smoke, but one of the never-break-them rules of firefighting was to never approach a fire from directly above.

As we neared the bottom, the brush towered over our heads and grew thicker. We began to hear the crackle and rush of the flames and see them a little. A few of the crew started to push through the brush to engage, but Willis called them back. "We need to cut a path in there," he yelled, "so we can get out when it blows up."

"You mean, if it blows up," I corrected him.

Willis had known me since I moved into the country fifteen years earlier. He gave me his best grin and said, "It's gonna blow. Look at all that old logging slash and brush upslope. We just need to get safe when it does."

By then two chain saw operators were cutting open a six-foot corridor through the brush, and the rest of us started cradling out the hacked vegetation so the path was passable. In thirty minutes, the first crew members started building fire line around the burn area, still less than an acre but building in heat.

The cutters with chain saws continued in the lead, followed by five men and women swinging Pulaskis, the unforgiving hybrid between an axe and a mattock that was most firefighters' favorite tool. Behind them came three of us scraping the path down to nonflammable mineral dirt with our McLeods. I heard Willis on the radio asking for another crew and for aircraft that could deliver a retardant drop.

It seemed to me that we would have the fire circled in an hour and be headed home by dinner. Willis's call for help and aircraft seemed overkill, but I said nothing. I was a timber cruiser who'd been more or less drafted to work with these regular firefighters.

Soon my part of the line was right up against the blaze. I started to reconsider. I was glad that we had the green and yellow fireproof clothes, but they were not heat-proof. They grew so hot that they stung our skin wherever the fabric touched us.

I remembered one of the women on the fire crew rambling on the day before about what T-shirt best protected her nipples from the heat. Another woman teased, "You just like to boast about those nipples," and I had discounted it all as loose talk, if provocative. Not anymore. It was hot.

Just then the breeze shifted upslope, and I saw that the brush on what should have been the cool side of our line was starting to smolder. Up ahead the saws stopped running, and the cutters came down toward us, with Willis behind them. "Move back out, over into those woods," he ordered, pointing toward the relative safety of the unlogged forest alongside the clear-cut. No one needed to hear it twice.

The air was fresher under the canopy of the unlogged patch when we got there. The sweat-soaked crew collapsed on the ground and began guzzling water. Soon a small aircraft, a spotter plane, buzzed overhead, and Willis began a radio conversation with the pilot about where a drop of fire retardant would work best.

Minutes later we heard the rumble of the retardant bomber overhead. Willis's radio crackled with instructions. The old bomber took a trial pass and then circled again for a drop.

I stood to watch as it disgorged a huge plume of thick red liquid from its belly. "Goddamn!" yelled the woman with the nipples. The load drifted dreamlike away from the burn and into the tall treetops over us. The firefighters dropped face down on the ground and covered their tools with their bodies.

Willis yelled for me to do the same. "Stop looking up!" he ordered.

I dropped and heard the shiny sticky retardant fall around us like a sudden rain shower. When it stopped, I opened my eyes, and the ground all around me was red. The backs of the crew were red. The back of my arms and most of my tool handle were red. A ripple of profanity grumbled through the crew.

The radio crackled again as the pilot asked Willis if he was on target. "Pretty good," Willis answered. "But we can use another or maybe two, a little farther west."

"No problem," the radio answered.

"Let's move up out of this stuff," Willis ordered, and we moved farther into the old-growth forest where there was little brush or other down fuel. Many of the giant trees formed dense closed canopies, which had damped the intensity of earlier fires. Old scars were visible on their thick bark, but the trees had survived. I began to hear birds that were alarmed by the smoke and our presence. We settled down in the shade for an extended break. I think I may have slept.

When I awoke, the radio was blaring out for Willis. He may have been asleep himself. Before he answered, he ordered one of the cutters to start up his chain saw. When the saw was running, Willis answered the radio summons.

"Headquarters, this is Willis. Just a minute. Shut off that goddamn saw. I'm trying to talk on the radio." The saw operator looked perplexed for a moment, but then shut off the saw and broke into a huge smile. The crew, scattered all around Willis on the ground, all grinned, but none laughed aloud.

I need to say that I met Willis a long time before I got drafted by the fire crew. I was still living at the commune, and it was sometime between the births of his kids Tonner and Shawnna when we hippies met Willis and his wife, Florence. They were camping near our camp on the North Fork Salmon. We had been picking blackberries all day and had car troubles when it was time to head home to Black Bear. Michael Tierra led us over to the campsite where Willis was roasting deer meat over the fire. Willis shared the cooked venison without hesitation. The hippies offered blackberries in return. If Willis and Florence thought it wasn't much of a trade to offer blackberries when you're stuck in a blackberry patch, they didn't show it. They just offered the Conrad hospitality that so many of us enjoyed over the years.

Except for Willis, it was not a friendly place here for hippies in those years. I'm not sure why Willis reached out the way he did. Maybe it was because he grew up in a world where Native Americans were badly treated. Maybe he was fascinated by white people like us hippies who were ranked even lower on the Siskiyou County pecking order than Native Americans. I figured Willis was determined to treat us better than he'd been treated growing up. It was just a bonus that most hippies thought the best thing they could be in the whole world was to be like Native Americans.

After that meeting at the blackberry patch, Willis became a regular visitor at the commune. He'd bring up his friends, other Karuks, from Somes Bar, sensing correctly that we had made few local friends. I remember many of them—George and Hambone Tripp, Norman Goodwin, Little Man Tripp, Blackie Harrison. Willis took us dipping for salmon at the falls, and eeling and hunting. He often would come to the commune with a truckload of salmon, thinking, probably, that it wasn't good to just live on blackberries and beans and brown rice. Once, when I was gushing thanks for all the fish, he said, "It's no big deal. Anyway, I just won a big bet. I bet those guys who came with me that we'd find hippies working naked in the garden."

CHAPTER 17

Pink Slips and Strawberries

I was a little surprised to get the invitation from the district ranger that spring day in 1988. There were no telephones, so it came as a hand-written note in the afternoon mail. But I hadn't even returned from the winter layoff yet and still had a couple of weeks to go. Why did she want me to come into the station?

It wasn't like this new district ranger was the pope. Our station was just a small clutch of buildings perched on a bluff above the Klamath River, about fifteen miles from my home. I'd often seen the ranger during work the year before and liked her for her gumption. She was the first of a wave of women rangers, the response to a big equal rights case in federal court.

Like all bureaucracies, the US Forest Service had a well-defined pecking order. I was a timber cruiser on a marking crew. We were on the bottom. We had a foreman; he had a forester over him; and the forester had a timber planning officer. Everyone had a number like GS-9 or GS-11 that bespoke their ranking in the federal system. It also indicated pay scale. Every department in the district was structured that way—fire, recreation, logging management, and timber planning (where I was). And the ranger was on the top.

The Forest Service had given me and my partner Von Tunstall $500 cash bonuses at the end of the season for our productivity putting up timber sales. Von teased me a bunch for hating logging and still winning a bonus for setting up sales. The bonus was an embarrassment, and I didn't ever boast about it, even to my wife, Sue. She's a fervent environmentalist. I guess I'm one, too, despite some of the things I chose to make a living.

Toward spring, during my seasonal winter layoff, I even wrote an article criticizing Forest Service policies for salvage logging after forest fires. Then Felice Pace, the firebrand environmental organizer from the big agricultural valley near Etna, invited me to a press conference in Yreka where we talked about why the salvage sales were so damaging to the river country. I was jumpy in front of the cameras, but Felice said it went great. At least I didn't feel so guilty about the bonus.

I hoped the ranger didn't want me to start two weeks early. I still had a lot of projects around the homestead to get done, and Sue was just finishing up the school year at Forks Elementary School. So I was nervous when I walked into the ranger's office. She swung around in her chair and greeted me with her usual smile. But instead of the ordinary stream of small talk, she said, "I've got some bad news, Malcolm. You're fired."

At first I thought I'd misunderstood her, but then, as it sunk in, I felt a huge sense of relief. I thought about the young forester they found the year before in his trailer, dead of some freak infection. His death had unsettled me. At least I won't die working for the Forest Service, I thought. I repressed a smile and said, "What's going on? I'm not even working yet. How can I be fired?"

"It wasn't my idea," she said. "People here think you're a great member of the marking crew."

Her endorsement was almost as unsettling as the idea of dying in a trailer. "So what's the issue then?"

"We're not exactly firing you. We're just withdrawing the offer to rehire. And it's not my idea. I got orders from the top guy in Yreka, and I've got orders not to say any more."

I suddenly remembered the public information officer from the Yreka headquarters of the Forest Service flitting rodent-like behind the cameras and the lights at the press conference. It's a free country, I thought at the time.

"I'll get a lawyer and contest it," I told the ranger. I don't know why that popped out of my mouth. I was pissed and happy at the same time.

"I hope you succeed," she said with a brave but rather hopeless smile. She was about as likable as any GS-13 I'd ever met.

I walked out into the Klamath River sunshine, looked both directions on the river and then up to the ridges where the last traces of morning fog were just burning off. I was a free man.

―――

My daughter, Erica Kate, who was then four, preceded me into the café. I'd been fired for a few weeks, and we were in Etna, a ninety-minute drive from the river. It was crowded full of cattlemen and loggers catching an early lunch. They were big men who'd grown up tossing hay bales and chain saws like they were no more than beach balls. Normally Erica Kate was shy of strangers, but she would have led me into the slums of Marrakech to get a waffle with strawberries and whipped cream. That's what I had promised her.

Despite the traffic, the service was quick. Erica Kate was speculating aloud, over the noise of the dining room, "Which is better, Poppa? Strawberries or catsup?" I started eavesdropping on the next table. Two uniformed piss-firs, Forest Service bigwigs, were talking, and a third joined them with introductions and much hand shaking.

The late arrival was a tall, baby-faced man with a commanding voice and a big smile. He began whispering about some public hearing of the state water board, but he had to raise his voice in the general din of the room. I heard only snippets of his talk.

"Felice was there hassling the loggers," he said. The others shook their heads in disgust. The next part was lost.

Then I heard him say, "There was this other guy, Petey Brucker from Salmon River. He was a real asshole." I didn't hear what Brucker did. Petey was a lovable community organizer from my hometown. I'd heard many descriptions of Petey, but never as an asshole. We locals loved him. Their voices lowered again.

Finally, in a louder voice, the tall, baby-faced man concluded, "But no matter what those loggers and the tree-huggers do to each other, the Forest Service comes out smelling like a rose."

His companions broke into raucous laughter so loud that Erica Kate looked up from her waffle to see the cause. They slapped tips on the table and pressed their way through the other tables full of ranchers and loggers. The faces of the locals flashed disapproval as the uniformed men departed.

———

It was the end of summer as I pulled into the parking lot of the store in Somes Bar. Somes is a town so small it is left off many maps. The store is an undistinguished cinder-block building that sits in one of the most beautiful places in the world. Towering behind the store is a wooded monolith of a small peak standing alone amid the weave of surrounding rivers and mountains. White people call it Sugar Loaf, and the local Karuk people in their language call it *á'uuyich*. I try to pronounce it, and it comes out "Ow-eesch." The Karuk tell me that their ancestors considered it the center of the world, and nothing I've learned or seen has made me doubt that interpretation.

Von, my partner before I got fired from the Forest Service log sale prep crew, waved and walked over as *á'uuyich* cast a longer shadow across the store parking lots. "Did you hear that they replaced that woman ranger down in Orleans, the one who shit-canned you last spring?" he gushed.

"What'd they dump her for?" I asked him.

"Dunno. Maybe cuz she went to bat for you after she fired you. Go figure."

"She went to bat for me? You've got it wrong."

"That's what everybody says," he said, with a manic grin. "'We need that mouthy hippie who can set up so many beautiful timber sales,'" he mocked in a woman's voice.

I hoped he was making this up. "Who's gonna replace her?"

"They already have some hotshot from Etna. Tall pretty boy with a loud voice. He's the best ranger this district ever had. Just ask him." Von flashed the grin again and rolled his eyes. I didn't miss marking timber, but I missed working with him.

CHAPTER 18

Beginner's Luck

I was running saw on a job up in Happy Camp, and headed home I made what I thought would be a short stop at the Somes Bar Store. The store sits just above where the rivers join. Just above that is a jumble of boulders in the Klamath so huge that even its vast flow is bent and wrapped into a riffle, a gray, grinding flood that has run there since the retreat of the last Ice Age and before. These rapids are called Ishi Pishi Falls, and the river has so much power that even the runs of many kinds of salmonids, as they return to spawn in their natal streams, need to slow in what backwaters and eddies they can find. For millennia, and maybe forever, Native people have fished at the falls with small nets strung between long poles. There was a village just above there that the Karuk people called Ka'tim'iin. That's the phonetic spelling offered by William Bright's brilliant Karuk Dictionary. The arrival of the white miners decimated the village just the same as it ruined so many others. The great fish runs were reduced in number from the sediments dumped by mining and by the generations of too many haul roads and too much logging that followed. Much of the Karuk culture was trampled in those years, but it is not forgotten.

Willis Conrad was the first person to take me to the falls. His family had had rights to a fishing spot there on the west side of the Klamath for countless generations, and he was justifiably proud of his skill maneuvering the net and poles. He had to do this perched on a wet boulder over the churning river, and the danger was not lost on him. He told me stories of people who had fallen in the water and were rescued by fellow

Willis Conrad, a member of the Karuk Tribe, was a traditional dip-net fisherman and a friend to the Black Bear Commune in the early days when we who lived there had few local friends. Photo courtesy of Shawnna Conrad.

fishermen. In one of the stories the person was swept away, and his body was found days later along the bank thirty or forty miles downriver in Weitchpec, being eaten by feral pigs. If the stories were to make me cautious, they certainly worked.

I should warn about the information I offer about local Natives. I am only half certain if it is right. Some of it I've been told by people I know. Some of it, I've read here or there. People on the river tell stories of academic ethnographers prowling around a hundred years ago and offering money to elders for stories. Elders are inventive by their nature, and money is an extra spur to invention. So my sources are suspect, I guess. You are warned accordingly.

But this I know: Willis had a certain kind of charisma. His charisma went beyond his ability to lead a fire crew, although he was certainly adept at that. Charisma, the way I define it, includes the ability to coax people into doing something they might not ordinarily do. Different people accomplish persuasion in different ways. Some browbeat you. Others guilt trip you or intimidate you. Willis's particular gift was to make you feel that some task was something you always wanted to do.

Charlie Thom, who was a Native doctor and a ceremonial leader among the Karuk, told me a story about Willis. It goes back some years to when the Karuk were trying to win official recognition from the feds. Charlie decided it would be useful, politically as much as culturally, to rebuild the ceremonial dance pit at Ka'tim'iin. He says he recruited Willis to the project because he knew Willis would know how to talk people into it. Willis must have told his friends, "You know how you've always wished there was a dance pit here again . . . ." The pit got built.

So there I was at the store, and Willis came in. Neither of us was still working for the Forest Service, and we exchanged greetings. To make small talk, I asked him when the next tribal Brush Dance would be. "It starts tomorrow," he said. I nodded appreciatively, and he added, "They're playing cards down there at Ka'tim'iin tonight. Let's go." Then, as I arranged my excuses in my mind, he added, "You always like that sort of stuff."

"Indian cards, with the sticks?" I asked, stalling.

"No. Regular cards. They're playing Ka'tim'iin Schmidt. You've played it, huh?"

Minutes later we were down at the ceremonial grounds even though I'd protested that, after a day running chain saw, there was nothing I wanted more at that moment than a shower. A summer day spent running saw coats your skin and your clothes with a fine film of bar oil and wood chips.

"I don't have any money, so I can't gamble," I said. This was not quite true.

"You don't need money," Willis said. "I have money."

Several other Native men were already sitting at the table when we arrived, and they greeted Willis enthusiastically. "Hah, now we'll get some of that Conrad *ishpuk,*" one of the gamblers said. I didn't know many Karuk words, but everybody knew *ishpuk* meant money.

One of them offered me a beer from under the table and then made a show of not offering any to Willis. He teased back and soon had a beer.

"Put your money out, Willis," the dealer said.

"I'm not playing. Just deal to my friend," he answered and dumped a handful of quarters on the table in front of me.

The dealer shuffled a fat deck—it must have been more than one set of cards—and dealt a small hand to each of us. I turned to Willis and mouthed, "I don't know how to play."

Willis only grinned, motioned my attention back into the game and slid a few of his quarters into the pot for me. Players laid out cards, and when my turn came, Willis made a gesture that I should play whatever card I wanted. It continued through the hand.

"Well, look at that. Hippie dude has won the whole thing. Who's this card shark you brought here, Mr. Conrad?" The dealer pushed the entire pot over into Willis's pile of quarters. I took a congratulatory sip of the beer and wondered how I'd won. Also whether this might be a clever hustle to get hold of any money I might have. Then another sip of the beer. Over the next few hands I won frequently, but not every hand. I started to think I understood the rules, but then something else would happen. It was as though the game was really three games overlaid, each with its own set of rules. As my pile of quarters grew, Willis pocketed a handful. No problem. It was his money. An hour went by. A few of the players, the biggest losers, started to seem annoyed, and that just made them the target of more intense teasing.

I was, by then, in my second beer, my usual limit, but the under-the-table stash had run out. A young Karuk woman, very pretty, had been sitting on the periphery, and one of the men instructed her to bring more from his pickup. When it arrived, he set one in front of me, even though mine was far from finished. I made a show of guzzling that one down and opened the new one. The game continued.

At some point, a Native woman of great age and great dignity approached our table. All of the men slipped their beers out of sight, and Willis nudged me to do the same. "Hello, Willis," she said.

"Hello, Elizabeth," he replied. All of the other players nodded with great respect, and so did I.

"Who's she?" I asked when she moved past us, and one card player said she was Elizabeth Case, an important medicine woman, come to join the Brush Dance ceremonies. Another said she'd been in declining health. It was a good sign that she'd come.

Beers surfaced again, and I was passed another. I didn't rush to open it. I still needed to drive home. The sun had dropped below the ridge, and one of the people near the dance pit preparing for the dances was looking around for a lamp. One of the card players said his wife would be pissed by his absence, and he left the table, in a shower of good-natured teasing. I turned to Willis, who still had not joined the game himself, and said I needed to leave too. Other players overheard me, and sour expressions crossed their faces.

"They're not gonna like it if you leave," Willis said.

"That guy left. Why not me?

"That guy hadn't won all their money. They want a chance to win it back."

So I played many more hands, winning some and losing others. Whenever my pile swelled with quarters, Willis would scoop up some and dump them into one of his pockets or another. Finally, I announced that I had to leave. Most of the players just broke into good-natured laughter, but one spoke in an angry tone, not to me but to Willis. He spoke in a mix of English and Karuk, so I was uncertain what he said. Willis answered in kind, and one of the other players leaned over to me and said, "If you're gonna go, you better go now." The rest of them, even the angry one, all broke into more laughing and louder teasing at that. I slipped away and could hear their voices as I wandered off into the approaching darkness, trying to remember where I'd left my truck.

Several weeks passed after the card game before I saw Willis Conrad again. He had a home not far from the ceremonial grounds at Ka'tim'íin, and I found him there. The house and its surroundings always fascinated me. A steep road descended to it from the main highway, and it was built on a forested bench, part of what I guessed was a very old landslide. There was a long line of abandoned cars in one direction and a full woodshed in the other. The cars were swallowed in blackberry canes, and farther away there was a small deserted cabin disappearing into the thickets of small conifers and more thorny brambles. When I stared hard, I could see signs of what I took to be another even older cabin, slowly sinking into the vegetation. That was just what I could see. I sensed that people had always lived at that place, close to the dip-net fishing places at the Ishi Pishi Falls. Even with the wrecked cars, it seemed as hallowed as an old country church.

But Willis's house was not so old. He had built a big add-on as his family grew. The new room was a source of personal pride; he told me the story. He had worked lots of different jobs over the years and eventually ended up with the US Forest Service. That was the period when I was assigned to his fire crew. He was not exactly in love with the agency. Lots of its employees felt that way, especially people who were local to the area, and this was even truer of Karuk people. All of the land that had once been theirs was now labeled National Forest. They were ticketed for cutting firewood, penalized for hunting deer for their families, and harassed for catching salmon, with the exception of the dip-netting at Ishi Pishi Falls, where the game wardens looked the other way. Eventually, when the tribe got federal recognition, there was much lip service paid by the government agencies to the new Karuk sovereignty. In this flush of "government-to-government" relations, it was agreed that the US Forest Service installation at Somes Bar should go to the tribe. Some of the structures were left for the tribe, and others were dismantled. One in the teardown category was what had been the main office of the Ukonom District. Willis made the winning bid for the demolition and then hauled the materials he could reuse to his own place, a half mile away. I could tell that he took great pleasure in tearing down a building that had been the source of so much aggravation over the years. He even reused the office doors, prominently labeled United States Forest Service, or propped them up in his yard like a hunter might hang a trophy head on his wall.

Willis was working under the hood of a car when I showed up, but he invited me into the house to visit. I wanted to tell him a story about my daughter, Erica Kate, who was then ten years old. When she was just a baby, Willis had given her a name in Karuk language, the word for mountain lion. Years earlier, Willis had named Slate, Erica Kate's big brother, *vírusur,* the Karuk word for bear. That made sense. Even as a child, Slate seemed bear-sized.

I always have trouble pronouncing the word for mountain lion, which is *yupthúkirar.* Try pronouncing that. Anyway, I told Willis that Erica Kate and a young friend had seen a mountain lion in the brush while walking home from the swimming hole at Grant Creek. Erica Kate and her friend had carefully backed away, and, as soon as they were out of its sight, they ran like crazy to get home.

Willis shook his head and said they shouldn't be afraid. "The mountain lion will protect Kate," he said. He called her Kate in those days. Everybody called her Kate.

He offered a beer, and I declined, but I thanked him for taking me to the card game. He laughed and said, "You thought you wouldn't do very good."

"I still don't think I'm very good."

"Well, all those guys who lost money thought you did okay," he said and laughed again.

"But really," I said. "How come I won so often?"

"Well, if you really didn't get the game, then maybe you were just lucky."

"Lucky? Nobody's lucky that much of the time." I could tell when Willis was being evasive. He'd get this sly smile and you knew.

He scratched his head and said, "I've been watching cards a long time, and luck plays a part. People don't give it enough credit. And beginner's luck is especially strong sometimes. Maybe you were having beginner's luck."

It was not a very satisfying explanation for me, but I finally said, "I have a couple of other questions."

"Fire away," he said. He was happy to change the subject.

"Is Ka'tim'íin Schmidt what people call Indian cards? I've always heard about Indian cards."

"Indian cards is different," he said, reaching across to the shelf behind him. He grasped a small bundle of sticks, untied the short deerskin lace that held them, and passed them to me. "You never seen Indian cards?" They were a little thicker than matchsticks and of sturdier wood, maybe hazel that's also used for baskets. They looked to be nine or ten inches long, and there were more than a dozen of them. I squeezed them in my hand to get the feel of them, and Willis nodded approvingly.

I returned them to him, and he showed me that there was a small black mark around the center of one of the sticks. Then he put them behind his back and divided them into both hands. He held both hands out and said, "Which hand has the marked stick?"

I picked a hand and was right. Next turn I was wrong. He passed me the sticks, and I tried, although I was really not certain myself how I'd divided them. Then he explained to me a long web of complex thinking that he used to outwit other players. My mouth may have hung open to hear such a maze of feint and deception for what, it seemed to me, was little more complex than flipping a coin heads or tails. On top of that, sometimes bystanders in real games were beating a drum and others might be singing or chanting with other people placing side bets or teasing or just generally making a racket. More than coin tossing, I agreed.

He wrapped the sticks together again with the deerskin lace and handed the bundle to me. "These are for you," he said.

I was touched by the gift and thanked him. Then I thanked him another time for the way he befriended us back when we lived at the commune. He pursed his lips and finally said, "You know what I think of white people. When I met you, you didn't seem white. Sometimes I watch you now with a job and a good truck and a big house, and I wonder if you're becoming too white."

I was unsure of what to say. Everything that came into my head was too glib or too defensive. So I didn't say anything and just stared down at the bundle of sticks he'd given me. After a while Willis said, "You said you had two questions. You only asked one."

"Yeah," I said, happy to stop reflecting on whether I was backsliding into some white-people cultural destiny. "What I want to know is what that guy said. The one who growled at you when I said I was gonna leave the Ka'tim'íin Schmidt game. He mostly spoke in Karuk."

Willis thought back for a minute and then another big smile crossed his face. "You don't wanna know," he said.

CHAPTER 19

Saloon

The bar upriver in Forks of Salmon was rarely full, but it was hard to find a table that particular day. No one had ever counted how many people still lived in Forks, but most estimates ran in the high double digits. I recognized nearly everybody as I walked in, although I didn't know some of them very well. A satellite television, high technology in those days, was playing a football game in one corner above the bar.

The waitress seemed engrossed in a conversation with the man behind the bar, so I looked for a table myself. She was animated, very pretty, and wearing far more makeup than one usually saw in a small town on the river. Story was that she and Billy Harling had bought the general store with money she had from a divorce settlement. Billy was the brother of Les Harling, the friend who'd gotten the broken leg on my first logging job. Billy was a charming guy, part gold miner and part real estate promoter, and he'd show up now and then on the Salmon River, and then disappear to chase exotic adventures. The store had been a cultural hub before the divorcee bought it, but certainly no big moneymaker. It was not clear that the addition of a bar added much to the cash flow except on days like this when the room, all eight tables, was full.

I saw two gold miners—hippie/loggers, really, who'd taken up mining—sitting in the darkest corner, and I gravitated their way. I'd worked logging with one of them and tree planting with the other but had not seen either of them in a long time. They waved me over and suggested I buy them a beer. I tried to get the waitress's attention and then gave up.

"She doesn't like Malcolm any more than us," one of them said. "Getting a beer in this saloon is a sobering experience. Hey, Malcolm, you still chasing after that pretty school teacher?"

Before I could answer, the other miner elbowed the first and said, "Chasing her? He had a kid with her. Where you been?"

The first man nodded sagely and said, "I can see chasing her. She's got looks would stop traffic, if we had any traffic." Then he turned to me and said, "But, Malcolm, you don't just like women cuz they're good looking," and he made a gesture with two hands to suggest a woman's curves. "You like women cuz they're smart. Now that is obsessive, if you ask me. Borders on sickness."

I grinned and said, "You guys getting any gold these days?"

"You should know better than to ask a miner that," Jerry Vessells answered. He was the guy who'd taught me to set chokers on that logging job a few years earlier when we worked road building for Rice Construction. He ran his fingers through his long, wavy, red hair. "If a miner's doing good, he won't tell a soul. If he gets skunked, then he'll claim he's in the best gravel of his whole damn life."

"C'mon, Jerry. Show Malcolm what you found," the other said. His name was John Albion, and he'd lived at the commune from the get-go like me and then moved down to the river.

Jerry looked me over, curled his lower lip suspiciously, and tugged a stoppered pill bottle out of his shirt pocket. On to the paper menu, he carefully poured a pile of fine placer gold, perhaps an ounce with a few nuggets the size of watermelon seeds. I sucked in my breath appreciatively, even though it was not an exceptional pouch.

Jerry grinned and said, "You know that ain't shit," and out of the other shirt pocket he pulled a second bottle. Out of it, he slipped a single gold nugget the size of the end of my thumb. It made a clunk as it landed on the table and both miners glanced around the room protectively. This time I gasped for real. The other miner handed me a jeweler's glass, and I hefted the shiny object in my hand. In its crevices, small crystals of native quartz were still embedded. I nodded appreciatively, and both miners grinned lasciviously.

Then Jerry fished a small manila envelope from the first pocket and slipped a small gold coin into his palm. It was well worn along one edge but otherwise intact. "Found it all in the same crevice."

Before I could comment, the waitress walked over to our table. They covered the gold with a battered hat. "Whatcha want tonight? You gonna order?"

I ordered hamburgers and beers for all three of us, and she moved to another table to collect the orders from a couple that had just seated themselves. They were tourists and looked around the room apprehensively. The other people in the room ignored them until a stout Native American man walked over to greet them.

"Welcome to Salmon River," he announced. "My name is Hoss. You folks can relax here. This a safe place."

The man introduced himself, and his wife and said they thought it was a fine restaurant.

"Yeah, there's some places where you can get hurt in a place like this. Be real careful, you head up to K-Falls in Oregon. K-Falls, that's Klamath Falls. I got in kinda a scrap near there one time in a town called Powers. Didn't come out so good."

The man tried to turn toward his wife in hopes Hoss Bennett would move on, but Hoss continued, "Yep, I was doing okay till some guy pulled a pistol on me, shot me in the belly." At that, he lifted his T-shirt and revealed a massive beer gut with a savage crisscross scar.

The man and the woman stared in horror, and Hoss broke into laughter. "Then, to make sure I was dead, the guy, he shot me in the mouth, and they all threw me out on the sidewalk in the snow." At that, he bared his teeth to reveal that the middle four were all missing. He laughed loudly again, but the waitress started in his direction. She didn't have a pistol, but she didn't need one. "I think I need some fresh air," Hoss said, as he ambled toward the door. "You folks enjoy your dinner."

The waitress brought us our beer and glasses of wine to the couple, then delivered our hamburgers and the same for the couple. Jerry set up a small balance scale on the table, and Albion began weighing the nugget and the powdered gold. I wolfed down my food, left money on the table, and headed toward the door. After I passed them, I heard the man of the couple ask, in a polite, plaintive voice, if he could have some catsup.

The waitress swung away from her conversation at the bar and snarled at the hapless tourist, "I'm not your servant." The rest of us pretended we hadn't heard it, and I slipped outside.

The Forks Store sat in the shade of two giant American chestnuts, a pair that was planted toward the end of the Gold Rush. Somehow, in their geographic isolation, the trees had survived the plague that killed nearly every other American chestnut in the country. Across the road was the Beer Tree, where a smaller walnut tree flourished, and under it was a worn picnic table, etched with carvings and initials. It was as much a cultural hub as the store.

Hoss was holding court there as I approached. Sitting with Hoss was another old man, whiskered and wearing a tattered hat that was more brim than crown. He said, "Hey, hippie dude. Care for a beer?"

Hoss interrupted to say, "That's my beer you're offerin'. Doncha think ya oughta check with me first?"

Before the other man could apologize, Hoss added, "What about it, Malcolm? You want a beer?"

I accepted, and the man with the hat said, "Hoss, tell the guy about you getting busted."

"Oh, Malcolm don't wanta hear a boring story like that."

The man in the shredded hat grabbed that as a cue and began, "Well, I'll tell him then. Bout a week ago, a Fish and Game enforcement guy was parked over there. When Hoss here started to get in his truck, he warned Hoss that he'd have to bust him for drunk driving if he drove off. So Hoss cursed him and came back to the table to wait him out.

"The fish cop was ready to wait, so in an hour Hoss gave up and went over and started his truck. Sure as shit, the cop busted him for drunk driving. But that was just the start. Then he had to radio out for deputies to haul Hoss off to jail in Yreka."

"Malcolm don' wanna hear the whole damn story," Hoss interrupted.

"Lemme finish. This is the best part. Took the deputies about two hours to arrive. They handcuffed him and were hauling him out over

Cecilville Road when Hoss here told 'em he had to piss. Now the cops were angry; they had to come all this way, so they just told Hoss, 'Fuck you.' So Hoss said he'd have to piss in their patrol car and that made 'em stop near the summit.

"Hoss told 'em they'd have to take off the handcuffs or else they'd have to hold it for him while he pissed, so they took off the handcuffs. It was dark by then, and Hoss walked up to the edge of the road where the bank fell off, so the two deputies stood either side of him. That was so he couldn't make a break for it. He pissed for a while, and then he reached out and grabbed both deputies and jumped off the cliff. They all rolled forty, fifty feet down the bank. That teach 'em to dick with Hoss."

"I guess it is a pretty good story," said Hoss. Great tectonic waves rolled through the flesh of his belly as he chuckled.

"How'd the cops take that?" I asked Hoss.

"I guess they thought it was a pretty good joke cuz they both only kicked me a couple times when we stopped rolling at the bottom of the bank. Cops ain't all bad." His visceral laughter continued.

Everyone turned as a weathered pickup truck pulled up to the tree. A familiar river couple clambered out. I hadn't seen the man since I'd visited him weeks earlier in jail. Hoss offered them both cans of beer and made a lewd suggestion to the woman, who only grinned and shrugged.

I said my hellos, and the man asked, "Did you get my letter?"

"I got it," I said. "Where did you learn such beautiful calligraphy?"

"I think I've always done it," he said. "I got good at it in the joint."

"My old man told me you visited him," the woman intruded.

"I was out in Yreka for lumber, and I remembered how much I hated the jail there," I said.

"Well, thanks for looking after my old man. If you ever need anything. . . . If you ever need anyone killed, you can come to me." She flashed an earnest smile.

My mouth must have fallen open.

"If the hippie can't think of nobody, I can give you a name or two," Hoss said. And he laughed again deep in his rolling mountain torso.

CHAPTER 20

Torches, Pitchforks, and Other Organizing Tools

It was not an unusual day in my ongoing political education. I drifted down to Kate George's place at suppertime back in those days when I still lived in that tiny cabin on the other side of the gold mine diggings. No one had mined there in two or three generations. By then, in the mid-1970s, the diggings were full of fruit trees, and above them was a small horse barn and corral. The horses would whinny and snort, and the dogs snuffled from their sleep as I approached but, for once, did not bark. I entered without knocking and found Kate playing her old upright piano with great enthusiasm. She did not notice me enter the room, and she bounced and wiggled on the bench as she played. I couldn't name the tune, but I recognized it as a jazz standard of the 1940s. Finally, she saw me standing there and swung around toward me to make a little mock curtsy.

"I never heard you play that before," I said. "It sounds great."

Kate smiled but shook her head ruefully. "I could play pretty good before I got the rheumatism in my shoulder. I can only move my arm this high now," and she lifted her arm a little with great effort. Then she reached quickly up toward the ceiling with the same arm and added, "I used to be able to lift it like this. C'mon. Supper's waiting for us. Just leftovers tonight, but they're hot."

We were both hungry and began eating without ceremony. Finally, I paused to praise her cooking and then asked about the old woman who had been visiting in the afternoon. The woman visitor was probably no older than Kate, who was approaching seventy, but Kate had something about her that made it hard to decide whether she was old or what. Kate said the woman lived up in Cecilville, near where Kate had raised her family. I recognized her name. "Didja like her?" she asked me.

"She seemed nice enough. You guys must be close friends."

Kate nodded and took a few more bites of food, then said, "Course, that's the first time we've talked to each other in thirty years," and she returned to eating.

I made a I-don't-get-it gesture, and she explained in a long and complicated story how the woman had long ago betrayed her and her family. But thirty years was enough, and she said she'd welcomed the woman when she came calling today as though the rift had never occurred. "But enough old gossip," she concluded. "What do you think people should do about the latest from Fish and Game?"

"Dunno. What's up with them?" I said, still trying to absorb the story of the Cecilville woman and not quite ready to hear about the latest affront from some distant state agency.

"I mean about their Wild and Scenic Rivers plan. What should people do?"

I confessed my ignorance, which was an invitation to another of Kate's lessons in her favorite subject: The Way Things Really Worked. Early on it had been hard for me to spot just how astute Kate George was at understanding local politics. Sometimes she sounded simplistic. In other situations, her river-brand of libertarian laissez-faire seemed to veer into the knee-jerk right wing. There was a stream not far from her house named Know-Nothing Creek after an anti-immigrant populist political party that had sprung up a little after the time of the California Gold Rush. But she was so often right that I learned at least to listen. "So what should we do about Fish and Game?" I said.

Kate explained that the state had declared the Salmon River a Wild and Scenic River, which was good because it meant no dams. But it was bad because it let Fish and Game write a management plan, although no one on the river knew quite what a management plan was. She told me that there was a big town meeting scheduled for a week from Tuesday at the Community Club, and everyone was going.

"But I thought all the gold miners hated the agencies," I said. "Why will they go to this one?"

"Fish and Game has some hot-stuff geologist presenting at the meeting, so the miners are gonna show up to see if they can learn anything that'll help them find more gold."

The Community Club was a spare frame building just downriver from where the North Fork Salmon River joined the South Fork. It had once been the town schoolhouse, and the night of the meeting it was packed to standing room only. The attendees, mostly miners from up and down the river, were dressed up, although that might have been lost on someone from a less rural setting. A few were already drunk, but not many, and even the drunks seemed on their best behavior. Finally, less than fifteen minutes past the announced starting time, some young agency person got the attention of the crowd and explained, in jargon few could follow, why the management plan was such a good idea. The crowd shifted restlessly, but finally the now-famous geologist was introduced and thanked the crowd for their patience. Town meetings had a checkered history of disruption, but the miners wanted insider secrets from this flatlander PhD. Members of the audience nodded to one another as if in congratulations on their good behavior. The geologist, recognizing that he had a captivated crowd, began by explaining his methodology in dense and undecipherable detail. Finally, he said, "And this is what we learned."

You could have heard the smallest fir cone drop in the woods, the miners were so quiet. "The rock types in the Salmon River," he intoned, "seem to fall into three main types. They are igneous, sedimentary, or metamorphic."

He paused for dramatic effect. It may have been more dramatic than he expected. A few miners chuckled. A few began to laugh out loud. One, in a loud voice, heckled, "Sheet. Just about every rock in the whole goddamn Earth is 'igneous, sedimentary, or metamorphic.'" He mimicked the exaggerated academic cadence of the speaker. "I reckon we won't find much gold on Mars, Jerry," he said to Jerry Cramer, a soft-spoken miner widely respected in the community. No one was quite sure what his wisecrack meant, but the entire crowd broke into raucous laughter. And did not stop. The geologist said a few other things into the microphone, but we couldn't hear him.

Another of the drunks, in a stage whisper, said, "He thinks we're dumb, and he's right. But we're not that dumb." The Salmon River miners were among the smartest people I'd ever met, but they enjoyed playing the hapless hick. The laughter accelerated. The geologist looked to the other agency people for help, but they only shrugged. The meeting was a short one.

———

Like the Fish and Game meeting, the Wild and Scenic management plan seemed to run aground, or at least we never heard of it again. But the meeting hall of the Community Club, or the Old School, as it was called, remained a cultural and civic hub for the Salmon River towns. There were dances with local bands that became wild parties. Kate George organized a dance band of local musicians like White Water Wally Watson. Some McBroom family members had a band called the Snipers. Other folks like Bob-O and Petey, both commune alumni, started a band called the Superfines. And both of those band names were gold-mining references.

I remember a town dance one rainy winter night. The hall was packed, and someone barged in between tunes to yell that the road was closed at Joe Miller's slide a half mile up the South Fork. This was the same Joe Miller who'd sold us the place at Butler Creek. Miller was no longer around, but his namesake rockslide was at his upriver residence, not at Butler, and it had closed the road many times before. The news meant that more than half the people in the hall couldn't get home until a skip loader cleared the road. That wouldn't happen until daylight, at the soonest.

People stared at each other in momentary alarm. Just then the band resumed playing with one of the town's favorite tunes. The crowd collectively shrugged their shoulders and strode onto the dance floor with the Salmon River Stomp, a dance step where all the dancers looked like people who had just stumbled on a nest of stinging yellow jackets, except that the kicking and arm waving was in perfect rhythm with the band.

The Community Club building also hosted more meetings of a political stripe. A memorable one came at the height of what we later called the Herbicide Wars. Like a lot of wars, it took us a little while to realize we were embroiled in one. In 1977 the Hog Fire swept the Salmon River, a blaze so large that climate scientists would later decide that it marked a grim benchmark in the history of global climate change. It marked the start of the period when America's vast western forests were no longer savings banks of atmospheric carbon, but instead were becoming smoky sources of it. Even larger fires have followed. The 1977 fire was also followed by a rush of salvage logging and reforestation. Reforestation turns out to be much more than just planting trees, although we did plenty of that. The trees preferred by the Forest Service, all conifers and mostly Douglas firs, have to survive competition from all the plants that usually follow a fire, plants without market value. That's where herbicides came in. The chemicals were, the foresters assured us, absolutely harmless. One government forester at the Salmon River station even claimed that he had drunk the stuff without ill effect, and, anyway, it was somehow needed to keep up the logging industry, which provided so many jobs in the community.

But stories were drifting back from Vietnam about the health effects of the chemicals our military had sprayed there, and also from toxicologists closer to home. Mavis McCovey, that well-known Karuk nurse, had alerted us about the newborn babies who had developmental problems that correlated to herbicide use. Mavis's discovery made such a stir that the state was obligated to send Sacramento investigators up to Orleans, where there had been much use of herbicides in the forest, including in the headwaters of streams that provided domestic water. The Bureau of Indian Affairs, as a precaution, sent Mavis to a conference in Montana so she'd be out of town when the investigators arrived. Over the next several years, few people on the Salmon River, whether they depended on logging for income or not, could cozy up to the idea of herbicide contamination of the water that their family would drink. A handful of us, mostly veterans of the commune who had migrated down to the river, decided to form an activist group and, after much discussion, named it Salmon River Concerned Citizens. We called it SRCC for short, although that's not too short. We wanted a name that wouldn't alienate the logging families who seemed to share our antiherbicide sentiments. It may have been unneeded effort because those families seemed even more worked up than we were at the rallies and public meetings. Each year the Forest Service would issue an environmental document listing their herbicide spray plans, and we'd write in our objections in great detail. The agency would reply with a letter thanking us for our input and proceed to spray anyway. Finally, one year, on the eve of one of the spray dates, SRCC set up a public meeting and invited the district ranger, in those days a man named Koenig. We had grown annoyed with the government's history of dishonesty and were determined to not let Ranger Koenig off easy. It was decided that I should facilitate the meeting, and I agreed if Ann Pullen agreed to co-facilitate. Ann was a pretty, sly piano player from Godfrey Ranch, where there had been plenty of spraying over the years. She was the person who'd successfully lobbied the top Forest Service officer in San Francisco to drop a few units near her water source from the previous year's spray plan. Together, Ann and I planned several tricks to keep the ranger on the hot seat. We had already heard enough of their propaganda to anticipate their pitch, so we developed a list of gotcha questions to deflate their claims. We would not let the public get fooled.

The day of the meeting, the hall was again packed to standing room only. But we hadn't anticipated just how tone-deaf Ranger Koenig was to the community sentiment. In his opening statement he thanked the community for its support of Forest Service programs and said everyone could rest assured that Forest Service expertise was more trustworthy than the flimsy criticisms of a few environmentalists. The crowd stirred but remained silent. I was reminded of the subvocal growl that came from Kate George's watch dogs when I approached the house. If I heard it, Koenig did not, and he continued talking about the priority of timber harvest over the unfounded fears about danger to human health. At that, one burly logger in the back row, said, "This jerk is full of crap." There was much affirmative nodding of heads.

Koenig may have missed the slur and taken the head nodding as agreement with his speech because he continued, clueless. "The Forest Service knows best what is good for the forest, and we promise to protect your health and your jobs," he said, his eyes turned toward the ceiling, as if invoking the deity.

A woman in the room, the wife of a logger, grumbled loudly, "Here we go again. Do they think we're stupid?"

I was confused. The crowd was substantially less fooled than we expected. I looked at Ann, my co-facilitator, and pointed at our list of loaded questions. She shook her head no. This crowd was so antagonized by the ranger that they could get ugly. No need to stir things up worse. But they got a little worse. The ranger seemed more and more arrogant and out of touch, and the crowd got louder and ruder. A few times I intervened to restore civility. That hadn't been part of the plan. Not one local spoke in favor of the spray programs, but several spoke against it.

Then a respected logger from Orleans took the floor. "My name is Roger Williams," he said. "I make my living and the people who work for me make their livings by cutting timber." Hearing this, the ranger broke into a broad grin. Finally, he thought to himself, a supporter. But Roger, a devout Seventh-day Adventist and highly respected in his community, continued. "What I don't see," he said, "is why you'd want to risk people's health just to set back some brush that's going to grow anyway?"

The crowd broke into their own grins, but the ranger's smile disappeared like a truck tire with a slow leak. Then the presentation ended, and several people lined up to talk with or growl at the ranger one on one.

I slipped out of the hall and wandered over to the Beer Tree. Everybody was welcome there, all ethnicities and all cultural roots. The regulars there were known for their wit and their willingness to share their twelve-packs of cheap beer. There was much conversation, ranging from local gossip to outrage about politics to teasing whoever was sitting across the table. As I approached the table, Hoss Bennett was once again holding court, as he often did, although I had seen him earlier at the public meeting. Hoss was known for his friendly nature and also for the way he could handle himself in a fight. He grinned when he saw me and offered me a beer, which I took gladly. "Well, hippie," he said. "You finally get sick of that ranger's lies?"

Hoss Bennett often held court at the picnic tables across the road from the Forks of Salmon Store. The location was called the Beer Tree, and the problems of the world and of the community were often parsed there. Photo by Hank Lebo.

"The ranger is a little hard to take," I agreed. "He talks to people like we're idiots."

"Well, we ain't that bright," one of Hoss's courtiers chimed in.

"We're a hell of a lot brighter than those piss firs," Hoss corrected, and he gave the man a serious evil eye for his clowning. He pondered a minute and then said, "Let's do something constructive about it. You gotta work within the system with these things. Let's go kill him."

The clown and two other men at the table nodded in somber, if not sober, agreement and started to get up from the table, no small thing because they were so drunk. I started talking as fast as I could to defuse things. Hoss furrowed his brow and studied me while I talked. Finally, he announced, "Well, if you won't let us kill him, then at least you got to buy some more beer. I gave you my last one." Hoss had great leadership skills because the men at the table settled back into their seats and started yelling their favorite brands of beer.

"Or some of that whacky-tabacky, hippie dude," one of them yelled. They all broke into gales of laughter. I realized that all I had accomplished that day was save the life of a district ranger.

———

One day I was lamenting the choreography of the herbicide wars to Jay Perkins, a young friend who was a rising star in the Forest Service downriver. "I don't get it," I said. "We write better and better appeals every year. It's clear that the sprays are toxic and that people around here are affected. But all we get are those thank-you-for-your-input letters."

Jay was a Forest Service company man, no doubt, but he had a lot of integrity and a lot of empathy. He shook his head slowly and finally said, "You're going at it the wrong way, with emotional arguments, no matter how heartfelt. The Forest Service has a mandate from above to spray with herbicides, and the only thing that will stop them is if you show them that they are breaking the law." I looked at him, puzzled and waiting for elaboration, but he said no more, and the look on his face made me realize that he might have said more than he meant to. The unspoken message had to be that we should sue the bastards, to use the formal language.

———

Salmon River was not alone in its public alarm at getting sprayed with toxic chemicals. Opposition was growing throughout the Northwest. Some opposition was loosely organized and fervent, if not sophisticated. Other groups were far more advanced. The Salmon River response in that era was loose and very fervent. Locals compared it to when the towns-people in the old movie get together and storm Dr. Frankenstein's castle with torches and pitchforks. But by the 1980s, the evidence and the public outcry was so great that environmental attorneys were launching well-written lawsuits to stop the spray programs. The level of sophistica-tion had come a long way since our bumbling attempts at stopping the logging at White Bear more than a decade earlier, when I still lived at the commune. As is often the case, the lawyers needed a local plaintiff, so our own SRCC stepped forward. Unexpectedly, at least unexpected by me, we won. Herbicide use throughout Forest Service Region Five—all of California—ground to a halt. We had helped win against a huge federal agency.

CHAPTER 21

"Thank You for Your Input"

It was then that we learned what it meant to win against a federal agency. David had it easy when he slew Goliath. Whereas before, every year we'd gotten the infamous thank-you-for-your-input letters, suddenly forty-four households—that's about half the residents of Salmon River— got a new kind of letter. It was the half who still lived on mining claims, and the letter informed them that their residency was illegal; they had to move and be quick about it. This wasn't picking on just one guy, as the ranger had done years earlier when Eldon Cott publicly disrespected him. This was half the town. Jay Perkins never warned me about that part of the process, but I guess Kate George had told me often when she was still alive.

There were two main kinds of people who lived on claims. There were, first, people who were mining or who had once mined but gotten too old, and, second, people who just needed a place to live, so they pretended to mine; let's call it mining theater. Many of the old miners were geniuses at their craft. In a richer river than the Salmon, miners might boast of how much gold they found, but from one little Salmon River town to another—from Sawyers Bar to Cecilville and from Forks of Salmon to Somes Bar—bragging rights went to the most inventive. Who could arc weld with a truck battery when the regular welder ran out of fuel or who could make a Grizzly rock classifier out of hog wire fencing when an ordinary mortal might need railroad rail steel. This fascinated many of us who'd been educated in schools and colleges. Many of these old miners had grammar that would hardly get you promoted to fifth grade, yet they could quote technical mining journals or old hydrology books on the mathematics of resistance in long runs of water pipe. They could also quote almost verbatim the paranoid political articles in the right-wing national mining magazines. They read those religiously. (I can't say with conviction that the Right is any more paranoid than the Left. Also, I need to remember that, when the curtains were pulled back just a little during the Watergate investigations in the 1970s, the real level of government-sponsored conspiracy outstripped anything we Wingers, Left or Right, could dream up.)

As time went on, many of the theatrical miners developed an interest in actual mining, and the old-timers were useful role models to the wannabes. Most of them actually did start mining, and they turned to the veteran miners as mentors. Their talk was suddenly filled with references to backhoe repair and sightings of platinum nestled in with the gold. The older miners were happy to welcome them into the fold and shared their know-how (as well as their right-wing magazines). But the eviction letters targeted authentic and wannabe miners alike. It was a crisis. The people living on claims tried to mobilize their old political structure, the Salmon River Mining Association, but it had fallen into disuse. Finally, the miners approached the most unlikely of allies, the forest activists, mostly veterans of the commune, who had some experience battling the Forest Service because of the herbicide wars. The main people they turned to were people like Kenoli Oleari and Petey Brucker, who were good at connecting with all sorts of people and also good at figuring things out.

I'm not sure which miner came up with the idea of this alliance, but it was probably Jerry Cramer. Jerry was a real miner through and through. Real machinery. Real earth moving. Real gold to show for it. Jerry had met the hippies on the commune when I lived up there and saw that we had potential, something we rarely saw ourselves. He would make suggestions about how to get electricity with water power as it flowed downhill, and it seemed like the easiest thing in the world when he explained it.

Among the miners, Jerry was one of the most inventive and imaginative. On one of my first visits, he showed me a big chest freezer that he'd rigged to run off a little waterwheel he'd made from the blade of a table saw. I asked him how he adjusted the temperature, and he jiggled a faucet that changed the flow to the wheel. That, in turn, slowed the compressor, which is the device that makes a freezer cold. "I just keep an eye on it and make sure it stays cold enough," he said, as though the whole artful contraption was the simplest thing in the world.

Jerry Cramer was such a genius at mining that he could "read" the gold like you might recognize someone's handwriting. He told us that he had been following a gold vein for years, and that pulling the gold out of the mine was just like scraping the cheese from between two slices of bread. Then he claimed that he could identify every vein that had been discovered in the area and seemed to think they had all been discovered. Apparently, it was not uncommon for the road crew to expose a vein when they were opening a new cut in the road, but every time it was identified as being part of a claim that someone had already made. Hard-rock claims, Jerry told us, are for a particular vein of gold as opposed to placer claims that are for a specific area of land. I hadn't heard that before, but, anyway, most of the claims with cabins being threatened were placer claims. You know the difference between vein gold and placer gold? It's like this. Vein gold, or they call it lode gold or hard-rock gold, squirted up when the original igneous rock was still molten rock juice. Then over the years, geologic years, erosion would eat away at the mountains, and bits of gold would get moved by rain runoff and erosion, especially when the ice ages thawed and the glaciers melted in big floods. But gold is so dense that it would redeposit here and there in pockets wherever the runoff slowed down. That's the source of placer gold.

So the miners, about as pro-gun-rights and libertarian as people can be, were suddenly allies with hippie environmentalists. Everybody involved was probably surprised, but there was some justice to it. Nobody in town liked the herbicides, but it was the hippies—with help from Mavis McCovey, the Karuk medicine woman—who figured out a path to make the Forest Service stop using them.

Little Jake, who could be very philosophical, gave me an explanation of what had happened. "They love it," he said, "when you play the game. You send in pleas and objections to their plans and they send you letters—Thank You for Your Input—letters practically dripping honey. But you win, even win a little bit, then it's hardball." It was classic Kate George analysis. Kate and Little Jake were mutual admirers.

New unlikely alliances are always tricky, but everybody worked to do their part. Once when we were visiting, Jerry Cramer was reading aloud from one of the articles with a bunch of anticommunist rhetoric from the Birch Society, real McCarthy-era right-wing paranoia. At some point Kenoli broke in and said, "You know, Jerry, I think I should let you know that I'm a communist." I don't think Kenoli was really a communist; maybe he said that for effect. Maybe he was a provocateur, if I can use the French word for a guy who makes trouble for sport. That was a common political stance at the commune.

Jerry stopped and reflected for a minute and came back with, "Kenoli, there are good people in the Communist Party and bad people in the Communist Party and good people in the John Birch Society and bad people in the John Birch Society, and we good people just have to stick together."

Another time, he gave Osha and Kenoli, both commune veterans, an article expounding about something, and every few lines there was an anti-Semitic slur of some sort. Osha informed him that he was a Jew. Jerry took the article back, and the next time he gave it to us with all the anti-Semitic slurs crossed out and told us to read the rest and ignore those parts.

The claim holders and their local defenders made effective use of the media—newspaper articles, television, and even a big spread in *People* magazine that showed photos of Sarah Hugdahl and her family at their claim at Indian Creek. Indian Creek poured into the South Fork Salmon River about a mile downriver from where Black Bear Creek entered. The Indian Creek cabin had become a sort of halfway house for families at the commune whose kids got old enough to attend the school at Forks of Salmon. It was also a real mining operation. Heavy equipment. Dirt and rock moved. Gravel washed. Most important, gold getting recovered from it all. I remember a picture in *People* magazine of Sarah's horse, a beautiful black stallion, ferrying her young son Miles Richardson across the river. When the Forest Service had harassed the miners in the past, the agency had always wilted from the adverse publicity.

The lead environmentalists, Petey, Kenoli, and Felice Pace, reached out to their allies in more powerful activist groups. At one point even the North Coast chapter of the Sierra Club was publicly defending the Salmon River miners. It might well be the first, and probably the only, occasion when the Sierra Club had ever supported miners. It must have seemed clear to them that the Forest Service was attacking the miners because the miners and the rest of the community had successfully opposed the use of herbicides.

I wasn't a bystander in this myself, even though I didn't live on a mining claim. We got word that the man who represented our district in the House of Representatives in Washington might decide to intervene on our behalf. But he wanted a word of support for us from George Thackeray, then the local county supervisor. Thackeray was a man I'd met years earlier when I lived at the commune, before he held office. He was a powerful rancher in Scott Valley. We knew he wasn't a fan of environmentalists, so we needed to hit the right notes. Also not boast that we'd won the herbicide court case.

It was decided that I should meet with Thackeray, even though I'd first met him when I still lived at the commune. I agreed but said I should take along a real miner who would dispel any doubts that the claim holders were both legit and also could pass any unspoken political litmus test. Lots of the miners were pretty libertarian, even antigovernment enough to leverage any Siskiyou County supervisor.

Finally, we came up with one candidate, a guy named Ray Rumrill, who really mined and who was a Vietnam War veteran besides. I figured that Republicans were always big supporters of that war and were always talking up support for the returning vets. This guy could be the one. There was one problem. Ray Rumrill had a frizzy beard and a head of crazy hair. He looked as crazy as I'd looked when I'd lived at the commune.

To bridge the culture gap a little, Lloyd Ingle also came along. Lloyd mined, really mined, on a claim up Know-Nothing Creek and had also planted trees with us at Ent Forestry. If you divided a group of people into the Talkers and the Do-ers, Lloyd would have been the King of the Do-ers. It surprised us all when he agreed to come along, but it was a good idea since Lloyd didn't look too crazy-hippie. He didn't promise to talk.

The Forest Service already had so much momentum with the evictions that time was short, so we made an appointment with Thackeray and headed out to meet him at his ranch along the main highway between the towns of Fort Jones and Etna. I always squirmed as we came down out of the mountains and drove through Etna. It was many years since I'd been charged with felony plumbing theft when I first arrived at the commune, but people still teased me about what they called the "Great Sink Heist." We drove many miles between broad expanses of alfalfa fields, all irrigated by powerful overhead sprinklers.

Thackeray's house was a tall, stately place, and he welcomed us graciously into a sitting room with a broad smile. He asked if I'd once bought hay from him, and I said I had, years earlier, when I'd lived at Black Bear. He got a faraway look and said he remembered hay buyers from the commune and especially a woman who clearly ran the place. "She was the Queen Bee," he said, admiringly. "All those men did whatever she ordered. 'Get those bales on the truck.'" That was Roselee, of course. I didn't tell him that I was probably one of her worker bees, and I wondered if he was privately fantasizing that he might have liked being one of them himself.

Small talk done, we shifted to the real business, and he began questioning me, and especially Rumrill and Lloyd, about their mining operations. Rumrill rose to the occasion and explained his claim, his water source, and his equipment. He talked about the history of the claim, which went back generations, and his plans for future development.

Thackeray nodded and asked if he found much gold. Rumrill answered that he got lots of fines, that is small flakes of gold, but here's what he was proudest of. He pulled a small can from his coat pocket and gestured to

Thackeray to hold out his hand. Rumrill dumped the contents into his hand: three nuggets. Two were medium-sized, but impressive, and the third was nearly half the size of Thackeray's thumb. Thackeray jiggled his hand to feel their heft, and an even fuller smile filled his weathered face. He reached out and hesitantly held them for a moment over Rumrill's can. Then he slipped them in, one at a time, with satisfying clinks.

"I'm convinced," Thackeray said, "but one other question. Do you have to live on the claim? Couldn't you live on private land?"

"I'd love to," Rumrill answered. "But there's almost no private land on Salmon River. It's almost entirely national forest. Plus, I need to live on the claim to protect it." He patted the can of nuggets, now squirreled away in his pocket.

Thackeray grinned, nodded in agreement, and patted the coat pocket himself. "I can see you have a lot to protect," he said, and he promised us that he'd talk to the congressman. Then he walked us out to our truck.

On the drive back to Salmon River I was optimistic and I told Rumrill, "Maybe politics isn't as hard as people make out." Rumrill looked over at me and didn't say anything. Neither did Lloyd.

I'd like to say that hippies were better at foiling the Forest Service than Jerry Cramer and the other old members of the Mining Association. It was not for lack of trying, but, when the powerful in this world decide it's in their interest to squeeze the weak, the outcome is not always pretty.

Kate George had always warned me that the Forest Service would shove all the people off their cabins on the mining claims, but I always tried to ignore her. It did convince me not to move to a mining claim, but I couldn't imagine that the agency would ever pull it off. When we'd argue, she'd always remind me of what she called "the First Law of Crime." The First Law of Crime, in Kate's formulation, was No Witnesses. So many people in the little Salmon River towns—Sawyers Bar, Cecilville, Forks of Salmon, and Somes Bar—lived on claims and there was so little nonfederal private land in the area that there would be few places for people to move if the evictions succeeded. Looking back, I often ignored Kate's advice, but she was nearly always right.

One afternoon the school bus from Forks of Salmon Elementary School was making its regular run returning children to their homes as far up the South Fork as Cecilville. The road is a winding, one-lane affair, half composed of gorgeous panoramas and half of blind curves. A few miles from the school, the road to Godfrey Ranch winds up the mountain, but the bus stays on the main river road. Just past the Godfrey turnoff, the driver slowed. A miner's cabin was in flames. Forest Service employees surrounded the structure, but they were not trying to save it. They were burning it down. The driver slowed but did not stop. The children, often noisy on the long bus ride, were uncharacteristically speechless. Many of them also lived on mining claims in cabins not much different from the one they had just seen being torched.

The river towns had long felt pressure from the Forest Service, an agency that is inexplicably a branch of the federal Department of Agriculture. There were a lot of good people who worked for them, most of them honest and many even pretty smart. But there were some others, too, who seemed that they'd do anything to get ahead in the organization. Maybe they were the problem. Still, some part of me thinks it's just another part, a small part, in the history of real estate.

Kate George, so often my mentor, had lived on private land, and the property we had just bought at Butler Creek was also private land, but many other friends still lived on claims.

Orion Marley, the youngest child of Richard and Elsa Marley, had lived at the Black Bear "townhouse" at the Indian Creek claim when he was school-aged. He remembers coming back home to Indian Creek as an adult between assignments abroad with the National Guard. He'd been working with a military crew after the 1989 invasion of Panama, building schools and houses, and had just returned in a giant C-5 Galaxy military transport to Travis Air Force Base near Oakland, California, two days earlier. By the time Orion got back from Panama, the Indian Creek cabin had been vacated, and he found a crowd of locals there when he arrived. They were busy demolishing the cabin. That was the best of bad alternatives. If a Forest Service crew had burned the place, as they had done for many other cabins, the claim owners would have been assessed the cost of the fire crew and the fire engine plus some other penalties that he labeled "administrative bullshit fees."

Plus locals were too practical to burn a cabin without salvaging all the reusable building materials—the windows, the siding, any metal roofing, and more. Orion remembered who was there when we talked later. The crowd included some of the tree planters: John Albion, Petey Brucker, Geba Greenberg, Danny Stanshaw, and Les Harling, several Bennetts including Hoss, Jack, and Son, and even a few of the newer hippies who then lived at the commune. There were some river people who were themselves getting pried off claims, including Jim Hensher and David Haley, whose dad, Dick Haley, had been a friend of the commune in those early days when we had few friends. Rex Richardson, a brilliant musician and miner, and Sara Hugdahl, a talented painter, had been living full-time at the cabin, but they had already moved to a place downriver. Orion named a few others—Wayne Huddleston, Don DeRoma, Steve Gunther, and Glenn McBroom. It was more than a salvage operation. It was a rally of a sort to support a neighbor in need, and the crowd crossed all the usual cultural and ethnic lines. That's code for hippies, rednecks, and Native Americans, groups that didn't always mingle. People rallied to protect the mining-claim residents the same way they had during big forest fires.

Once the salvage and the ruminations were done, the remnants of the cabin were burned by locals. Days later, when I got there, only Sarah Hugdahl was around. She was sifting through the ashes with a rake, and she turned to greet me, with a melancholy shrug. When I asked, she said she was looking for any small objects that might have survived the demolition and then the burn. Everyone remembered the stories of people with metal detectors finding small stashes of gold on abandoned claims, so I teased her about caches of nuggets under the floor boards. She said people had, of course, looked, but found none. She gestured to a small pile of doodads on a nearby boulder—a broach, some metal buttons, a silver dollar—and she said she might use them in an art project. "I just don't get why they did it here, why they did it so many places," she said. She said that she'd heard that Mike Lee, then the Forest Service ranger for the Salmon River District, had made a trip to Washington, DC, where he'd lobbied congressmen and other officials. His message was that the mining-claim residents were mostly big pot growers, not miners. I said the pot growers I'd heard of lived on private land, not claims, and she nodded agreement. Then I explained my theory that it was a hardball response to the community's success in the herbicide lawsuit.

Sarah said, "But everybody was against the sprays for years. Everybody. Why did they finally get so heavy?" She paused, pursed her lips and answered her own question: "Maybe it's because we won." Then she turned back to raking the ashes.

———

I didn't see George Thackeray, the county supervisor, for about a year after that visit with Lloyd Ingle and Ray Rumrill. Things had gone badly for the families who lived on the claims. The worst was on Salmon River, but people also lost their homes along the Klamath. At the advice of Morris Udall, then a congressman from Arizona, we had proposed buying the claims. He'd suggested using a law called the Townsite Expansion Act, for communities surrounded by federal ownership. We wrote a formal proposal and started to line up financing, but midlevel Forest Service apparatchiks tossed it on a technicality. The word "apparatchik" comes from loyal members of the Soviet Communist Party, but it applies well to bureaucratic subordinates who are unquestioningly loyal. There was plenty of publicity that favored the claim holders. A few claims were exempted, but only a few, and the people that lived on them were never certain why they were skipped. In an act of futile protest, the Forest Service head cop's house in Yreka was torched. Usually, when there was an event like this, we all heard rumors, possibly true, about who had done it. Not in this case. Not a peep. Not a guess. The Mafia called its code of silence *omertà*, and it clearly applied here.

I finally crossed paths with Supervisor Thackeray at a small public event in Forks of Salmon months later, about a year after our lobbying visit to his ranch. The local volunteer fire department, Salmon River Fire and Rescue, had built a barn-like fire station next door to the Forks

Elementary School, and the event was to celebrate the milestone. I wasn't sure why I was invited. I'd been off on a job and hadn't had time to help with the construction or had the money to contribute much, but we were all big fans of the volunteers, so I went. The crowd was small, and we sat outside for what ceremony there was. Mike Lee, the district ranger who'd been the judge and executioner for forcing the families off the claims, was there. I'd just read an article about some act of genocide in Eastern Europe. They called it "ethnic cleansing," which may have made it sound more sanitary. I wondered if Lee's actions qualified as a war crime, but, in fact, it had instead earned him a promotion in the Forest Service. Jimmy Bennett, the man who'd hired me on my first firefighting job back at the start of the Hog Fire in 1977, was there. He'd worked for years for the Forest Service and was also fire chief of the volunteers. Jimmy was a driven man and opinionated, although I never knew which way the opinions would swing. We all respected Jimmy, and he had been a key force in the completion of the new firehouse. A few short speeches were delivered, and people politely clapped for each speaker.

Finally, Thackeray rose to speak. He had a winning smile, always an asset in a politician. He thanked Jimmy and congratulated the community for their accomplishments. First, he listed the building of the firehouse and gestured to the tall frame structure. Then he said that things had gotten much better on the river "since we drove all that scum out of town." Locals traded nervous glances and said nothing.

When I talked to Little Jake after hearing Thackeray at the dedication, Jake was less offended than I had been. "He promised to help us," I protested.

"He's a politician. You used to be a reporter at the *Los Angeles Times*. When since then did you start believing anything politicians say?" I started to sputter an answer, but Jake continued, "Besides, Thackeray has a tradition to live up to. His ancestors won their land fair and square, by carving it out of the wilderness and killing most of the Native Americans who lived there when they first arrived. He grew up hearing from his father and from his grandfather that he had to fight for the land just like they had, whenever it was threatened. When we hippies moved nearby and then started meddling with things like herbicide policy, he knew which side he was on. He didn't even kill you and burn your village. You got off easy."

Then Jake stopped and waited for my response. I didn't have one.

CHAPTER 22

Cooperation, Collaboration, and Other Four-Letter Words—An Epilogue

When I was a young reporter in Los Angeles, I would go drinking after work with the older reporters, whom I revered. The conversation would sometimes turn to people who had studied literature in college, a slur that was grumbled with disdain in that journalistic company. We reporters wrote about real life, real people. I learned later that a significant fraction of my colleagues were secretly writing novels in their off-hours, maybe even in their on-hours, if our editors weren't pressing them for copy. But all that smack talk about our literary betters stayed with me.

Through it all, there was still always one element of literature that I admired—the epilogue. There is no equivalent in newspaper writing, unless you count obituaries. I wrote many obits over the years about people I didn't know and, lately, a few about friends, but they all lacked that stitched-up quality of an epilogue. Certainly, when you look at your own life, there is no point where you can say, this is how it all worked out. But books can do that.

So you are owed an epilogue.

For starters, we ask if there are still Diggers, that dazzling gang that captured and also defined the hippie ethos of San Francisco in the late 1960s. They were wildly idealistic and also transparently self-serving. Maybe they weren't different from a lot of us, except that they did it brilliantly. And publicly. They were the darlings of the media. By the mid-1970s, they seemed to have dispersed, but many stayed active in politics and environmental advocacy. One of the best-known Diggers,

Peter Coyote, emerged as a talented actor in film and television and later wrote a book on the sixties titled *Sleeping Where I Fall.* I thought it a very good book. In the last few years, veterans of the Digger movement began small-scale fund-raising among themselves to support a few members of their old cohort who were down on their economic luck. There is a certain pleasing symmetry that, after many decades of diaspora, Diggers who offered to make everything free—food, clothes, sex, everything— would join together to help support old comrades.

—

Our unsuccessful lawsuit to stop the White Bear logging, our victory in the fight to stop the use of herbicides, and our resistance to the mining claim evictions were not the end of our community organizing. Many local activists, a number of them either residents or alumni of the commune, formed a regional coalition to counter the breakneck pace of old-growth logging. Appeals were submitted, lawsuits filed, and one by one there were victories. The group organized itself as the Klamath Forest Alliance, and Felice Pace and Petey Brucker emerged as highly effective activist/organizers. The list of cases grew long, and wins by KFA and kindred environmental groups started to counterweigh the rubber-stamp approvals accorded timber sales by the Forest Service.

It was not always an easy path. Local groups made highly effective alliances with regional and national enviro organizations, which gave us both funding and access to sophisticated legal teams. But moneyed timber interests began a campaign across the Northwest that intentionally pitted local logging families against their environmentalist neighbors.

These lawsuits grew more and more sophisticated, and the enviro filings prevailed more and more of the time. Set-asides for northern spotted owl and for President Clinton's Northwest Forest Plan seriously reduced the pace of logging on federal lands.

One part of that that is most evident to me: only one of the many timber sales I helped prepare in those years in the mid-1980s as a US Forest Service timber cruiser ever got cut. It was a tipping point. If there was ever a stretch of my life where I wanted my energies squandered, it was those three years. The best thing about the job was that I got to work much of the time in near-pristine stands of old-growth conifers. The worst thing was that it seemed at the time that I would be the last person to see them in that condition.

The other focus of groups like KFA became the health of the region's rivers and the survival of the once vibrant salmon runs. In this they had another set of allies, the local tribes. There are several tribes in the Klamath Basin, and the one around us was Willis and Florence Conrad's tribe, the Karuk. The tribe has about thirty-two hundred enrolled members spread along the Klamath Basin from Yreka downriver to beyond Orleans. They were granted federal recognition in 1979 and with it some sort of sovereignty. There was much talk of government-to-government relations between the tribe and their neighbor, the United States, from the start. I was uncertain if the federal agency types at the time would pay it anything more than lip service, but over the following decades the Karuk leadership has used this status to leverage genuine power. It for sure brought funding for social services, housing, and employment for tribal members. But for the Karuk and the other tribes in the basin it also represented an opportunity for a growing measure of influence in natural resource issues. At the top of the list was protection and growth of salmon populations and ending a century of knee-jerk suppression of wildfires. The Karuk and the other tribes favored a transition back to their traditional practices of periodic intentional burning. The choices, they said, were prescribed burning at a safer time of year or devastating conflagrations at the driest and hottest times of summer.

Another specific target was the removal of four hydroelectric dams in the upper reaches of the Klamath River, and the tribes, including the Karuk, began a high-level negotiation that offered some water supplies to upper-basin irrigators in return for dam removal and restoration of conditions that favored the fish. Many but not all of the tribes and many but not all of the environmentalists supported a proposed settlement hammered out by the power company that owned the dams, working with NGOs, government agencies, tribes, and other interested parties.

On the timber front, Forest Service timber planners recognized that the balance had shifted because of litigation, so they tried another strategy by the early 1990s. Let's call it collaboration. The idea was to sit down with all the interest groups and come up with timber sales that everyone could live with. The first such effort in our area was called "the Cooperative Working Group." The CWG, to use its initials, was designed to advance more logging in the old Monte Creek Sale area, which included Butler, Duncan, Monte, and Somes Creeks, the tributaries from our house down to the mouth of the Salmon River. I knew the area well from my timber cruising work the season before the agency fired me. The CWG held many meetings, and some parts of them seemed useful, but it was hard not to notice that the deck seemed stacked. The district ranger who set up the "collaborative approach" was the same man I'd first seen in Etna Café a couple years earlier, the one who boasted, "But no matter what those loggers and the tree-huggers do to each other, the Forest Service comes out smelling like a rose." Whenever during the CWG proceedings a local with an environmental bent made a strong point, he made a habit of standing where his staff could see him and rolling his eyes. My wife, Sue, was always making strong points and smart ones, but I don't doubt that any Forest Service specialist in wildlife or geology or any branch of science got a clear message: "Discount whatever this woman says."

The ranger with the eye-rolling discounted my wife, Sue, at his peril. She may not have had a forestry degree, but she had done her homework and much more. She was still, in those days, the teacher at the Forks of Salmon Elementary School, and she was very good at it, even brilliant at it. She was one of the first teachers in the region to develop a curriculum for watershed education. That's an approach that teaches science locally, not globally. She brought in experts, working professionals, to her class and on field trips to explain local botany, geology, hydrology, forestry, fire, and more. The kids wrote in observation journals, did interviews, studied local history, filmed underwater, monitored water quality, did fuels reduction work around elders' homes, and honed wilderness skills.

Her favorite evaluative tool was to have the kids write their questions about a topic before they studied it (which she would then send to the experts who had agreed to visit the class so they would know what level to aim at). Then at the conclusion of that area of study the kids wrote the questions they had after their studies, which clearly showed the deepening of their level of understanding and engagement and left them with ever-widening curiosity about the subject. It may have been a small class, grades 4–8, but its content would have done well in an undergraduate natural resources program. One measure of her effectiveness is that so many of her students eventually studied some branch of environmental science at the college level. A second is that so many of them came back to the river to make use of their new skills.

Besides that, Sue was already very familiar with the area. An earlier ranger had tried to set up a sale on the same ground just a few years earlier, and Sue knew the turf. She got copies of the environmental assessment documents, maps and all, and read them cover to cover. And she had walked the ground. Predictably, the "Ologists," our shorthand for geologists, hydrologists, biologists, and so on, were wary of the negative impacts clear-cut logging would have on such steep, decomposed granite slopes. Sue noticed that a number of the many geologically unstable areas shown on the maps had straight lines and right angles for boundaries. How could a geologically unstable boundary be defined by straight lines and right angles? So Sue bought some Mylar plastic sheets and traced the boundaries of geologic instability. Then she placed them over the map that showed the units slated to be logged. This was in the days before GIS would have made the same work a snap. Sure enough, the Forest Service had conveniently drawn the geologically unstable boundaries to avoid the units where they wanted to log. So much for building trust between the Forest Service and the community.

It would have taken more than a few fraternity-boy gestures of disrespect by a district ranger to shake people's confidence in Sue's homework.

Besides that, the meetings always seemed to be discussing side topics and not talking about where new roads would be pioneered or about what acres would actually be logged. When we asked when all we "cooperators" would decide that, he kept saying it was coming. Finally, at the meeting where we were supposed to get to the nitty-gritty of the sale collaboratively, the ranger came into the meeting with a completed plan, roads, logging units, everything. When we complained, he responded that our meetings had taken too long, so he had taken things into his own hands. The timber company reps had long since stopped coming to the meetings. We decided that it was time for us to walk out in protest. The timber sale never happened.

Many years later, another district ranger launched another round of faux collaboration. They called it the Orleans Community Fuels Reduction project, or OCFR. This one was linked to a theory popular with timber companies: that the big increase in wildfires was because there were too many trees. The industry has a solution for that, of course. This new ranger wasn't big on eye-rolling, but we noticed that the Forest Service had drawn the footprint of the sale before there was any community collaboration. Although it was billed as a community fuels reduction project, the harvest units were almost all on the ridges where there was still big timber volume, not down around the community where the residents could get some real protection from a wildfire. We also spotted that the district ranger was altering the minutes of each community meeting. Somehow, many locals and the Karuk Tribe did sign on to OCFR, but operations were stopped by court order when it became clear that the logger, with the acquiescence of the Forest Service, had broken the agreements that would have protected certain tribal spiritual trails.

Most recently there is still another attempt at collaboration under way, this one called the Western Klamath Restoration Partnership. As of this writing, I have hopes that this one will really work. First off, local activists from both the Karuk Tribe and from two local restoration groups called the Mid Klamath Watershed Council and Salmon River Restoration Council are leading a lot of the initial planning. MKWC leader Will Harling and Bill Tripp from the tribe are working closely and cooperatively on the outcomes, along with dozens of diverse locals, agency people, and a few gifted facilitators from the Nature Conservancy. There are even a few people with distinctly pro-logging sentiments, but they jump in and do their share in the planning. In the past, that initial stage had been handed down to the community like the Ten Commandments. In this round, the community is leading the way. Another factor that keeps me hopeful is that the current district ranger, Nolan Colegrove, and also his boss, Merv George Jr., Six Rivers forest supervisor, are both locals and, besides that, both members of the Hoopa Tribe. They seem to have an inclusive outlook that we have not seen before. If it works, it may warrant another book, although I may not be the guy to write it.

———

Not all the people in this book whom I've loved and respected so much are still alive. A couple of them still talk to me in my dreams and still coach me like they did before they got to the spirit world or wherever they are now. To two of them in particular—Willis Conrad and Kate George—I owe a special debt. I was not planning to stay long when I first came to the commune in 1968. Immediately getting busted for the kitchen sink heist and then waiting for a court date kept me around. But the hostility to hippies from so many Siskiyou County locals would have probably driven me away if not for the friendship and help of Willis, Kate, and a few other locals.

When Willis Conrad, the early friend of the Black Bear hippies and my mentor in card playing, died, his wife, Florence, asked me if I'd do part of the eulogy. I was honored by the request and especially when I learned that the other person she'd asked to speak was Julian Lang, the university academic who was also a respected tribal spiritual leader. I wrote my words beforehand for the approval of Florence, who was by then a member of the Karuk Tribal Council. She accepted all but one thing I'd written, a reference to the years in his youth when Willis was forced to attend the infamous boarding school for Native Americans called Chemawa, a place where students were beaten for speaking in their native language. She read that part to herself twice, then shook her head in disapproval. "He suffered that enough when he was alive," she said. "No need for him to hear it now." The day of the memorial the tribal hall in Orleans was packed. The overflow crowd was even bigger. The stream of arriving cars blocked traffic on Highway 96 for a long time. I'd coaxed Julian to tell traditional stories when he spoke, and he told several. Then many others told their remembrances of Willis, many of them incredibly funny. Much of the day remains a blur in my mind. Mostly I remember people—men and women alike—weeping as I spoke. Many people rose to tell their own Willis stories afterward, some very funny. We all seized the excuse to laugh, and the laughter blended well with the tears.

When Kate George died, her daughter-in-law Marge George also asked me to deliver the eulogy. Once again, I was surprised, also honored. Marge was part of the community that often seemed distrustful of the hippie transplants who'd come to the river. The event was at the George Ranch up in Cecilville, where Kate had lived long before I'd met her. The family graveyard was on an especially Spartan plot of land, with few trees and even little grass or brush. A few years earlier, Kate had said that family cemeteries were always built on land unlikely to be worth mining and too barren for a garden, fruit trees, or even pasture. A cold wind blew down from the snow-covered Trinity Alps. I told stories from my life with Kate and stories from the old days that she'd told me along the way. At certain stories, many people would nod in agreement, and many also wept. Marge George ran the Forks of Salmon store in those days, and she was there when I walked in a few days later to buy some groceries and beer. Marge thanked me for the eulogy, and I said that I was honored by the request. She acknowledged my comment with a nod, then said, "We all talked about who to ask and we couldn't think of anybody else who wouldn't mention God. Kate would have wanted it that way."

———

Black Bear Ranch, the commune, also still exists. People still come there to live for a while in a style not too different from what we tried nearly fifty years ago. I still visit there almost every year; it is not too far from where I live now along the main stem of the Salmon River. I find the people there friendly, more industrious than we were, and certainly more skilled at surviving in a remote mountain hideaway. The commune still gets the attention of the police; recently sheriff deputies came by and dutifully recorded the license plates on every vehicle. No tomato plants were seized.

There are many miracles, large and small, that attend the survival of a cultural enterprise like Black Bear Ranch. Many communes sprang up in the late sixties and early seventies. Hardly any still exist, but Black Bear is still around—with a crowd of new young hippies.

One particular miracle always sticks in my mind. Remember that Black Bear was originally purchased by a handful of Diggers who raised money from rock stars then prominent in Los Angeles. I was invited along, although I was a Haight-Ashbury newbie. I told them that I knew a lot of music biz luminaries because I'd just spent a couple years managing a momentarily popular band. More likely, the Diggers took me along because their only transportation was the Coors beer delivery truck I'd kept from my brush with show business. It had been our equipment truck for West Coast shows.

We did raise enough for a down payment, but our new property required the formality of an owner. Somebody's name had to go on the dotted line. This was a complication for a crowd who preached that everything should be free and scrawled "Property Is Theft" on every untended

Richard Marley, left, could sing a rousing version of the *Internationale*, but his voice ascended to the operatic on the day in 1987 when he formally passed the ownership of the commune over to a community trust. Here, he is accompanied on fiddle by John Salter, an anthropologist who often stayed at the commune and developed deep ties with Karuk tribal elders. Photo by Jeff Buchin.

wall they could find. Or else they glued up iconic posters that showed two nineteenth-century Chinatown gangsters and the enigmatic Digger slogan: "1% FREE."

It was decided that the best name on the title would be Richard Marley. Marley and his wife, Elsa, had thought up the whole enterprise and pitched it to a small crowd upstairs at the big Victorian just a few days before we were arrested there. But Richard Marley was not the kind of person you'd expect to be a founder of such an enduring movement. We might have expected it from his political DNA. His mother was secretary of the British Communist Party, but Marley carried little of that legacy beyond the ability to sing a rousing version of the *Internationale*. Before the Diggers, he'd worked in the Merchant Marine and then on the San Francisco docks as a longshoreman, both classic proletarian jobs, but he was an unemployed beatnik/hippie with a back-to-the-land vision by the time I met him. Also, in the style of the times, he had developed an affinity for addictive drugs, especially speed.

Some of the Digger theorists made a distinction between good drugs and bad. The "good" list included marijuana and the psychedelics like LSD, peyote, and psilocybin mushrooms. These were drugs that promoted awareness, a trendy goal of that era and never a bad idea. The "bad" inventory was headed with highly addictive drugs like heroin and speed, the street word for amphetamines, plus their pharmaceutical cousins. The marketplace for the bad drugs, and the urgency of the users' need, promoted an anything-goes set of ethical standards.

Richard Marley was a visionary and a community organizer, but he was not immune to the corrupt pressures of his bad habits. One part of him surely treasured the isolation of the commune as at least partial protection from his own drug use, but another part convinced the midwives at Black Bear not to leave anything in the collective medical cache that could remotely be a painkiller. Inga Troutman was a woman who lived at the commune in those days, a blonde so pretty that I grew tongue-tied the first time I met her. Inga once told me about a time down in San Francisco when Marley dropped her off at the apartment of a man she barely knew and promised to come back soon to retrieve her. Later, she realized that he had picked up a package of drugs with the intent to sell most of them retail and keep a little for himself. "I figured out later that Richard left me there as a deposit to convince the dealer—that's whose place it was—that he'd return with payment for all the speed. I was the collateral!" Yeah, Richard returned.

It's worth mentioning that Elsa Marley, Richard's widow, tells a similar story. In Elsa's case, she was left by Richard at the Grateful Dead House on upper Ashby Street. Before we race to be unsympathetic, remember that in many business deals the transactions are guaranteed by credit checks and other safeguards. Think of the plight of a hapless drug wholesaler. If he wants security on a loan, the deposit of a pretty girl for the afternoon seems minimal. I'm not sure what either Inga or Elsa thought about it at the time, but each of them told me their stories decades later with a detached amusement.

So here was a man who was at once saint and sinner in an uneasy mix. Maybe a lot of us are a mix like that. But few of us have our name on the title of a piece of real estate where hundreds of people have lived, many spouting slogans like "Free Land for Free People." In the early years Marley's name on the title of the commune was less a blessing for him than a pain in the butt. The worst was that whenever government people came prowling around—county zoning enforcers, sheriff deputies, even the FBI looking for radical fugitives—the first person they'd ask to see was Richard Marley. After all, he was the property owner. As consequence, as we were fanning out over the wooded landscape to build our cabins, Richard and his family moved into a nearly invisible hollow far from the downtown metropolitan hippie commune. After that, whenever law enforcement showed up and asked to see him, we'd say we hadn't seen him. It was no small irony that mapmakers several years later published a new area map, and Richard's secret hollow was suddenly labeled Marley Gulch. Maybe the FBI helped in map design.

In the years after I left the commune, some others in the extended family of commune alumni started hatching plans to switch the title into some kind of community trust. The first effort won lots of support, including from Richard. But at the last minute, Richard pulled the plug.

A rumor circulated that somebody had approached him when he was very sick, perhaps mortally sick, and lobbied against giving up the place. "What else will you have to leave your kids?" was their argument.

Years passed. Richard healed. Another group developed a trust agreement. Andrew Getz, one of the ex-communards who helped develop the proposal, remembers that Richard would talk about "signing away the ranch." Each time Richard used that phrase or showed any other twitches of hesitation, it would unsettle Andrew, but this time things held together. It was decided to hold a celebration to observe the transfer. The date was obvious. The best time would be the next summer solstice. I've heard that there were Christian communes and Hindu communes, but religion never found much of a foothold at Black Bear. No surprise that Druid holidays would be observed as much as the ones we'd grown up with. Lots of former communards always showed up every summer solstice. The roads were free of snow. Camping out was easy.

When word of the title transfer spread in 1987, hundreds of us showed up. Late morning of the solstice, we gathered in a huge circle on the knoll that overlooked gardens and the commune Main House in the foreground, and the towering Trinity Alps, still caked in snow, in the distance. We called it the Sacred Knoll, part for the grandeur of its setting, but also because of the celebrations we'd held there over the years. There were overnight LSD trips in the early years when the space was caked in three feet of frozen snow. We'd have a bonfire, but it barely warmed us. Those sessions were hardly Dionysian. There was the circle to mourn Alan Hoffman, the anarchist leader, when he lay comatose and mortally wounded in a Redding hospital. Allen had been driving to the commune when his truck was rear-ended by a huge logging chip truck headed to a sawmill. There was even the time on the knoll when Zoë Leader, my partner back then, cut my hair there, and people showed up impromptu to play drums and dance in a circle. That one was barely worthy of a ceremony, but it was my first haircut in three years, and I guess people couldn't resist. If a regular hair cutter could offer conga drum players and naked women dancing in a circle, I guess people could start calling it the Sacred Barbershop. I could really grow hair in those days.

Zoë Leader was my partner in the years when we lived at Black Bear. She gave me my first haircut in three years one early summer day on the knoll that overlooked the commune's center, and, while she snipped, drummers and naked women spontaneously encircled us to dance. People, half-mocking, called it the sacred knoll. Photo by Hank Lebo.

Food prep on the day of the 1987 solstice had begun early, and the morning was full of buzz. People were there from different generations of residency at Black Bear plus no shortage of just plain visitors, some from the Salmon River towns and some from farther afield. Around the circle, people would say who they were and maybe tell a story from their life at the commune or from where they lived and what they did there. The stories were good, and no one seemed impatient.

Finally, when they were done, Richard Marley approached the center of the circle. The crowd fell silent. I recalled the day at the Victorian house in Haight-Ashbury, decades earlier, when Richard had coaxed us all into raising money to buy a place in the mountains. On this day, years later, Richard walked slowly, looking over the crowd. Then in his sweet

The commune held many gatherings over the years on the knoll, including this one, Summer Solstice 1987. People had gathered to observe the transition of the title to the land from private ownership to a community trust. Photo by Don Monkerud.

New York wise-guy voice, but loud so all could hear, he said, "The truth is out. I never did own it. Some of you always knew that."

People got his metaphorical joke, and there were chuckles in the crowd. Then his voice switched to the purest operatic, and he began a song, almost a chant, that had been a favorite in the commune sweat houses, going back to when I'd lived there.

"Blessed am I," he sang, even shouted, to the treetops, and he paused and stepped in another direction.

More opera and even more powerfully: *"Freedom am I."*

Another step and trumpeted to the treetops: *"I am the infinite within my soul. I can find no beginning; I can find no end. All this I am."* If the birds overhead had stopped in their flight, it would have been no surprise.

So the commune is still there. People come for a few hours or a few years until they find what they need there. I've come to think of it as some sort of feral graduate school. And the title to the land is vested in a maze of trustees and beneficiaries whose main mandates are to protect the place and, incidentally, to keep it out of the system we call property.

I have no idea what John Daggett, the man who started the Black Bear gold mine there in the 1800s, would have thought, but I feel certain that Willis Conrad, the Karuk fisherman who befriended us early on, and his downriver sidekicks, would be both amused and somehow impressed by this outcome.

Methodology and Acknowledgments

I want to share how this book was written. My mentor in newspaper writing was Sherman Miller, retired from the world news desk of the *New York Times*, and our professor at the Journalism Department at the University of Arizona in the early 1960s. He taught us many things, all of which I still observe—all but one. He said the reporter should never be part of the story. It is a rule often broken nowadays, and I break it myself in this book.

I may have taken the world's longest hiatus from writing. I left my job as a reporter at the *Los Angeles Times* in 1967 and quickly got talked into becoming business manager for some friends at UCLA's music school who had started an avant-garde rock band called United States of America. We cut a record with Columbia Records, made the charts, and had bookings on both coasts. After a year-plus of that we were playing San Francisco, and I got talked into joining a nascent hippie commune in the mountains of northern California. I was easy to talk into things in those days. For many reasons, I stopped writing.

But decades later, I started to realize that there were stories on the river that were as readable and as worth remembering as the ones I had covered in Los Angeles. The first sparkplug for these stories was my daughter, Erica Kate. Even as a child, she would pump me for stories. Then, in the mid-1990s we traveled to Haiti as school teachers. Haiti is a remarkable place, and I started posting weekly dispatches to friends; it reminded me how powerful and how exciting writing could be.

Our friend Peter Coyote was then writing his brilliant memoir *Sleeping Where I Fall*. After supper he'd read aloud to us all from his latest chapter and I was hypnotized, both by the voice and the power of the old stories. I started writing, and at the next dinner together, after Coyote finished reading his latest, I asked people if I could read next. Following an act like Coyote, with his gorgeous resonant voice, was like a band asking to go on stage after James Brown, but our friends were generous and encouraging.

Next, Sue and I both grabbed jobs as public school teachers in Santa Cruz in California. Before long the Santa Cruz High principal sweet-talked me into teaching journalism and becoming adviser to the school paper. The students were full of excitement, and, a bonus, Erica Kate was already editor of the school paper.

Jane Hundertmark, editor for the California Federation of Teachers paper, heard that I'd been a news writer and started feeding me assignments. When we returned to our place on the river, I started writing features for the *North Coast Journal*, a juicy Humboldt County weekly. Hank Sims, the editor, Heidi Walters, and later Thad Greenson and Jennifer Fumiko Cahill were all smart, demanding, and supportive. Then, closer to home, Allie Hostler, editor of the *Two Rivers Tribune*, got me writing every week for her. The *Trib* is a weekly published by the Hoopa Tribe. All of them would improve my copy. When I was at the *LA Times* I'd hated my editors; now I love them. Don't know what changed, but I'm grateful that they all got me writing again.

So I began writing down the old river stories I'd told and retold Erica Kate as she grew up. I had many helpers along the way, too many to recall anymore. Let me name a few. Jerry Martien, Olivia Camenga, Nicholas Marrow, Pat Messer, Bill Ayers, Bernardine Dohrn, Jim Mosher, Creek Hanauer, Edna Watson, Efrem Korngold, Harriet Beinfield, John Salter, Carolyn Niethammer, Ford Burkhart, Frank O. Sotomayor, Kari Norgaard, and Yeshi Neumann. For spelling of Karuk words, I've depended on the *Karuk Dictionary* by William Bright and Susan Gehr, published by the Karuk Tribe of California in 2005.

And more. My son, Slate Boykin, and my daughter-in-law, Shawnna Conrad, Phil Slater, Molli White, Hawk White, Gene White, Don

Monkerud, Carol Hamilton, Susan Keese, Peter Coyote, Linda Ronstadt, Tina Bennett, Dorothy Moskowitz, Rachel Dewoskin, Brian Tripp, and Susie Terence (my sister). And my mom, the late Rose Terence. Every phone call for years, Momma would talk about my latest article in the *Two Rivers Tribune* and then ask me how this book was going. (She'd also tell me about the romance novel she and my sister Susie were writing.)

And also all our dinner guests for years who, as the dishes were being bussed, would coax me to read one chapter or another aloud. It didn't take much coaxing. And the anonymous reviewers from Oregon State University Press who both supported my work and then peppered it with detailed lists of substantive suggestions. They filled the gaps in my understanding of the different demands of newspapers and of books. And especially Mary Elizabeth Braun, the OSU Press acquisitions editor. She was head coach and guardian angel.

More than anyone, I'm grateful to my wife, Susan Ring Terence, and to my daughter, Erica Kate Terence, for their untiring smarts to complete the stories that fill this book. They were unsparing in their critiques when that was needed and gushing in their praise when things were right. When the OSU Press reviewers sent back draft after draft, their comments seemed to boil down to an unwritten subtext: this work has promise, but it may be hopeless. Erica jumped in as a resident editor for months, improving my manuscript line by line and every day left me long lists of items that needed attention. Then more the next day.

To all of you, I say thank you.

I need also to address a few conventions. The book is true as I remember it. A few names are changed, to spare people who may need to protect their privacy. Also, I have honored a request of activists I respect, that, where appropriate, I have used the words "Native" and "Native American" instead of the word "Indian." A few of the chapters have appeared in earlier forms in other publications. Chapter 4, "White Bear," first appeared in the *Los Angeles Free Press* in 1972. Chapter 2, "The Recipe for Chimichangas, or How I Saved the Commune," appeared in the anthology *Free Land, Free Love*, written by commune alumni and self-published in 2001. Chapter 7, "Playing with Fire," and Chapter 18, "Beginner's Luck," both appeared in the *Two Rivers Tribune* in 2013.

There is another area where I have departed from the lessons of Sherman Miller, my long-gone but never forgotten journalism professor. I have not always embraced objectivity.

I am openly proud of the river communities, of their diversity and their vitality. I am proud of the evolution of relations between the peoples in our communities—white and Native alike. We are not at the destination, but we are on the path. Sherman Miller, my professor, told me once that he started the news bureau for the *Times* at the United Nations when it opened in New York. I think Miller would approve of my bias, my embrace of our communities.